FORTY THOUSAND
AGAINST THE ARCTIC

Russia's Polar Empire

by

H. P. SMOLKA

*With 53 Illustrations
and 2 folding maps*

THIRD IMPRESSION

HUTCHINSON & CO.
(Publishers) Ltd.
LONDON

Made and Printed in Great Britain at
The Mayflower Press, Plymouth. William Brendon & Son, Ltd.
1937

TO
T. G. S.

CONTENTS

LIST OF ILLUSTRATIONS

LIST OF ILLUSTRATIONS

All photographs taken by the author except where otherwise stated.

In the Text

ACKNOWLEDGMENTS

My thanks are due to:

Professor Otto Yulievitch Schmidt, head of Northern Sea Route Administration, for allowing me to intrude into Russia's Arctic Empire.

Professor Rudolf Lazarevitch Samoilovitch, Chief of the Arctic Institute, for hammering into me the scientific aspects of Polar research.

The Editor of *The Times* for allowing me to express again some of the thoughts first published in my series of articles in his columns.

Sir Harry Brittain for his many acts of encouragement.

Mr. Iverach McDonald of *The Times* for acting as physician and surgeon to this book in its infancy.

And to my wife—for letting me go.

FORTY THOUSAND AGAINST THE ARCTIC:

Otto Yulievitch Schmidt, 46, Professor of mathematics, Polar explorer, member of Council of People's Commissars, head of Central Administration of the Northern Sea Route, Commander-in-Chief 'Polar Army'.

Rudolf Lazarevitch Samoilovitch, 56, professor of geology, Director of Russia's Arctic University.

Valerya Petrovna Ostroumova, 43, official of Communist Party, political chief of Port Igarka (which is the newest and the largest Polar city in the world) and of the surrounding district above the Arctic Circle, a district sixteen times the size of Great Britain.

Abram Abramovitch Stukater, 47, Managing Director, all industrial and transport enterprises, Central region, Arctic Asia.

Mark Ivanovitch Shevelyov, 32, head of the Polar Air Force, commanding 125 machines.

Dr. Shlakhman, 45, Professor, Medical Faculty, East Siberia University, Irkutsk, the author's travelling companion on Trans-Siberian express.

Maxim Isidorovitch Nurik, 31, clerk at ticket office, Avyo Arctica Air Lines; and

Tassya Alexeyevna, his wife, 27, the author's hosts in Krasnoyarsk.

Galina Dimitrevna, 24, girl mechanic at repair base for Arctic aeroplanes.

Vava Nikolayevna, 23, wife of Arctic pilot.

Grazianski, 29, pilot on Arctic Air Lines.

Sadkov, 27, pilot on Arctic Air Lines.

Vodopyanov, 38, Polar air ace, 'hero of Soviet Union', candidate for trans-Polar flight Moscow-San Francisco.

Moses Isaakovitch Sack, 32, chief at Podkammenaya Tunguska, isolated North Siberian air base.

Smirnov, Smirnova, 31, 22, young married couple, geologists for Nordvyk, future Polar salt-mining and oil-boring centre.

Boris Vassilyevitch Lavrov, former Soviet trade diplomat, now founder and builder of towns in Arctic Siberia.

Nadeshda Grigoryevna Strelyakova, 14, daughter of exiled peasants in Igarka, co-author of book on children's life in Polar towns.

Antoni Klimov, 26, one time among 2,000,000 homeless children after Civil War, now explorer, writer and teacher in Far North.

Sakhari Yegarovitch Goshkov, 37, champion saw-mill worker in Igarka.

Claudia, 19, girl registrar in Polar city.

Charlie, 47, stoker on British tramp steamer carrying timber from Arctic Siberia to European ports.

Bogomolkin, 39, chief of department of Arctic agriculture, responsible for growth of cucumbers and cabbages under Polar ice.

Voronin, 41, captain, ice-breaker *Yermak.*

Borovikov, 42, head of Dickson Island, 'Arctic Radio City'.

Olga Pavlovna Gamel, 21, girl meteorologist, Dickson Polar station.

Young explorers, scientists, Red missionaries, women radio operators, doctors, sailors, miners, engineers, hunters belonging to nomad tribes in Arctic Siberia, young Samoyed, Tungus, Dolgan, Ostyak, Yurak natives, studying at the Institute of Northern Peoples and local schools in Polar regions, exiled peasants and Trotskyites, murderers, thieves, inmates of G.P.U. convict camp in Norilsk-Dudinka district, building coal and nickel mines, and northernmost railway in the world; Polar farmers, actors and actresses and teachers.

CHAPTER I

TWO MAPS

THERE are two maps in this book—one at the beginning, one at the end. They belie each other.

One pretends that the whole northern edge of Asia, the Arctic, cannot be developed. No civilized people (it declares) can live there regularly. Its earth cannot or will not yield its treasures to mankind; modern travel is impossible. A death sentence is put upon a Continent.

The other says it can be done. There can be life. Ships can travel along the shores during part of the year; they can be guided with ice breakers. Aeroplanes can link the centres of man and keep up contacts throughout the year. Plants can be made to grow on the soil. Precious minerals can be lifted from the earth, factories constructed, towns built. Thousands can live there.

It goes further. All this (it says) is being done already. There are ports by the mouths of the rivers. Radio stations are working. Man has developed his technical abilities so highly that he can bring life to the 'land of white death'. This map issues the birth certificate of a new world, and issues also the passport for man into it.

.For me, it all started in London. The Ambassador of the Union of Soviet Socialist Republics 'requested the pleasure of Mr. H. P. Smolka's company at tea to meet Professor Otto Yulievitch Schmidt, Chairman of the Northern Sea Route Administration at the Council of People's Commissars'.

I bought the latest economic map of Northern Asia and, armed with it, arrived at Kensington Palace Gardens.

'Is this the Soviet Embassy?'

The butler's face was enough to tell me the answer.

15

'This is Lord Rothschild's residence. The Russians live next door.'

In a gold-and-white drawing-room stood Dr. Schmidt. We already knew his rich black beard and his gleaming blue eyes from news reels and photographs.

He is Russia's Arctic Hero No. 1. In 1934 he gained the sympathy and admiration of the world. 'First circumnavigation of Northern Asia in Cargo-Passenger Boat', the headlines proclaimed when he and 120 men, 6 women and 2 children set out on the *Chelyuskin* from Leningrad in July, 1933. 'North-east Passage crossed in one season', they announced at the beginning of November, when the ship sent its radio message: 'We are in sight of Bering Straits.'

'Premature winter imprisons Arctic Expedition six hours before final victory', came the announcement a day later. The Chelyuskinites had been caught helplessly in the embrace of heavy pack ice. The wind had turned. The temperature fell. Ice floes came dangerously near. Arctic night came on. Ship and passengers were enveloped in frost and darkness. Their ship drifted back north and west —back towards the place whence they had come. The rapidly freezing East Siberian Sea was not to release its victims. In February we were reading: '*Chelyuskin* sunk. Passengers marooned on drift ice.' For sixty days they camped on the ice. It broke here and there; it almost split the kitchen hut in two. Once they had completed clearing a landing field on the ice for their aeroplane and that of rescue parties, the treacherous ice gave way, and a narrow lane of water cut across the field. This happened twenty times. From day to day the radio operator, living in a tent at 15 degrees of cold, reported to the world the agony of life in Camp Schmidt. During these two months the bearded Professor kept their spirits up. Being atheists, they were debarred the consolation of prayers. All they could trust was the skill and courage of their comrades ashore and of others all over the country who struggled to

come to their help. The leaders saw to it that everybody
kept fit in spite of the cold and the darkness; regular exercise was compulsory to keep off scurvy. And Schmidt gave
them lectures on science, on history, mathematics, on
modern theories of psychology. Illiterate carpenters from
the backwoods of Karelia, who had joined the Expedition
to build houses on Polar islands, were taught to read and
write and were initiated into elementary arithmetic. In
March the first aeroplane succeeded in landing near the
camp, which was then hundreds of miles away from the
shore, and always in danger of melting into the sea with
the warmer winds. The aeroplanes brought the means of
rescue.

To save space, men were packed into the petrol tanks of
Lyapidevski's machine so that as many as possible could
be carried away in each flight. Nobody knew when, or
even whether, the machines would return, and so it was
agreed that rescue should be by rota, with the women,
children, sick and weak to be taken first. On April 13 the
last batch was brought to safety. Russia made holiday.

Remembering these events, I expected to hear Schmidt
tell romantic accounts of Polar exploration, of the thrilling
struggle in the Far North, of the discoveries and achievements of scientists in Nature's last unconquered reserve.
Instead, he spoke of the Arctic, as Rhodes would have
spoken of South Africa or as an eighteenth-century pioneer
of America, as a land of promise. He held out to us a prospect of wealth and beauty beyond dream—a prospect that,
he said, was to be a reality, waiting to yield at last its
virgin pride to man, now that he has armed himself with
the latest technical inventions. He unfolded his own map
of Arctic Asia, so widely different from the one I had bought.
He kept us all in eager suspense. We wriggled between the
vision of Siberia as the America of to-morrow and our gnaw-
ing incredulity at the fairy-tales of a Red Columbus.

Here are some of the things he said:

B   17

'Russia has embarked upon a great scheme of industrialization, navigation and aviation in the Arctic. We are building towns and ports in the Polar regions, factories, mines, vegetable plantations, aerodromes, schools and hospitals. People believe that the Arctic is waste land, incapable of development, useless to mankind, a frozen desert. They are utterly wrong. The cold is no obstacle against human habitation. Usually the winter temperature in the Arctic does not fall below 40 minus. Such temperatures are quite usual in other parts of Russia, long recognized as industrial centres; the Ukraine, the Urals. The lowest temperatures do not occur in the Arctic at all, the pole of greatest cold lies only 90 miles away from the Okhotsk Sea in the Far East. The climatic characteristic of the Arctic is the cool summer. But this is bearable. Even plants find that the continuous sunshine which prevails day and night during the Polar summer compensates them for the chill in August. Beautiful flowers grow in the Arctic—violets, marguerites, forget-me-nots, they grow even bigger than here, because their growth is not arrested overnight. The same applies to our cabbage plantations. We get larger cabbage leaves in the Arctic than on the Volga. The people in our Polar towns eat fresh vegetables, which they grow themselves in the open air in hotbeds and hot-houses: tomatoes, cucumbers, radishes, cauliflower. Now we are experimenting with wheat and oats. Our geographic position demands that we should look north. The whole northern coast of Asia is ours. It is our only independent coastline. We own half the Polar basin, half of all the shores of the World's Arctic Sea, 6000 miles of it. There is coal, oil, gold, silver, platinum, nickel and plenty of other valuable metals underneath the ice, precious tin, delicious fish and excellent timber—we are going to get them. Our largest rivers flow north into the icebound sea, the Obi, Yenisei and Lena. They are the longest rivers of Asia, among the longest of the world. We are going to take

products up and down these rivers, change them over to ocean vessels at their mouths, and thereby establish communication from Europe and America, the Pacific and the Atlantic to Siberia, which was formerly regarded as the backyard of Asia.

'We have lined our northern coast with radio stations to assist our Arctic navigation and aviation. At difficult spots we have stationed ice-breakers. They guide our shipping caravans through the drift ice. We have fifty-seven Polar stations. Their staff are young and courageous scientists. They stay there summer and winter and keep us and the world informed of the meteorological conditions in the Arctic—the weather-shop of the world.

'Our new Polar towns grow rapidly. One, Igarka, has up to 20,000 inhabitants during the summer, the permanent population is 12,000. Their life does not differ very much from that of other Russians. They have cinemas and theatres, dance halls, restaurants, kindergartens and clubs. In the summer of 1935 they were visited by forty foreign ships which came to take Siberian timber away.

'Our Polar settlements are linked by air lines—we have a fleet of over one hundred Arctic 'planes, 10,000 miles of regular passenger lines.

'We have opened the North-east Passage for navigation during three months of the year. An old dream has come true now that this new shipping route between Europe, Asia and America is established. It links our European territories to the Far East. In three hundred years not more than nine little boats have passed Cape Chelyuskin, the northernmost tip of Asia. In the summer of 1935 eleven of our cargo boats assembled there simultaneously.

'Our Government has formed a special company with the task of organizing this great enterprise in the North. Its name is Glavnoye Upravlenya, Severnovo Morskovo Puty —we say Glavsevmorput—it means Central Administration of the Northern Sea Route. All territory in the U.S.S.R.

beyond the sixty-second northern parallel has been chartered
to this company for exclusive exploitation. It is a modern
socialist equivalent of the East India Company. It owns
a territory fourth of the Soviet Union, one and a half times
the Indian Empire, thirty times England. Forty thousand
men and women are employed by it. They are the pioneers
and organizers of this modern colonizing enterprise. It is
a very sparsely populated territory. Only about a million
people live in it, one man to every six square kilometres.
In England 251 live on a square kilometre, in the United
States 13. We do not regard this Arctic Empire as a land
of immigration. We have plenty of free land in more
moderate zones. But another million people will probably
go to our Far North in the next few decades to organize
industry, agriculture and transport.

'We are greatly concerned with cultural work for the
Arctic natives. Before the revolution they were on the verge
of dying out. Now their birth-rate increases again. We
shall save them. Their cultural level will rise as we give
them modern methods and instruments of production.
They will be the future masters of this great dominion.

'All the men and women who have gone to the North are
unanimous in praising its beauty—its colours and shapes
the particular charm of the landscape—summer as well as
winter. There are no diseases; the air contains no germs,
it is the ideal country for tuberculosis nursing-homes and
holiday hotels. We fully believe the word stamped by the
American Polar explorer Stefansson: 'The friendly Arctic.'
But we do not only believe in it, we are really making friends
with the Polar world, we are bringing it to life and life to it.'

My daily work often brings me into a conflict between
two emotions: first, an exalted enthusiasm at the discovery
of really valuable and important news, something worth
noting and reporting; and then, secondly, the cold shower
when I remember that I have to reduce what I hear to the

realism of facts and figures, without which the world will not accept anything. It has been cheated too often.

So in the end I could stick Schmidt's tales no longer, and I said : ' Do you think, Professor, that an unbiased observer without party tickets, and a layman as far as Polar science is concerned, would find the same picture if he were to visit your realm?'

Schmidt answered quickly: 'Why don't you go and see for yourself?'

There were some thirty people in the room. I could not back out. We fixed an appointment for the coming summer, 'either in Moscow or somewhere in Arctic Asia'.

I had doubts about it all later that evening. Was I the right person to penetrate into this new field of Soviet activity? I have the not uncommon habit of drawing back like a snail and hiding in a house of stiff disbelief as soon as I suspect that anyone is trying to feed me with propaganda. And then, would the people have confidence in me, seeing that I would go without party tickets of any kind? I knew my Russian to be fair-to-middling from former travelling in the Soviet Union, sufficient to make myself understood and to get the meaning of what people would say to me. Curiosity was stronger than modesty, and so I spent the next months reading accounts of Arctic explorers, descriptions of Siberia and the Polar regions. While Germany marched into the Rhineland, Haile Selassie lost his Empire, and Downing Street adopted an attitude of wait and see, while I cabled what 'was authoritatively reported in diplomatic circles about the future of Abyssinia' and telephoned what 'was learned in usually well-informed quarters about the British Government's policy towards Germany and her claims for colonial expansion', I had at the back of my mind pictures of future Arctic towns, centrally heated, illuminated day and night throughout the Polar winter. Week-ends were spent refreshing my Russian, and certain afternoons reading dusty parchment volumes in the archives of the British Admiralty. There I learned details about the earliest Elizabethan ambitions to send ships over and round the top of the world. . . .

The spiritual ancestors of the Bolshevik *polyarniki* I found had been the English merchant adventurers.

In the sixteenth century Portuguese and Spaniards had occupied and monopolized the southern oceans. It was a risky thing to butt in on them and try to snatch a slice from the cake of discoveries for which they were just then reaching out greedily.

To find an alternative route to India, which would save the hot and stormy trip round the Cape, Columbus sailed west. His journey was regarded as a failure. 'North America revealed no treasure, no useful commodities but fish.' Soon it was found out that the spice island he had discovered was really no half-way base on the journey to Cathay at all, but a barrier blocking the road to the treasure chamber of Asia.

But the century had set its heart on finding far-off lands, full of sweet perfumes, silks and precious stones, of balms and spices worth their weight in gold. Whoever found a new route round the world, a shorter route to the Fairy East—they thought would grow enormously rich, King, tradesman, or nation.

In 1527 an English merchant who lived for a long time in Seville, then centre of Spain's world-discovering activity, wrote a memorandum to Henry VIII imploring him to finance and godfather such enterprise. 'Most Excellent Prince', he addressed Henry, 'experience proveth that naturally princes bee desirous to extend and enlarge their dominions and Kingdomes. That natural inclination is cause that scarcely it may be said there is any kingdome stable nor king quiet but that his owne imagination or other princes his neighbours do trouble him.' After this statement—as valid to-day as then—good Mr. Thorne proceeded to say that he regarded it his 'bounden duety to manifest a secret which hitherto hath been hid. That with a small number of ships there may bee discovered divers new lands and kingdomes in the which Henry VIII shall winne perpetuall glory and infinite profite.' Mr. Thorne's magic word was 'The North'. 'For that the four parts of the worlde it seemeth three parts are discovered by other princes. For out of Spaine they have discovered all the Indies and Seas Occidentall and out of Portingall all the Indies and Seas Orientall. So that now rest to be discovered the sayd North parts which it seemeth because of the situation of Henry's realme it was this excellent prince's charge and duety to do. The cost therein will be nothing in comparison with the greate profite. Shippes in Northern Seas may passe and have in them perpetualle clerenesse of the day without any darknesse of the night: which thing is a great commoditie for the navigators. . . .' In case this monarch was just then thinking of his Anne or Catherine, Mr. Thorne rubbed this wisdom of his in twice and thrice, exclaiming finally: 'I thinke there is none so ignorant but perceiveth this more plainely than it can be expressed'—a very tactful way of telling a king what one thought of his mental capacities.

According to Mr. Thorne, all one had to do to get to Asia from England was 'to passe two or three leagues before the pole and as much more after the pole and thenceforth the seas and lands would be as in these temperate partes—a pleasure to the mariners'. He promised access through this route to 'Tartaria, the lands of the Chinas and Cathaio Orientall, to Malaca and all the Indies Orientall, once over the pole to the backside and south seas of the Indies Occidentall and continuing their voyages through the Strait of Magellan home again or right towards the Pole Antarcticke and then between the Tropikes and the Equinoctiall without doubt finding there the richest landes and Islands of the Worlde of golde and precious stones, balmes, spices and

23

the thinges that one esteemeth most, which come out of
strange lands and may returne the same way'.

Mr. Thorne even drew a splendid little map of the world
to illustrate his arguments. Nevertheless it took another
twenty-five years before the first attempt was made. In
1553 under Edward VI an expedition was equipped and
dispatched to the north-east of the world. His Majesty
had ordered home from Seville Sebastian Cabot, Chief
Navigator of Spain, and made him Grand Pilot of England.
Cabot organized the 'companie of the Merchants adventurers for the discoverie of Regions Dominiins Islands and
places unknowen', became its governour and sent Sir Hugh
Willoughby and Mr. Richard Chancelor with three boats
on their trip; the *Bona Esperanza* had 120 tons, the *Edward
Bounaventure* 160 and the *Bona Confidentia* 91. (They are
now building ice-breakers of 10,000 tons and 12,000 h.p.
in Russia to blast the same route open for three months in
the year.)

So sure were the courageous men under Cabot—admirable for their powerful imagination as much as for their
courage—that they would get to India round the north,
that they had their ships lined with lead outside, because
they had heard that certain worms living in the hot climate
of India 'were destructive of wooden sheathing'. These
were probably the first English ships coated with metal.

Unfortunately Sir Hugh perished off Lapland. Mr.
Chancelor got to Archangel and from there walked down
to Muscovy. He established contact with the Grand Duke.
The practical outcome of the generous enterprise was the
first British-Russian trade agreement. The company soon
satisfied itself with developing her trade with Russia and
was shortly only known as the Muscovy Company. The
Dutch tried later and so did more English sailors. But
although Count Herberstein, Habsburg Ambassador in
Moscow, had sworn in his treatise 'Rerum Muscovitarum
Comentarii' in 1549 that Asia would be found just round

the corner as soon as one passed the North Cape, even the brave sailors of that age found the Kara Sea so full of ice and fog when they approached it that they thought they had reached the end of the world.

The British beat the Spaniards off the world's seas later on. There was no more need to sail round the north and over the Pole. In the seventeenth century the Russians pushed forward east and in the eighteenth north by land instead of by sea. Tsar Boris Godunov forbade the use of the Arctic Sea because the merchants, jealous of their profits on land-transported goods and the bourse in Nijhny Novgorod, and the Cossacks, anxious to preserve their grip on Siberia, had warned him that as soon as foreigners would come to the mouths of the Obi and Yenisei they would snatch away the trade with China from him.

The nineteenth century brought the Suez and the Panama Canal. The trade route round the north as a means of getting to India and China had lost all importance. But as access to Siberia itself the vision never died completely. Somehow or other the English always took a fancy to it. Captain Wiggins tried the Kara Sea route sixty years ago and lost a good deal of money—some of it collected for him from the public by *The Times*. In 1876 Nordenskioeld completed the circumnavigation of Asia for the first time in history. But he as well as Amundsen and Vilkitski (the only three people to succeed before the Russian revolution broke out) took two years and had to winter half way. That deprived the whole idea of any commercial importance. Shortly before the War, however, a Norwegian merchant concentrated upon the venture to establish regular trade with the eastern and western halves of Arctic Asia by sea. By a mere chance I was able to dig him out in London, where he lives now and is engaged in other commercial activities.

Now what has the twentieth-century business man to say about it? After a few conventional words over a glass of whisky in his Pall Mall flat Mr. Jonas Lied looked at me with his grey eyes—an odd mixture of shrewdness and melancholy. 'I envy you your journey', he said. 'Who has been to the Arctic once will always be craving to return. And I have been in love with Siberia since 1907. I have gone through the Kara Sea five times, and have brought cargo from England and America. I have unloaded from ocean steamers into river steamers in the Yenisei estuary, and have been stalking for reindeer and wild geese in the tundra. . . . You will have a grand time.' He spoke with a very slight Scandinavian accent. 'And apart from the beauties of nature, Mr. Lied. Do you believe in the practical, economic possibilities of what the Soviets are doing? Do you think that Arctic shipping routes will become a factor of importance in world trade and in Russia's strategical position?'

'We invested almost a million pounds in that belief as far back as 1916. Of course we lost it all. Not because the idea was unsound. It was the revolution. Sixty of our river steamers on Yenisei and Obi and one hundred and seventy of our barges were confiscated; the State took over what was our monopoly of transport on the two large Siberian streams. We had already established canning factories, wood-pulp works. Work had begun on a shipyard for river craft near Krasnoyarsk. Equipment for the first modern timber sawmill on the Yenisei was brought from Sweden. Large forest concessions had been obtained from the Tsar's Government. In 1912 I had founded the Siberian Steamship, Manufacturing and Trading Co. Ltd. in Oslo. All our plans were based on the use of the Kara Sea route. Up to that moment nobody had yet been able to make a commercial success of it. Our first expedition failed. In 1913 the Company found fresh capital and dispatched a larger vessel, the S.S. *Correct*. This time we invited Fridtjof Nansen to accompany us and give his opinion as the foremost authority on the Polar Sea on the practicability of this shipping route. He was doubtful when he set out. After his return he wrote the famous book *Through Siberia, Land of the Future.* He was convinced. The journey was a success. In 1914 I sailed again, this time with a fleet of eight vessels from England, Germany and Norway. They all returned safely with Siberian cargoes. After the outbreak of the War our activities were curtailed. Nevertheless, in 1915, we brought a caravan once more from the Yenisei and the Obi and shipped Siberian butter to the value of £350,000 to London. For the first time arrangements were made for the use of aeroplanes to ascertain the position of drift ice. We made a substantial profit. In 1917 we brought the most valuable goods at that time to Russia : shoes, clothes, coffee, typewriters. We sailed to Siberia from New York between Greenland and Iceland round Scandinavia to avoid German submarines. We had to land in Archangel. The revolution had broken out. Our cargo was confiscated by the Soviet Government.

'I lost everything. Yet somehow, you know, this is not what I resent. I managed to get on an even keel once more. But I could be happier with £100 made out of a timber mill which I personally lay out somewhere in virgin taiga than with ten or a hundred times that amount on the London Stock Exchange. Perhaps you will think me crazy. But in 1923 I wrote a letter to the Soviet Government offering them my services as an expert and organizer of the Northern Sea Route for 500 roubles a month. I was willing to go through all the hardships they had to endure; prepared to give up everything else and, of course, exclude all motives of private profit. They had no confidence in me. They could not believe that all I really cared for was the development of that route, the opening up of that country. What did they know of the trouble one has with shareholders when trying to get them to put up more money for a pioneering effort ? Their mistrust was too great to let them see that I often thought it would be better to have a Government charge me with this work rather than a group of people who were primarily interested with getting a quick and bulky return on their investments. On the other hand, of course, I was quite aware of the dangers of wastage involved in Government enterprise where considerations of profit do not count and do not act as a brake on avoidable expenditure. Anyway, what is the use of going into all that now. It is history to me; no longer daily work. And yet, you know, there is hardly a day when I do not think of the Northern Sea Route as my dearest baby.'

It was the first of several conversations. We started in a bachelor flat in Pall Mall. From dimly lit, bronze-coloured walls a portrait of King Oscar of Sweden looked down upon us; the room was full of souvenirs of my host's days in Russia. Looking at my *vis-à-vis* and listening to his words I somehow forgot our surroundings. Back came the figures of the merchant adventurers. Here was a man similar to those early pioneers, to whom building, construction, exploration, and production meant more than their reward, men who got their fun out of the work itself. Who thought of growing life and not of growing dividend. He is of the type that made the *bourgeois* epoch great and pushed the world ahead. I learnt to understand him—late-comer of capitalism, standing between two eras, no longer in harmony with the world he helped to create.

Seeing all that, unable to alter it, Jonas Lied longs for Siberia, for the Arctic, and envies me about to go there.

CHAPTER II

POLAR ARMY, HEADQUARTERS

' St. petersburg is not Russia', the critics of Tsarist times
used to say when foreign friends praised the beauty of the
capital and forgot the misery and filth of millions behind
the façade.

'Leningrad is not the Soviet Union', the Bolshevists ought
to announce to visitors who enter their country by this port.
When I embarked at London Bridge, I left a city of matter-
of-fact houses. Five days passed: North Sea, Kiel Canal,
Baltic, Gulf of Finland. . . . American millionaires and
emigrating Communists were among my travelling companions. And then came the first view of Russia's greatest
port, awakening thoughts of rococo mistresses deserted by
their royal lovers; down and out. . . . The broad open
spaces with which Peter and his descendants lavishly endowed their new capital are still there. But the palaces
of Grand Dukes and the patrician houses of the merchants
have lost their glamour. Their richly adorned façades
look grimly defeatist. Some appear not to have been re-
painted since the revolution. Others, with broken windows
and missing bricks, seem to recall street battles as though of
yesterday, not of twenty years ago.

Everywhere else in Russia the picture of new life outshines
the evidence of past shambles. In Leningrad the old
phantoms still exercise an eerie power. They hover over
the young gardens and the sports stadiums, choke the
breath of life in the workers' housing estates and industrial
plants. You feel that they hate these witnesses of a busy
present, these heralds of a better future. They almost
succeed in crushing and silencing all demonstrations of a
new and different power. Caryatides with broken noses,

29

crumbling stucco, plaster architraves coming off in bits and threatening to fall on workers' demonstrations—such is the first impression of the city's appearance, and I have almost to force myself to reproduce the picture of newness that is present in Leningrad, as it is anywhere else.

One of the palaces with an exterior worse than many others is the former residence of Count Sheremetev. Inside : a labyrinth of back-stairs and dark corridors. Wooden partitions have divided bedrooms, dining-halls and ball-rooms into halves and quarters. From the walls little plaster angels and cheap copies of Florentine Renaissance sculpture look down, covered with dust that gives them an oddly puzzled air. They had seen well-dressed people collecting curios, holding banquets, fostering little intrigues. Then, suddenly, came years of darkness and cold. And now: what funny goings-on. Young men and women, clad in blue and white uniforms bow over desks and map tables. They peep through microscopes, hold test-tubes against the light, tap little hammers on samples of stone and earth, make calculations and draw diagrams. . . .

In glass cupboards stand ships' models and stuffed animals. On the walls, where the red silk tapestry is bleaching and falling to pieces after years of moisture and dust, hang photographs of Mongolic fur-clad humans, utterly different to the elegant officers who danced here a generation ago, and even very much unlike the less fashionable but still European-looking youths now at work in these halls—the halls of the Arctic Institute.

Russia's University of Polar Science could not wait for new and worthy buildings to be erected for its laboratories and reading-rooms. Work is driven forward all over the country under the impatient command of the second Five-Year Plan. Ever-conscious is the feeling that construction and development are racing with an approaching war.

I walked through the rooms. A girl explained to me her study of the chemical composition of sea water. Samples had been brought from different parts of the Arctic Ocean. Their salt content varies in accordance with the quantity of fresh water poured out by the great rivers, the composition of the floor of the sea and the currents. And the salt content in its turn influences the ice formation.

Her friend opposite was comparing meteorological data, the strength and the direction of the wind, temperature, fog, moisture. Elsewhere stones and earth were being analysed by geologists from samples sent by expedition centres in the Far North of Asia. White owls, stream-lined gulls, miniature penguins, foxes, hares and squirrels stand on the shelves in the biologists quarters. The naked embryo of a Polar bear, as small as a human hand, grins out of the bottle of spirit in which he is preserved for eternity, half-finished.

Geology, geophysics, geodesy, oceanography, biochemistry, biology, hydrochemistry, ice analysis. . . . To the three hundred and fifty members of the Institute they are elements of strategy in a war of conquest against the ice cap of the world. Behind their books and preparations they see a *fata Morgana;* a greater yield of Arctic mines, safer shipping in the Polar sea, the extension of flying seasons into the winter, flying hours throughout the night, more certain weather forecasts for the world from the centre of its meteorological moods, increases of fur from the forests and steppes of the North.

'We supply the scientific armoury for the battle against the Arctic. Our team of research workers and scientists form the cadre of officers to our Northern Army.' So the work was explained to me by Professor Samoilovitch. The close contact and intercourse between theoretical investigation and practical construction in the Arctic is a chief point of satisfaction to him and his brigade. The greater the economic yield and progress in the North, the deeper their consciousness of having contributed to the increasing wealth of the nation.

More and more women apply for vacancies in this Institute from year to year. It has become a fashionable ambition for university graduates to be a Polar explorer.

Applications for lecturers to leave the Academy for a few hours pour in daily. I was shown a letter signed: 'Study Circle of the Red October Factory for Artificial Rubber Products, Resino Trust, Leningrad', asking for an expert in zoology: 'We would like to know about the latest progress in precious fur breeding in Northern Siberia.'

A clumsily written post card read: 'Please can Professor Wiese come and lecture on the history of Arctic exploration. He or somebody good. We can send a lorry to bring him down. (Signed) Village Soviet Collective Farm named Vera Figner, Leningrad District.'

.   .   .   .   .   .

While the new occupants of Count Sheremetev's residence look after the sea and land, the heavens above and the treasures under the earth, the flowers and mosses, the swimming, creeping, running, jumping and flying population of the Arctic, their colleagues at the Institute of the Northern Peoples (housed in a former convent) devote their attention to the human beings. Count Sheremetev liked to be in the midst of fashionable St. Petersburg. The monks of the Alexander Nevsky monastery preferred the quiet of the suburbs. The chapel is now a lecture-room. The dormitory is a classroom; the refectory a gymnasium. As I walked through the Institute, a man was making his bed in one of the cells, a man with extraordinarily high cheekbones, receding forehead, protruding jaws and a leathery dark brown skin. The Russian Jew who was with me addressed him in Tungus. 'I am his teacher', he added to me. 'He has a great talent for literature, and so I translate his poems into Russian. Incidentally I learn as much from him as he gets from me.'

In the Institute altogether are 223 men and 87 girls, aged

between 18 and 32. All the twenty-six different nations and tribes of Asia's North are represented. Each student was picked for his intelligence and inclination for modern Soviet ideas. Communists travelling as Red missionaries in the tundra and taiga of Northern Siberia made contact with them and now they are being studied by ethnologists and linguists. Scholars are coming from America—led by Professor Boas—to hear of new theories and scientific findings about these nations, many of whom were more legends than men to the civilized world until yesterday. In return, teachers and political agents give to the natives the gist of Red Russia's civilization. Their childhood was spent in tents, in continuous travel over the vast expanses of the North. And now this modern city is like a fairy tale to most of them. After two, three or four years they still look at it more or less as an enchanted world, calling their school 'Chudesny Chum': The Tent of Miracles.

I saw them practising the foxtrot, getting ready for a visit to the cinema, writing a report about an excursion by aeroplane, listening to a lecture about the engine of the motor car, and relating their impressions of factories and mines. They were taking gliding and parachute lessons when I visited their summer camp on the Estonian border. But yet, with it all, these same people still fall back upon superstitious beliefs of witches and demons at times.

'Who knows', they argue, 'perhaps the dead machines, which can move without human or animal force, are driven by mysterious spirits which the Russians have learnt to master. They call them coal and petrol. But the teacher does admit, doesn't he, that these fuels were once trees and plants before they had lain in the ground for thousands of years? Why should the spirits of the trees, whom we have learned to respect in the taiga, not preserve themselves even for many centuries of sleep underground? Who can define the difference between the gods of plants and animals and the spirits who draw cars over roads and lift steel birds into the

C

clouds? Who is right, the Shaman who used to put the fear of all these spirits into us during his dances in Arctic nights or the Soviet encyclopedia?'

I saw and heard much among those students and their teacher-friends who think that the jump from Stone Age to the twentieth century is possible at a few years' notice. Yet the full encasing of what I was told was brought home to me only when, a month later, I reached their actual country and met their countrymen in the Far North.

. . . . . .

In Moscow I spent a fortnight interviewing all the chiefs and vice-chiefs at the office of the Northern Sea Route Administration. Here again: 'Our new offices ought to have been ready by now, but then it was found more important to give our floor in the Palace of the Council of People's Commissars to another organization, and so we have to wait.'

To wait means crowding five people into an office for two and keeping seven visitors who called to see the Chairman within fifteen minutes waiting among the clapping typewriters of his secretaries.

Each morning at ten I arrived at Glavsevmorput, as the organization is called, and was given a room to myself, a privilege I fully appreciated. A battery of bottles of iced Narzan mineral water, plates of caviare and ham sandwiches, tomato salad, chocolates and sweets, and a box of cigarettes were waiting for me on the desk. In the perfect order of a perfectly arranged schedule the chiefs and sub-chiefs appeared, sat down, helped themselves to the delicacies, answered questions, put facts and figures before me. There was Papanin, chief of the fifty-seven Polar stations, a stout little fellow, decorated with the Order of the Red Banner for his deeds in the civil war and with a golden watch for his work on an expedition to the North. There was Comrade Geze, a former Hungarian mechanic, now in charge of

all the naval operations in the western half of the Arctic
Ocean. Bogomolkin, the head of Arctic agriculture, unfolded his diagrams and maps and showed how far up
north one could drive wheat culture, vegetable plantation,
potato growing. The chief of the 'Culture Sector' went
with me through his records of educational activities and
of the number of schools, colleges, libraries erected in the
Arctic. The political department gave me samples of local
newspapers published in villages or on boats, on a Polar
station or on ice-breakers, and they opened the archives
where the best wall-journals are kept for an annual All-
Union prize.

.   .   .   .   .   .

Opposite the offices of Glavsevmorput is a cellar: a mouldy
little hole. Down there I went to get my costume for the
North. It is the store of Arctic Snab, the outfitting department of the Polar organization. Hanging behind curtains
and on raw wooden shelves there were furs, leather coats,
shawls, sweaters, and high boots, half-boots, low boots, all
made of rubber, felt, fur and leather; gloves reaching to your
elbows, pilots' overalls, sleeping-bags. I had received a
voucher entitling me to a summer outfit: a long leather coat
with a lining of brown lamb's wool, which is detachable in
case of an Arctic heat wave; a headgear, also of brown lamb's
wool, with ear flaps that can be tied over the top to form a
pleasant sort of crown or brought down over the cheeks
and tied under the chin; a pair of leather boots, well oiled,
which can be drawn almost to the hips or rolled down
concertina-like. (I was to have continuous trouble with
these boots later, because I did not share the Siberians'
pride in having them flapping round the feet at every step.)
I was also given a pair of white felt boots, which I carried
half-way round the north of Asia without ever needing them,
and finally left them at the most outlying point of my
journey with a local engineer. He had forgotten to take

35

some out for his two-year stay and gave me a slip of paper torn from my note-book as a receipt. The most fascinating pieces of equipment, however, were the gloves. Three kinds of leather and two qualities of fur were spent on them. They could be worn as gloves pure and simple or, by loosening a few straps and buckles and releasing a little hidden sack of more fur, as a muff.

I may admit that it was difficult to find the proper sizes for me because I am not exactly slim. Neither, for that matter, is the average Russian and so I got what I wanted after an hour and a half trying on and putting off. True, the boots were two sizes too large and the coat one too small; but three pairs of socks and a pair of stockings brought my feet up to the dimensions of the boots, and a belt safeguarded the coat on my back.

Then I went on to order some foodstuffs from the 'Gastronom', which sent them to my flat just half an hour before I left. I bought tinned fruit, chocolate, cheese and some of Russia's delicious vegetable and meat preserves, all completely unnecessary as it turned out, for the dining-car on the train had quite good provisions this year. Finally, after eight days of fuming and waiting while red tape was unravelled, I got my Arctic *visa*, confirming that the journalist Smolka was entitled to go to the otherwise closed regions of the Soviet North, thanks to this special permit issued by the Foreign Department of the Moscow section of the Commissariat of Interior (the late G.P.U.). I folded it neatly so as not to break the photograph and found it exactly in that position when I cleared my wallet a week after my return to London. Nobody had asked me for it during the whole time in the North.

CHAPTER III

TO-MORROW'S AMERICA

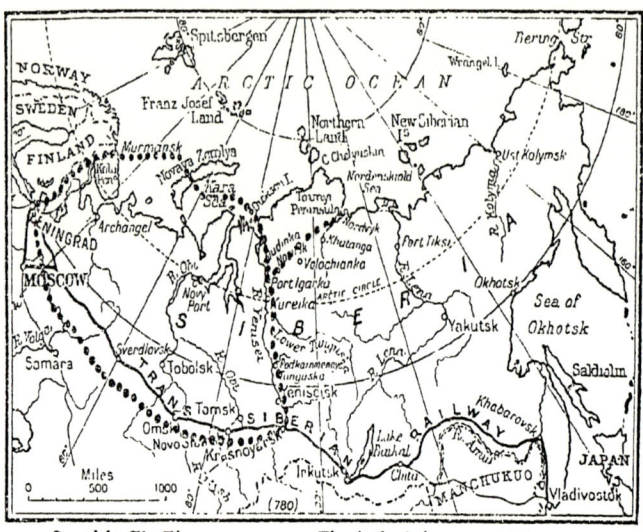

Copyright *The Times*.   The Author's journey. ●●●●●●

A JOURNEY on the Trans-Siberian can be exactly as romantic
as you want it to be. Your coach is like any European
sleeping-car, though a little larger because of Russia's
wider gauge. Stay in your compartment, read a crime
story, and nothing extraordinary will happen. If you
have never been outside Europe, you may be surprised to
hear the conductor asking you whether you want a bath
every morning. Should you travel on an all-Russian express
(as I did) instead of an International train the attendant
will offer you a chessboard and men, or dominoes—and a
partner will not be lacking. The attendant is equally proud
of his lending library, an institution first started on the
Polar Arrow—the train which links Leningrad and Murmansk, the Baltic and the Arctic Sea.

Here was I then on the longest railway line in the world. It stretched back as far as Lisbon. Ahead it goes on to Vladivostok. I look out of the window and take a lesson in contemporary agrarian history: In France, in Germany, in Poland, I had seen small plots of land, a chessboard, every man's property fenced off against his neighbours. Now long stretches of continuous fields swing slowly by; they belong to collective farms.

At every stop I do as my travelling companions: step off the train to stretch my legs. The others run for the free hot water supply, the *kipyatok*, with tea kettles in hand. I loaf through the waiting-rooms. There are hundreds of peasants camping out—waiting for local trains which will take them along. Besides his ticket every traveller must have a *platskart* entitling him to a sleeping-berth. There are more people who want trains than trains to take them. Goods trains of wheat and machinery, guns and aeroplanes have preference over passenger trains. Hence the crowds on the platform and behind the scenes of every station. Greybeards with long hair, looking like apostles, hang around for days. Women lie on benches and nurse their babies. Youngsters sleep on the floor. There were five times as many four years ago, they waited then for weeks where now they wait for days: the industrialization campaign has set millions of people wandering; travelling, to new places of work, to towns, and towns to be. At Kazan I heard the loud speaker relaying gramophone music—*Carmen*. At Omsk it is *Rigoletto;* at Novosibirsk the Internationale. There is music at 4 a.m.

A signboard—'For mother and child'—above a door at Sverdlovsk, in the Urals, attracts my attention. An ante-room behind it is called 'Sanitary Filter'. Women and children who come out of curiosity, or because they know its meaning, are examined by nurses, sent to the bathroom and have their clothes disinfected before passing further on to a rest hall with divans or to a kindergarten with Liliput armchairs and painted toys. Red spots on a toddler's skin are the sign for a woman doctor to be called; the child is examined, the mother told what to do. A suite of white painted rooms combines hospital, bath, kindergarten—and the inevitable bureau for cultural propaganda. The most backward women who fear and distrust doctors and progress are caught in an atmosphere of friendliness and, once disarmed of their shyness and suspicion, exposed to a frontal attack of popular education in hygiene. A 'milk kitchen' supplies clean food for the babies.

At Omsk I wanted to buy a picture post card and was sold a colour reproduction of old Persian miniatures instead of a view of the town. My complaint was met laconically by the sales girl: 'Our travellers can describe in their messages what they have seen; a good example of art will stimulate their interest for culture. And, besides, we are sold out.' At Taiga, a day further east, I battle against my suspicion of some wild strawberries and cream offered by peasant women at stands along the platform. 'Don't worry, citizen, it's all clean and fresh—they are official representatives of collective farms, their goods are inspected', a fat Mongol officer assures me, while his fingers dissect a roast chicken.

Travelling for hours without coming to a stop, I compare the map in the corridor with the landscape outside the window. On my left the green-grey billiard table of steppe and prairie goes on for two thousand miles northward to the Arctic Ocean. So far the plain has not risen to more than 240 feet above sea-level. Below the horizon on the right is Central Asia, Afghanistan, India. Another day and we shall be over against Mongolia. No railway goes up north, none down south. Only aeroplanes and tracks for horses, mules and camel caravans. One thin railway line—single track until a few months ago—cuts through this continent. More than one-third of it runs dangerously near the frontier, continuously open to be attacked by enemy aircraft in case of war.

A friend of mine once wrote that trains were to the Russians what cafés are to the French: meeting-places, debating clubs, social centres, where political ideas are passionately thrashed out and engagements rashly entered into. A foreigner in a Russian dining-car is a very welcome target for searching questions about conditions abroad and frank declarations on life at home. Escape is possible only if a heated debate starts among the hosts themselves. That provides an easy opportunity for unnoticed retreat to one's own compartment. But I did not always want to escape.

Rumbling over a steel bridge into Novosibirsk, the new capital of Western Siberia, we were again busy discussing the future. Doctor Shlakhman, who went to take up his post as chief of the new medical faculty in Irkutsk, pointed to the town that rises from the banks of the Obi, and said: 'This is Asia's Chicago. Junction of the east-west line of the railway; the cross-road of the north-flowing river; the link between iron and coal of Kuznetzk, cotton of Turkestan, wheat of the wide plains around. You can get off here, and go by rail to the Pacific or to the Atlantic, or by river to the Arctic or to the sub-tropics.'

I had Nansen's book with me. I opened to the page at which he described Novo Nikolayevsk as it was twenty-three years ago. Nansen had taken a photograph from the window at the spot we were passing now. The picture showed wooden shacks, one-storey houses. The text gave the population as 79,000.

Dr. Shlakhman looked up his 1935 guide book, and read out: 'Population 300,000; plants for mining and agricultural machinery; clothing factories; centre for mechanization of agriculture; railway repair shops . . .'

'But why are there so many skyscrapers?' I asked. 'There is plenty of space in the steppe all round the town to build extensively.' He stopped for a moment, and looked at me as if he were a bishop whose faith was being attacked. Then he said: 'Because all this is to-morrow's America!' Although as an answer it was not quite to the point, I did not doubt the statement. I believe the contention that Siberia is 'the land of the future'.

The towns we passed through were bristling with new life. Since the revolution they have grown like mushrooms after the rain. Sverdlovsk, for instance: 1920—90,000 people; 1936—500,000. And there are new centres such as Magnitogorsk with 37 families in 1926 and a population of 160,000 ten years later. The country is enormously rich in natural wealth. It has the largest gold deposits in the world, although as for producing gold Russia ranks only second. Siberia's forest is quantitatively and qualitatively supreme. In the Kuznetzk basin it has coal enough to supply the whole world for three hundred years, according to an estimate by a French scientist. In the Tungus basin it has at least as much again. It has more platinum than the rest of the world all told. Its iron ore, its oil deposits, its untapped metals, its rare earths, its tin in the north and its copper in the south, and its waterpower of 128,000,000 kilowatts, single it out for the mightiest and most prosperous industrial area of the future. In the Far Eastern provinces alone seven hundred various deposits of gold, platinum, silver, lead, zinc, copper, tungsten, coal, oil, iron, manganese, have been located so far. The figure goes into thousands if one includes west and central and southern as well as far northern Siberia. An area the third of the whole of Asia and twenty-five times as large as France, it lacks only two things: men and transport. Since the completion of its conquest by Russia in the first years of the eighteenth century this huge country has only been settled by 23,000,000 people as against the 260,000 counted at the start. Its native population was decimated in these two hundred and fifty years. During the last century exiles came to Siberia at the rate of one every forty-five minutes, 800,000 within sixty years. But who cared to come voluntarily into this land? It had the reputation of being a wild and unhospitable backyard of Asia, a vast prison. Yet out of the blood of political and criminal prisoners has sprung up in Siberia a sturdy race of keen and energetic people. They carry many of the characteristics which we know from some Americans and some inhabitants of one or two British Dominions (those which were at one time convict colonies). These people have endurance, broad-mindedness, a sense for opportunity and the will to use it.

They suffered from the curse under which the country lived. It is a geographical freak: the richest and least accessible area in the world. Only now that Russia has given up all thought of territorial expansion and concentrates on the development of its own riches are they given support in exploiting the wealth. According to conservative estimates of non-Russian economists, Siberia could house something like 300,000,000 people and nourish and provide them with all modern comforts.

This I pointed out to my dining-car companions as the train continued from Novosibirsk, and we all felt the greatness and emptiness of the country through which we travelled.

'You are complaining of a lack of workers, and on the other hand you do not open your frontiers to the unemployed of the world. Why don't you settle the overpopulation of the world here?'

'It would not solve your own problems, it is the economic system that's wrong with you, not the disproportion of space and men,' one of them said, a party instructor named Stolaroff on a speechmaking tour to Trans-Baikalia.

The waiter butted in. He was 'off duty' since we had all finished our meals. 'Problem or no problem', he said, 'why don't we let them come to us. Don't we need an extra six men on this very train? Does not my brother complain that his *Kolkhoz* is dangerously understaffed. Are not the steel plant at Kuznctzk, the power station on the Angara and the truck factory at Chclyabinsk, all advertising in the papers for workers. The factory at Omsk, where my wife is employed, has sent three hundred circulars to all the farms in the district to ask them at least for seasonal workers, and the women in the plant were offered commissions for each girl friend whom they could induce to leave their children in kindergartens, and join the factory.'

· Stolaroff reprimanded him. 'It is no solution for us and none for the world if we take over their unemployed. An army of saboteurs and spies would come with them. The Japanese from the East and the Germans from the West would not only send us workers. They would send agents to disorganize our construction and to help their own ambitions of expanding at our cost and becoming virtual neighbours, perhaps with a little Russian buffer state between them at the Urals or on the Yenisei. It is our duty to settle this country and develop it. The world does not suffer from a wrong distribution of land between the nations, but from a wrong organization of the distribution of wealth within the nations. We must have more children —that is the lesson to draw from our journey to-day. Thus you will understand why the Government and the Party say that abortions must become illegal now that the fundamental means of subsistence are guaranteed to every family. We want to turn these steppes into wheat fields and gardens, to build roads and towns, factories and mines. Siberia is to be no colony, but an integral part of our country, exchanging goods with other provinces and primarily supporting its own people.'

Land of the Future. To-morrow's America, a new Siberia . . . all that depends on effective communications. Britain has conquered and opened for mankind the richest areas of the world, while her own soil was comparatively poor. Her Empire is not much older than two hundred years. She knew how to use her position in the centre of the world seas. Russia possessed the riches of Siberia for almost three centuries. The conquest which was begun by Yermak took hardly sixty years from the Ural mountains to the shores of the Pacific ocean. It was effected by miniature armies, or bands of Cossacks, and met with almost no resistance. Their vast colonial empire, however, remained sterile, giving prosperity to a ridiculously small number of *entrepreneurs* because (apart from all questions of social organization) the country was landlocked. Its only independent link with the world's oceans is the ice-bound Arctic sea. Its large rivers all flow into it. The solution of the crucial problem is to open the frozen window to the north. Even America carries trans-continental home trade in bulky commodities by sea and river and not by rail. For Russia and for Siberia the necessity for using the sea is even greater.

I get off the train on the fifth day. From now on I shall travel on without railway or roads. Aeroplanes, boats on the rivers, ice-breaker and steamers on the sea will be my vehicles.

CHAPTER IV

ARCTIC VESTIBULE

I STEPPED out on to a chilly railway station. The coach, with its enamel plate 'Stolpce—Moscow—Manchuria', faded into the mist of the early morning. 'Three o'clock', said my watch. 'Three o'clock', concurred the clock on the station building. In fact it was seven here in Krasnoyarsk. I had forgotten to put my watch forward in accordance with the eastward course of the train, and railways use Moscow time all through the Continent. When a train reaches Vladivostok at 'midday', people are already dining, and the sun has set.

I looked round. They had promised in Moscow to send a wire to their local office. 'The Consul of our North Asia Company will fetch you from the station', they had declared heartily. But here was only a sleepy station master and a bearded porter. The first suggested I better put my luggage into the cloak-room and try to get in touch with the man I wanted to see in the town. The porter, true to type, advised me to take a car and find a place in the hotel right away. He wanted to make some money before breakfast.

A blue-coated *isvostchik* was just having an argument with his skinny horse outside the station.

'How much to the hotel?' I asked him.

'Twice ten roubles', he said.

'Once ten roubles', I said automatically.

'One and a half times ten roubles', we agreed.

His horse would go to straw without dinner to-night because of my meanness, he sulked.

The *isvostchik*, by the way, is about the last private business-man still tolerated. Together with a minority of the peasants and such people like the cobblers who wander from market to market with a portable shop of wooden boxes, he is

45

represented as a narrow white sector in the red circle of Soviet statistics showing the process of socialization. He owes his opportunity to survive in 'stubborn capitalistic psychology' to the scarcity of taxis. In a few years time nobody will be prepared to pay his fares any longer. He will die out like his symbolized effigy in the recent Russian film, 'The last coach driver'. Meanwhile he charges four or five times as much as the municipal taxi trusts. The reason: he has to pay for stable and fodder, the prices asked by other 'ghosts of capitalism'. Socialized motor cars are fed on socialized petrol and housed in socialized garages. Capitalist horses must eat hay bought from private peasants, and sleep in stables rented from the last remaining private house-owners.

I dumped my luggage on the box. The driver enthroned himself on top. My fur and boots, a burdensome parcel wrapped in brown packing paper, had to be placed on the floor of the tiny Siberian hansom. My legs rested on the back of the driver's seat; in fact my position as I rolled into Siberia was oddly like that of the Prime Minister in the House of Commons when the Leader of the Opposition attacks the Government.

Tattle-ti-rattle—the wheels, more oval than round, bumped over the cobbled station square. A minute later we were ploughing through dust, hoof deep. The town was still asleep. Occasionally we overtook a delivery cart bringing foodstuffs from a *Kolkhoz*, with the farmer dozing behind his horse, which in its turn took its job rather easily under the wooden troika. When an army driver flashed by in his open Ford car, a smoke screen would flare up from the dusty ground and give him a strategic shield from inquisitive eyes. Where my pre-War guide-book indicated the site of the Hotel Gadulof, my driver stopped. The sleepy woman hall-porter of the new 'Guesthouse Red Trade' apologized: 'I am sorry, citizen. There is not a single bed left in the house. The steamer for the North is leaving in a day or two. We have fifty-six more people

46

staying here than we can really accommodate. They are all waiting to embark for the Arctic' . . .

I paid my carriage off at the offices of 'Arctic Air Lines', a set of two-storied block-houses near the banks of the river—or near where I imagined the river to be, for my eyes peered only into a drab nothingness. In the hut an old man in polar uniform was busy dusting desks and type-writers. He suggested that I should go to the bath house—he would watch over my luggage—until the chief of the local Avyo-Groupa turned in. It was a welcome idea. In spite of the double windows on the Trans-Siberian train, the red dust finds its way through the tiniest fissures of the wooden coaches.

When I returned, thoroughly steamed and scrubbed, the Yenisei had condescended to start its day's work. Flowing majestically, it was now fully visible in all its curves. With the mountain background of Krasnoyarsk it reminded me strongly of the Danube near Budapest. But its dimen-sions were truly Siberian. The Tokmak, local equivalent for the Schwabenberg, reclined lazily in the dim distance. A red painted railway bridge has been flung across the river here, and the Soviets are just presenting it with a strongly built twin brother. They fear a few Japanese aeroplanes might after all get through outer Mongolia and bomb it, interrupting communications between Eastern Siberia and the chain of industrial bases along the line to the Urals. A single track railway bridge crossing a river, almost two miles wide and full of treacherous rapids, whirlpools and shoals, is certainly a very poor strategical contrivance.

The Russians firmly believe that the martial programme of Baron Tanaka envisages Japanese conquest up to the Yenisei. I often heard the joke repeated in Krasnoyarsk that the bridge would become the frontier between Germany and Japan, were Hitler and the Black Dragon society allowed to have their way. 'But the Red Army and Air Force and our new defence works in the Far East, which are double the size of the Maginot line between France and Germany, will

47

prevent the Nipponians from getting in.' Five aerodromes around the city are further proof of the strong strategical importance which is attributed to it. I also saw a new face among the photographs of Bolshevik leaders displayed in shop windows, public offices and social centres in Krasnoyarsk: the face of Field-Marshal Blücher, Chief of the special Far Eastern Red Army. His headquarters are in Khabarovsk; the campaign to make him popular starts here, and goes on increasingly towards Transbaikalia.

Business had started when I entered the office of 'Avyo Arctica' again. A young man in white uniform studied blueprints at the desk in the main room. Opposite him a dark-eyed official wrote out aeroplane tickets. He was clad in a grey linen blouse, brown embroidered, worn outside the trousers and held round the waist by a leather belt. A workman's cap hung over his left ear.

I produced my documents, including a letter, which was solemnly read out aloud:

'The bearer, foreign journalist Smolka, is going to the Arctic to acquaint himself with our economic activity in the Far North. He needs information for a book he is writing about our Polar work.

'Mr. Smolka is to be shown what he wants to see and to be given all necessary information as well as permission to make personal contact with the local population on his route: Krasnoyarsk, Port Igarka, Cape Chelyuskin, Dickson Island and Murmansk. His transport is to be facilitated by all means available.

'(Signed) OTTO YULIEVITCH SCHMIDT,
Chief of the Central Administration of the Northern Sea Route at the Council of People's Commissars,

and
'(Signed) O. M. SERKIN,
Vice Chief of the department of Political Administration.'

48

This paper seemed to impress my *vis-à-vis*. He got up, shook my hand and said, apparently without suspicion at seeing a foreigner in an otherwise well guarded part of the Soviet Union: 'Good. First of all we shall have to secure a place for you to sleep in. There is no room at any hotel. Comrade Nurik has a spare room. You will be his guest while you are in Krasnoyarsk. Is that O.K. with you?' (He said that last sentence in English.)

'Quite O.K.,' I replied.

Comrade Nurik was writing out aeroplane tickets. Now was his turn to get up and shake hands with me. 'Unfortunately', he said, 'I speak no English. Only Russian . . . and a little Yiddish, if that would be of any help?'

During the next few days we spoke an odd mixture of languages at Nurik's house. When I used a wrong expression in Russian, I repeated it in German; when I could not make out what he meant, he said it in Yiddish, whereupon my knowledge of German allowed me to grasp the meaning. His wife spoke Russian only. But she was very imaginative and took great pains to make herself understood. We could converse over the most difficult questions without ever needing recourse to dictionaries or interpreters. In the evening I was introduced to my host's father.

Nurik senior quickly put a coat over his shirt-sleeves when I entered the room, got up formally and introduced himself in immaculate English. He spoke German and French as well. 'I am delighted to meet you, sir. You come from London, my son told me. I have a brother there. Perhaps you know him. He is also Nurik, of course. Isaac Nurik, 33 Bedford Place, was his last address. I have not seen him since 1921. Then he left for Constantinople and I returned to Russia, where my family had been without news from me throughout the civil war.' Mrs. Nurik, or rather Tassya Alexeyevna, as we called her in Russian fashion, asked whether he would not continue his speech sitting. She brought a quickly prepared dinner, obviously cooked with special generosity in my honour: Bouillon of beef with noodles, meat with rice and potatoes, tea and jam, which Nurik ate from a little plate, whereas Tassya put several spoonfuls into her cup. Cake and cream finished our fare.

I asked Nurik where he had learned his languages.

'Oh, I was a wealthy man before the revolution. Do not judge me by my clothes. I come from Odessa. I was manager of a great firm of grain shippers. I have travelled abroad, have been to Paris and London several times before the War. But, by the way, do not misunderstand those references to the past. I am not grumbling at my present fate. I am still working. It would not do to live on my children's earnings although they could and would willingly keep me. It would not suit my sense of independence; I am not broken by the turn of history. You must not think that. . . . I am very happy. My children have all done well. . . . My eldest son is in Vladivostok. He is a member of the Party, and occupies a position of responsibility. . . . Have some more of this jam. It's really good. There was not any three years ago. . . . You must excuse me but my memory fails me sometimes, or if I get confused. After all I have had a very moved life. . . . Oh, yes, now I know. I was talking of my children, of course. . . . Well, my eldest son has made a very nice career. He is a Communist. I was always keen on giving my children a good education. That is worth more than leaving them a fortune, my wife used to say. And developments proved her right. Knowledge was worth more than money when the revolution came. You cannot confiscate a brain, can you?'

He leaned towards me and added in a low voice: 'It is queer. All my children are married to Russians. I am not a Russian. I am a Jew. So is my wife. But our children, like all the young people nowadays, do not think anything about getting married between the different nationalities. Oh, inter-marrying is the word; I am sorry. My daughter's

husband is a Russian. My son's wife here, she is not a
Jewess either. A very good girl nevertheless ; I like her.
Keeps his house decently and looks after him nicely, although
she has a job herself. And Rudolf is always tidy. Have you
seen Rudolf? That's my grandson. Not my only one,
no, no, do not believe that. . . . My father, of course,
would have killed me or himself if I had married a Christian
girl. But then times have changed. There are different
beliefs now. I am a very happy man nevertheless. I see
my children are all healthy and I have five grandchildren.'

There he paused for a few seconds: 'The Nuriks were
always ones to get on. Since Stalin said: "Non-Party
Bolshevists are to be respected as much as Party members if
they do their work properly", I think there is nothing to
worry about any more. Even I cannot complain: When
I got to Moscow from Odessa I got a job within two days.
The same in Krasnoyarsk. All I have to do is think "timber"
instead of "grain". The work is the same: export. A man
with brains will find work in all circumstances. Do not think
that it applies less to-day than fifty years ago. Look what a
nice house they have given my son! Of course, you must
judge it by comparison with local standards. They bought
it for him from an old merchant. It is made entirely of
stone. Look' (he got up and hammered on the wall with
a spoon) 'that keeps it just as warm as the log cabins in the
winter, and it is much nicer than all the others.'

I nodded consent. He went on: 'You must not think
that I am telling you all that because I am an old gossiper.
But after all I have not spoken to anybody from abroad for
a long time, and I do not like them to think out there that
all the old people from good families and with a proper
education could not hold their own under the new régime.
. . . There is a room for the boy and his wife, and behind
the kitchen a nice place where I live. You will sleep here
in the dining-room; they have brought this iron bed for
you in the afternoon. Rudolf has his little bed in the

51

parents' room during the day, and at night Babushka, the
maid, takes him out to the kitchen where she sleeps, so
that she can keep an eye on him and talk to him in the morning when he starts crying. He sings at four when the cock
in the farmyard next door gets up. Hope he will not
wake you up, this Ganef. Great God, now I have kept you
almost an hour with my talk. It was a nice change; thank
you. We shall see each other every night now until you
leave. But I will not always take your time so long. You
must not believe that.'

Krasnoyarsk is the jumping-off point for the central region
of Arctic Asia. To me it was the vestibule to the Red Empire
in the North; a large waiting-room, an assembly place. It
is the centre of the 'territorial administration' of Glavsevmorput. Other such bases are Leningrad, with a branch
in Murmansk; Novosibirsk on the Obi; and Irkutsk, with
a branch in Yakutsk on the Lena. The territory administered from Krasnoyarsk is almost 800,000 square miles,
772,000 to be exact, more than eight times the size of Great
Britain, or a quarter of the whole United States. River
transport on the Yenisei, the spine of Eastern Siberia, is
organized from here. It covers a distance of altogether
4000 miles (including tributaries and short distances on
both sides of the estuary). A mine for coal and nickel,
1500 miles down-stream, which is being built at present,
is provisioned with machinery and food from here. The new
Arctic air lines operating in North-eastern Siberia have their
administrative offices and repair base here. Fishing, fur-
trapping and wood-cutting are organized here. There is
a wharf for river steamers, a factory for gold-washing
dredges, timber-sowing machines, a paper combine, graphite
works. State farms for agricultural produce, cattle and
reindeer breeding belong to it; some of them are right up
in the Arctic, others are in sub-Arctic regions. They
provide food for 1400 industrial workers, 1000 river sailors

and roughly a thousand ocean sailors and up to 1500 scientific and manual workers engaged on Polar stations and radio outposts.

It has seen a good many changes, this Krasnoyarsk.

At the end of the sixteenth century a Cossack leader, who had good reason to put some miles between himself and the capital, set out with a small band of men eastwards from the Urals. Not more than 2000 started with him. Yermak Timofeyevitch himself was drowned on the way in the river Obi, and later, when his history was written, his figure presented a difficult problem to Russia's scholars. They ought to have condemned him because he lifted the sword against the will of the ruler. But he was in fact the first conqueror of Russia's vast colonial Empire, the first to dare out into the fairy wilderness behind the Urals. By 1626 the Cossacks had reached the Yenisei. At the end of the century they stood at the shores of the Pacific. Where it was necessary they carried their boats across land from one river to the other. Krasnoyarsk, 'the red ford', was founded by them as an outpost on the Yenisei red sand shore. Their watch tower on the yellow sand hill overlooking the valley is still there, and nowadays lovers hide in it on hot summer nights.

About a century after the Cossacks came the traders. They imposed a fur tribute upon the natives. Ostyak and Tungus princes were kidnapped by Cossack gangsters and kept in dungeons. Once a year the fur racketeers allowed the tribes' elders to come and look at their hostaged elders. If they paid ransom money in grey squirrels, brown sables or white ermines, they assured another year's board and accommodation for their princes. This congenial system lasted until the eighteenth century drew to its close.

Soon gold was found round about Krasnoyarsk. There is much fine gold in the rivers and mountains of Siberia, and, although the Russians have kept secret the figures for their gold production during the past few years, it is known that theirs is potentially the richest gold country in the world.

At the end of the nineteenth century Krasnoyarsk gained a new lease of life. The Trans-Siberian Railway was built, and here was an important junction for rail and river transport. Coach drivers, stage inns, repair shops for saddlework and wheels—all went bankrupt. Contractors for food supplies to the convict gangs who built the track made tons of money. So did the bridge builders. They put a splendid steel construction up at one point where the Government inspectors looked at it. Then they copied the bridge in wood at fifteen other places. A few years later the bridges were ruins, and the rails screwed on to rotting sleepers had to be replaced. Crooked people had a fine harvest. Yeniseisk, the old patrician trading centre a few days' journey down the river, fell into decay. The merchants then had got so rich that every large family built its own church.

During the Great War more than 20,000 Austrians, Hungarians, Czechs, Poles, Croats, were brought to Krasnoyarsk, Russian troops having taken them prisoners on the Eastern Front. A few thousand died of typhus. Several hundreds starved or froze to death. The stronger boys seduced the peasant daughters on the farms where the Government made them work while the Russian men were at the front. Many married, and I met some who have forgotten their native language by now. When the Reds came into the town the private soldiers joined their ranks. When the Whites came, the officers—particularly Czechs— joined up with them against the Bolsheviks. Partisans and Red Army finally drove Admiral Koltchak to Irkutsk, where he was executed. This White Russian leader had dreamt of the Arctic Sea route before the War. Siberia sees his dreams come true fifteen years after his death.

To-day most houses in Krasnoyarsk are hidden behind scaffolding. New floors are put on to old houses; wooden extensions and improvised shacks extend into the backyards as temporary accommodation for the swelling number of factory hands and administrative workers. In the midst of deafening noises, rhythmical hammering, out-of-tune riveting and nerve-racking cries of rusty winches, students are at work in the half-finished new college for agricultural science. I wonder if they feel this as a symbol for their own psychological transformation: peasants into land-workers. Their future is in organizing tractor stations, supervising the building and running of grain elevators, instructing 'older elements' in the careful treatment of agricultural machinery, controlling repair shops for all the puffing, rattling and petrol-drinking monsters who invade the Siberian plains and promise to wring more food from the soil in shorter time.

The side streets are still lined with blockhouses full of carved window sills, reminding one of Swiss and Tyrolean architecture. Pavements: wooden boards. Half an hour's rain turns the dusty valley of a road into lakes and waterfalls. Hours afterwards the place is still an expanse of slimy mud. Horses sink in over their hooves, men to their ankles, motor cars to their axles. The asphalting of the main street holds out a promise of general modernization at a later stage.

'When the second Five Year Plan is completed and the war danger perhaps removed, then we shall have money and time to reconstruct old towns. Meanwhile too much of our energy has to go into armaments to keep the Japanese and Germans out.'

The monastery on one of the suburban hill-tops has been turned into a barrack for part of the local garrison. On the grassy slopes gypsies have put up a tent and have settled for a few months. They offer you prophecies in French and German, for they have been as far as Lille and Vienna during the last twenty years. In the church a priest is still celebrating divine service, but the secretary of the local Young Communist League asked me not to photograph

55

him doing it: 'The new Constitution affords liberty of thought to everybody. That implies respect for other people's feelings. They are dying out anyway. Why spoil their last years by annoying them with cameras?'

I needed a gauze hood to protect me against the mosquitoes which, the local paper reported, were particularly vicious in the North this summer. Hoods were sold out in the stores. The commission shop, where old-timers gradually dispose of their china, furs, silver, cutlery, 1906 Kodaks, embroidered table covers, pianos, brass and silver samovars, could not get me any either. 'The old merchants never went up to the North themselves', the Red sales girl remarked sarcastically. So I went to the bazaar on a free day. (Every sixth day is free day in Soviet Russia now. Only rural communities hold on to their Sunday.) There at the outskirts of the city on a flat plain near the banks of a poorly watered river-bed, a primitive form of private trade is going on. Whoever wants to sell anything pays a few kopeks admission fee, plants himself in what he thinks a favourable position, and holds out his goods. You can get embroidered shirts made by peasant women in spare days, nicely finished boots made by industrialized cobblers after the seven-hour factory day is over. Gramophone records are sold second-hand. Someone who has to move to another part of the country gets rid of his library to save the cost of transport. Old editions of Tolstoy and Turgenyev, pamphlets on foreign policy, mathematical and physical text-books (natural science is always in demand) wait to be bought by eager readers. Chinese cobblers do odd jobs while their customers wait, with naked foot in the air. Anybody can sell the product of his own labour. Employment of workers for productive purposes is forbidden; organized trade and industry are State monopolies.

The market is a ghastly caricature of dying capitalism. Walking shadows of a defunct economic system—returned to infantile primitiveness. In other countries you go to the market to do your shopping more cheaply than in shops; here it is the contrary. Prices are in no relation to actual values. They are much higher than in the 'competing' State shops. But because there are still certain products which cannot be bought in the shops occasionally, when supplies lag behind increasing purchasing power, this bazaar can still hold out; sometimes speculators will buy up small quantities of boots, or coats, or stockings, as soon as new deliveries arrive from the factories. Then they wait until the stocks are exhausted and use the interval before fresh supplies get down from the factories to dispose of them in the bazaars as 'second-hand goods' at twice or thrice times the price of the new.

There is a large whitewashed building with thick high walls in Krasnoyarsk. Bolsheviks pass it with mixed feelings. To them it is a relic worthy of sacred respect. At the same time it holds some of their deadliest enemies now. Lenin, Stalin, Sverdloff, Dzerjhinsky, an honoured roll call of revolutionary leaders spent nights and even weeks in this half-way house. They had come from Russia by train. Here they were kept until sufficient numbers of exiles were assembled to justify a further convoy down the Yenisei, the old highway of whole generations of State enemies or of courtiers fallen in disgrace. By foot or in barges, on roads and by monotonous rural paths, they travelled on to outlying Siberian villages. Now Krasnoyarsk prison is still in use. Last year two Japanese spies were executed in the courtyard. The speculator at the bazaar who sold me a black gauze hood for six roubles may sit behind these whitewashed walls to-morrow, waiting his turn to leave for a prolonged stay in the country.

CHAPTER V

SHALL WE JOIN THE LADIES?

'How do you people in Krasnoyarsk spend your free evenings?' I asked young Nurik once.

'Well, there is a cinema and a theatre. Tassya likes to go to the Park of Culture and Rest or the restaurant at the "Red Trade" where they have got a jazz band now. I myself do usually still a little work after the meal. You see, the office is only next door and the others are also there most of the time. We do want to get things into proper shape this season. So we mostly put in an extra two hours or so each night.'

I went with him. The officer in white was there, and greeted me with another merry display of his golden teeth.

'Everything O.K.?' he asked. 'Everything . . .'

'What are you doing to-night, Comrade Shevelyov?'

'Oh, there is a *sobranye* after nine. The pilots' wives meet to discuss a few things. It won't interest you. Just a few routine questions, you know.'

'Does that mean you would rather have no foreigner around when they come?'

'Not at all. By no means. If you like please stay and listen. Only do not blame me if you are bored. Should you stick through it to the end we could go and have a spot of supper towards eleven. Have not had a bite since this morning.'

'A good Bolshevik, eh?' I teased him. . . . 'Too busy to think of himself.'

'A bad Bolshevik', he replied seriously, 'too inefficient to organize his time properly.'

So we went on to a whitewashed room in the log house, lit generously by a shadeless 250 candle-power bulb. Soon all the chairs were occupied. The newcomers had to sit on desks and window-sills. Two by two the women had come in. A young Ukrainian first, pretty in her red silk dress, her nationality easily betrayed by her accent and chestnut hair. An Armenian, velvet-eyed, olive-skinned, and with long shining black tresses, had brought her little boy. He had the flax coloured hair and water-blue eyes of his father, whom I met a week later flying in the machine on which he served as mechanic. Indefinable was the origin of a conspicuous young woman with hair bleached to platinum blonde, and face richly made up with lipstick and black dye for eyebrows. She wore a white raw silk dress with red buttons and a flaring patent leather belt. Unlike the others she wore stockings, and her shoes were arrogantly conspicuous among the tennis slippers and sandals of the others. All of them seemed to regard this meeting as a welcome opportunity to show off their good clothes to the Siberian provincials.

The officer in white opened the meeting with his typical grin, and said:

'Comrades! We are meeting here to-night to discuss questions affecting our every-day life. As you know, a movement was started all over the country last year under the name "The Technicians' Wives". It enjoys great popularity by now. Many districts of our wide country—outlying places where villages, tiny towns, deserts and swamps are now rapidly turned into great industrial centres—are coming to life under the hands of Soviet workers, directed by pioneer technicians. Everywhere into these bustling turmoils of socialist construction, faithful Soviet women have followed their courageous husbands; nearly always they have to take upon themselves hardships and discomforts. These are unavoidable amidst the rapidity of progress in the battle for new life in formerly forgotten lands. The movement of the technicians' wives—which you, brave companions of our heroic Arctic airmen, have now joined—has a worthy object. It is well in harmony with Comrade Stalin's inspiring appeal: "Live better, comrades, live happier and more cultured".

'The technicians wives do not often take part in the active work of construction to which their husbands are devoted. But they are going to assist it indirectly in the most effective manner: by collective effort they have resolved to bring more comfort, beauty, culture into the daily life of their hard working husbands, officers on the front of construction. They want to make it pleasant for them, to relieve monotony, to inspire new strength and create new enthusiasm out of material improvement, better and more tasty food, nicer surroundings, cleaner clothes, more amusing social activity. They are assured of the full support of the Party and the Government, who are concerned for the happiness of the community. Our Culture Department has ear-marked 300,000 roubles for this purpose. Your criticism of existing conditions is as much welcome as your initiative for improvement. Above all do not forget, it is yourselves who have to build the new life.

'I now call upon you all to participate actively in our discussion and put your views forward keenly.'

Applause. Silence. Then a fair-haired girl gets up. She could not be more than twenty-two.

'Mark Ivanovitch, you have made a good speech. We appreciate your words. I am going to put my views before you right now and without restraint. My living quarters are very bad. My husband comes down from the North for two or three days every fortnight. The children are too small to understand he needs a rest. The two of them and my husband and I have only got a small room next to the museum on the Yenisei. With the best of intentions, I cannot secure the comfort he needs to regenerate his strength. How can we change that?'

A shadow passed over the chairman's brow.

'You are not telling me anything new. I agree with

you; such conditions must not be allowed to persist. We are very much concerned about it. On the other hand, you know their causes as well as I do. It is difficult to find good lodgings in Krasnoyarsk. The town has grown too quickly. There will be a marked improvement as soon as our house at the air base will be completed. Meanwhile, I have only a stop gap suggestion. Find out when a family will leave here. Let us know of it—we shall press the town Soviet to reserve their apartment for you. Beyond that, all of you go on criticizing housing conditions and talk your grievances round the town. Especially urge the people who are in charge of the building activity at the air base—not only Smirnov—he knows his responsibility as chief. The smallest and seemingly most unimportant labourers on the job must be made to understand that their utmost energy and resourcefulness are needed to turn the life of their comrades into a better one. They must understand that they have to put all their strength into their work; go on telling them that the people for whom they build the house are risking their lives daily in the struggle against the forces of the Arctic, which is going to make the whole community richer and happier. Write of your discontent on the wall journal of the building brigade—make them realize that their slackness means unhappiness to you, their efficiency a better life for all.'

The pretty Ukrainian got up next.

'The whole place on the island looks sad and dirty. There is nothing but sand and mud round the air base. Couldn't we get some flowers to make it all a little more cheerful? It would put a stronger love for his work into everybody.'

The eagle-nosed Armenian woman nodded support.

'But where are you going to get the flowers?'

'I did not think of that', the speaker admitted.

'You can drive out to a collective farm and get bulbs from them. I'll give you some money from our culture fund', replied the chairman, and added Point 2 to his notes of the proceedings.

'Since we are all supposed to talk freely here', the lady-like woman, whose make-up was proverbial in Krasnoyarsk, started, 'I might say that I think it most uncultured how all the men are running about unshaven at our centre. That's my own point of view, anyway.'

Everybody laughed.

'I do not defend the sloppiness of my sex', the chairman added to the general amusement. 'Care for one's own appearance is certainly an essential condition for a cultured social life. I have a suggestion to offer myself. If you like, I shall have a room reserved at the air base for a barber's shop. You write to Moscow and get a hairdresser to come out here, or hire an apprentice from the town. I notice, by the way, that the women barbers here are more efficient than the men. There will probably be a sound commercial basis for a hairdresser's establishment at the air base, with all the mechanics, engineers, pilots and ground staff about. If you like, you could even see that you get somebody who is trained for tending women customers as well, with permanent waving and all that.'

While all this talk was going on two children who had accompanied their mothers to the meeting played hide and seek between the chairs and desks and behind their mothers' skirts. They made quite a considerable noise and certainly disturbed everybody. But no one really took any notice of them. Now suddenly we saw a narrow wet spoor trickling suspiciously across the floor. The Armenian woman blushed and, swearing softly, rushed her baby out of the room, telling him obviously what kind of culture would have to be adopted first.

The young woman doctor who wore the jacket of the Polar uniform, with shining golden buttons, raised her voice now.

'I wanted to raise a problem at the end of the meeting.

But what we have just watched is tempting me to bring the point up immediately. Comrades, it is not good to take your children along with you wherever you go. It is also bad to leave them alone, because that arrests their intellectual development. Not all of us can, or want, to hire permanent servant girls. Now that the Government has asked for more children, and made abortions illegal, sixteen-hour kindergartens will be organized all over the country. But funds for additional staffs will only be provided in sufficient numbers to secure places for mothers who go to work themselves. So my suggestion to you is that you should organize among yourselves a rota by which one of you would do service at the kindergarten and crèche one afternoon or evening a week for the children of all the others. That is certainly a sacrifice worth while, considering the improvement which would be gained for the children. And I would even like you to take a resolution that the women who have no children of their own should equally offer themselves voluntarily for that service. Maybe'— she smiled, ' the contact with the toddlers will make them wish for an increase of population themselves.'

There had been a little dissent among the women when the girl doctor had mentioned the new abortion laws, which seemed to be less popular where housing conditions are bad than among women workers whose factories provide good accommodation for parents and children. But the suggestion was accepted, and by the time the Armenian woman came back with her newly dressed little boy, they hurried to communicate the news to her.

A fiercer attack was launched next against the restaurant at the air base.

'It hardly deserves the name of a restaurant', a quiet little woman declared. 'They boil the water for tea in open pots. Why, think of the dirt that can get in with all the building and engineering going on around. It is a scandal, comrades, a real scandal. They have not even

63

got a decent samovar. Nobody can tell me that they cannot get one because we are in a pioneer town in Siberia. The Sunday market is full of good secondhand ones. Nobody cares about it, that's the truth. And the food? Is that perhaps satisfactory? It is rotten, in my opinion. There is no proper hearth to cook it on, and when my husband came in the other day he swore that the petrol space on his 'plane is bigger than our whole kitchen. That is why they get the products half-finished from the eating-house in town. And those wise fellows at the Ulitsa Lenina send the worst stuff out to us at the air base because they want to keep the good pieces for their customers who would kick a row at the table.'

'Who runs the kitchen at the air base?' Shevelyov interrupted.

'A committee of women are supposed to exercise control over the staff.'

'And what has that committee done so far to remedy this impossible situation?'

The women looked at each other in silence and from the background roared a male voice: 'Nothing!'

'We have told the cook she is no good', the original plaintiff corrected him, 'but she puts the blame on the people in town.'

'What have you done to put the supply side of the matter in order?'

'Nothing yet; we wanted to ask your advice.'

Shevelyov gave them an *ordre de bataille* which proved his experience at such problems. 'First go to the *stolovaya* people and tell them what you think of them.'

'Do you think that will help much?'

'No, I don't, but you have to do it to be able afterwards to say you gave them a chance. If it does not help, you send a letter to the town Soviet, who are the body responsible for the eating-house, and complain. Should that not do the trick you can form a demonstration and march through the town to the Soviet, putting them up for public criticism. If that should still do no good, then I, in your place, would write a juicy letter to the local paper, the *Krasnoyarski Rabotchi*, and send a copy of it to *Pravda* in Moscow. It is a shame that our people should not even get proper food, if they take all the other discomforts of pioneering upon themselves. Such deficiencies are unnecessary.'

There was genuine appreciation for his diplomacy when he had finished. 'We are going to build a real scandal', the women laughed. 'You rely on us!'

The debate went on three hours. Once the women understood that their worries were given serious consideration they developed a holy zeal of criticism and new ideas. There ought to be soft furniture, easy chairs and settees in the waiting-room of the aerodrome instead of the wooden benches at present in use. One ought to buy heavy curtains for the winter and—to be safe—lay in a small stock of the material for later repairs, so that they would not have to be done in different colours, which is so often the case in view of the short life of early factory patterns. There ought to be curtains in all the bedrooms to make them look cheerful and 'cultured'; two sets would be better than one, because then one could always wash the light ones and keep the heavy ones to shield the room from inquisitive eyes without.

The tennis courts ought to be repaired—mountains and valleys, that was what they resemble. And how many rackets are there for eleven regular players and a whole Siberian province waiting to be initiated into this sport? Three good ones, and one with half the cords broken. Of two dozen balls which had been delivered seven months ago, nineteen had meanwhile disappeared in the waves of the Yenisei. Tea-parties should be organized so that all should get to know each other more intimately, and not always keep in cliques of two or three. The similarity of interest among the men should constitute a bond of friendship and solidarity among the women. And, in the end, Shevel-

E   65

yov was asked to order a big box of gramophone needles from Moscow. The local store had run short of them and for over a month the issue at the air base club had been to renounce the pleasure of music or ruin the records systematically by using worn-out needles on them.

. . . . . .

Tassya Alexeyevna had not been to the meeting. I met her afterwards at the restaurant.

'I am a working woman', she insisted. 'It is not good if women do no work. What do you imagine the people here think of these pilots' wives who walk about in nice dresses and amuse themselves while their husbands risk their lives every hour of the day and night in the Arctic storms and fogs? They make a lot of money—three times as much as a university professor, and spend nothing of it on themselves up there in the North. All goes to their wives. In a small place like this every movement of these women gives rise to all sorts of rumours. Even if there is nothing in it, gossip will spread nasty tales if they go to a dance with a student of the Agricultural College or walk along the Yenisei in the evening with an actor.'

She worked herself up. 'If all of them had children at least, that would give them something to do, and their lives would not be entirely useless. But look at them. I have worked out that less than 25 per cent of them are mothers. Only one has two children. Of course, there is no prostitution in Russia. But don't you know about the wives of the hard-working and much-earning technicians in Moscow, who live idle and alone for the greater part of the year because the men are always on some out-of-town job? Do you think that they have no friends? Why, it would be superhuman if they had not. And the more fashion goods appear in the shops, the more they want. And the stuff is still expensive. If a friend makes them presents they are certainly not reluctant to accept them. It is a bad thing, in my opinion. A woman ought to do something, especially in these difficult years, when we need every able-bodied worker more than anything else. These idiots, who boast that they can now afford to keep non-earning wives because wages for specialist work have gone up, think that a young girl will just sit and wait for them to come home late in the evening or even only once in three months. What do they imagine that their good girls are doing meanwhile? Just reading a novel, rearranging the furniture and polishing their finger-nails? Phoo!'

I put the problem to Shevelyov.

'Yes, it is true', he admitted; 'there is a certain small section of women who have been observed to develop erroneous tendencies these last two years since economic conditions have grown better all round. We realize that those of this type do also sooner or later exercise a bad influence on their husbands, and the men in general. My own wife has kept her job in the manometer factory, although we have a daughter, a nice apartment and a car, and I earn about six times as much as she could get. But it makes our relations more interesting, because she moves in different circles than I do, and it also brings a serious outlook on life to our little girl and stabilizes the foundations of our family life. Anyway, you have seen yourself to-day what we are trying to do. We attempt to harness just the tendencies towards comfort and enjoyment of life—which are decidedly negative if they remain individual—for service towards the community. And we have had practical and good psychological results. Some women have later resolved to put these activities on a planned and remunerative collective basis. They became interior decorators, organizers for kindergartens, fashion designers, window display specialists for department stores, club and dance leaders; some even found their way into serious artistic professions. But since you seem to be so interested in our women's lives—come along to my office early to-morrow morning. There you will see

67

a different aspect. An aeroplane mechanic, a girl of twenty-five, comes to consult me on her career. Stay in the room inconspicuously when she comes and pretend to read some papers. Then she will not be embarrassed, and you can listen how frankly she will speak to me.'

Galina Dimitrevna is Ukrainian. For three years she has been a mechanic on light aeroplanes. She has been a member of the ground staff at Krasnoyarsk base for eighteen months. I had noticed her the first evening outside the town office of the air lines. She wore a nice summer dress of light coloured satin, was powdered; her lips painted. When we went into the meeting she was just walking off arm-in-arm with a student of the Timber Institute, holding his hand and a little bunch of edelweiss, which grows as abundantly on the plain round the town as on Alpine peaks in Europe. Now she wore a blue overall; her face looked energetic and a little coarse without make-up. As I glanced over the edge of my book I saw a few tears in her eyes which were not at all in harmony with her self-confident bearing. '. . . That's what worries me, Mark Ivanovitch,' she was just saying to Shevelyov. 'I am making 450 roubles a month now. Of that I send 200 to my mother, who lives in Samara, and is too old to earn enough with her own work. My boy is eight now. And I keep him from my own wages. His father does not worry about us. And here I sit for eighteen months with no career ahead of me at all. This work of repairing light machines is not very interesting. You have seen yourself that I can do it almost in my sleep. There are no more problems in it for me. My life has become empty. I am a Stakhanovist; I have increased my productivity to 173 per cent above plan. There is no more room for improvement. Do you want me to go on like this for the rest of my life? Why don't you put me on to a heavy machine as a mechanic. I would enjoy work up there in the Arctic much more than sitting around here, simply overhauling machines, lubricating propeller bearings, clean-

ing and exchanging plugs and repairing carburettors. I
need not explain to you how sick I am of it.'

'Sorry, Galina Dimitrevna, it cannot be done.' Shevelyov
looked straight at her. 'Do not believe that ridiculous fairy
tale which—I know—you girls have put round about me.
I am no woman-hater at all. But flying in the Arctic is
the most difficult section of all our aviation. Sometimes a
machine will be *en route* for a week without getting to a repair
base. A board mechanic may even have to do a job in
mid-air.'

'It is not my fault that I am a woman, is it?'

'Be sensible, comrade. Look. You know there are
different types of machines. Some for this kind of service,
some for others. Surely you will never think one is better
and the other worse because they are built on different lines
for different purposes? The human body is also a machine.
And man and woman are quite different models. A woman
has other functions besides her work. That puts her out of
condition at times. We cannot let her do the heaviest and
most responsible kind of work in such circumstances. Either
she will overstrain herself and fall ill, or her work will suffer.
One side will always suffer. I am not telling you anything
you don't know. I just want you to realize the reasons for
my attitude. You will understand when I say you have
to put this idea of becoming board mechanic on a heavy
Arctic machine out of your head, won't you?'

'Well, Mark Ivanovitch, since you are the *natchalnik*
anyway, it is no use trying to make you change your last
word. I take it as your final ruling as chief and so I will
not discuss it any further. But that does mean, doesn't it,
that I have no more prospects in my profession?'

'Not at all.'

'I do not see any.'

'Why don't you study to become an aircraft constructor?
Your brain is certainly as good as any man's. I even think
that women are often better at work that requires exactness.

69

You have acquired a great proficiency in practical engineering. Do some theoretical work and you can secure more interesting and also more remunerative posts. There lies your chance to reach a higher intellectual and cultural level.'

'How can I go to the technical high school, since I cannot afford nine months' preparatory study, when there is no chance to earn enough money for my mother and child?'

'That I can arrange. We have a preparatory school now. I can get you a scholarship. You will have your uniform, which will save you from buying clothes. A room will be provided where your child can live with you. Food and books are, of course, free and, if you will sign a contract with us that you will work in our organization after you complete your studies, we can give you a monthly allowance of 250 roubles.'

'That would be enough', she agreed. 'I could send 200 to the old woman in Samara and 50 ought to suffice as pocket money. I suppose I could do some odd jobs occasionally, or earn premiums for good work, couldn't I?'

'Probably you could. At any rate, once you have passed your preliminary exam. and are admitted to the technical high school you are secured for six years until you get your diploma. Of course, your colleagues will have their whole stipendia money for themselves, whereas you send most of it to your mother. I do not want to discourage you from doing that, although I feel that she could probably live on her pension. But if you are keen on the work and eager to get ahead in life, you should not mind having to restrict your budget a little during a transitory period.'

'Well, that is a possibility. I'll have to work out a decent plan for my life. Let me think it over. I was getting all mixed up the last few weeks, when I saw that you would not give me a chance up North. I'll give you my reply in a few days. So long.'

No 'Thank you', and Shevelyov did not seem to expect

any. Triumphantly he turned to me: 'Well, Mister, that is another type of woman, don't you think?'

'I think that it will be damned hard on the wretched woman. She is twenty-five, has a boy of eight and a mother to keep, and that scoundrel husband of hers does not show up. You expect her to go to high school for six years and live on pocket money exactly one-fifth of that of her colleagues who have not got the responsibilities that she has. There are more temptations in Moscow, with clothes and dances, as you yourself have told me.'

'I am sorry if we don't understand each other on that point. I have worked myself up under much more difficult conditions after the civil war. In comparison I am offering this girl a sinecure. Perhaps you judge us too much from your Western standards. This girl is typical of the heroic young generation in our country. And at any rate I have my doubts as to how many mechanics are offered university training with pay in your Western Europe.'

CHAPTER VI

FLYING NORTH

GRAZIANSKI held the control column loosely; he wanted to show off. He was always talking of his new machine: 'a country cottage with a veranda to enjoy the view', he would describe it; or as being 'more comfortable than any other aeroplane in the Arctic'. Only a week ago he had fetched it from the hydroplane wharf at Tagan Rog on the Sea of Asov. It had no landing wheels, only floats. Nevertheless he had flown it over 2000 miles of land from the Southern Ukraine to Eastern Siberia. And now his immediate job was to impress me, his first foreign passenger, with the safety and comfort provided to Arctic pilots by the Government.

Leaning lazily back in his seat he let his fingers play occasionally with the controls. From time to time he looked out of his cellophane window to compare the course of the river below us with the hand-drawn map of the landscape which I held on my knees, a map ten feet long and a few inches wide, with 'Arctic Air Line Krasnoyarsk-Dickson Island' written in block letters across the top. While the country below unfolded its forest vastness, I wound the map up steadily on its cardboard spool. We were heading North.

Just when I began to appreciate the cosy warmth of my fur cap, and had decided I would soon tie the ear flaps down as well, Grazianski discarded his cap entirely. The strong air current whirled through his flaxen hair. He was a hand-some man; young, tall and broad-shouldered, with a forehead firm and clear like a warrior's shield. There he sat in his fur-lined trousers, woollen sweater, and black boots, enjoying every minute of his triumph over the air and looking for all the world like the symbolic poster displayed to Soviet youth to-day as its ideal: 'Knight of the Sky'. I wondered if he, too, had already sacrificed the refreshing naïvety common to the best type of Russia's young men to the spoiling consciousness of belonging to the country's modern stardom. He started singing. Steadily he grew louder, finding a new pride in being able to raise his voice just a little over the roar of the engine. I picked out the tune. This song he was singing out into the wind above the Siberian taiga had been in the mouths of all Russians last summer. Red Army men and school-children sang it; the teacher of Marxism knew it by heart, as well as the peasant girl on the collective farm; the jazz bands of the Café Metropole and the Savoy Hotel in Moscow had snapped it up; it was meant to sweep the country with its new spirit:

> ' Splendid land of mine so full of glory,
> Lakes and rivers, mountains, fields, so free;
> Do you know of any other country,
> Where the people are as glad as we? . . .'

Then he leaned across to me and shouted into my ears: 'Only an airman really knows what this song means: only we, who fly over our lakes and rivers, high above the fields, can appreciate how beautiful it is. Just look, there and there. . . .'

The earth was a huge disc. All around, its edges touched the sky. With its millions of trees the forest covered the land like a rich fur coat. The broad grey back of the Yenisei carried long timber rafts straight down its course; it knew its way well after thousands of years. Like a compass needle it cut through the plain: pointing north. Here and there a little lake, a tiny pool reflected the glittering light of the sky.

We had flown for several hours. Starting at three in the afternoon from Krasnoyarsk we took tea an hour and a half later at Yeniseisk, while Shevelyov, who was with us, inspected the new air base. Mighty glad to get to the Arctic after nine months of office work, he assured me: 'Who travels North takes the day with him. The sun stays longer the nearer one gets to the top of the world.'

When, at eleven p.m. we came down for the night at Podkammenaya Tunguska, we were 400 miles away already from the thin foliage of civilization that clusters round the railway line. The air base where we slept was in the midst of the virgin taiga. A full moon stood crystal clear in a sky which, from here onwards, became never fully dark again for me in many nights. The sturdy pine trees threw green shadows across the silvery cupola that roofed the earth. The air had the vigour and exhilarating freshness of high alpine peaks. Dark figures in sheepskins came down the steep hill towards the water where we had brought our 'plane to rest. We rowed ashore in a fisherman's dinghy, to be greeted by a pack of Ostyak dogs. Every move, gracefully elastic under a thick pelt, betrayed their parentage; through the first half-hour of sleep, I heard them howl to the moon an oath that they would never forget they sprang from the noble stock of free Siberian wolves.

We had some caviare and black bread for dinner; and a fish soup (quite as strong as Monsieur Prunier's Marseillian Bouillabaisse) and biscuits and whipped cream before we went to bed. The six of us slept in a large room, keeping the door to the kitchen open to let in the warmth of the huge brick stove.

At five in the morning I was up again. The chief of the station—a Jew, whose father had sold collar-studs, lent money and repaired Sabbath-chandeliers as the occasion demanded—told me of his childhood in the ghetto of Warsaw. Because of his tuberculosis, nurtured in damp basement lodgings during the first six years of his life, the Government had given him this job in Northern Siberia. I have never heard a more sincere appreciation of a political

area. Now our education authorities administer thirty-three schools from here and eleven of them are for my countrymen. The Tungus are now called by their own name once more: Evyenki. We are building a hospital centre; we have an air ambulance; next year our plan is . . . in the future we are going to . . . in the future in the future . . .'

While my companions are having a second round of lunch—their appetite has also grown to Siberian dimensions—I take a stroll through the place by myself. There is a hut bearing a wooden commemoration plate: 'Here lived Jacob Sverdloff, first President of the All-Union Executive Committee, during three years of his exile.' That reminds me of a letter of Sverdloff's which I had read and which is kept as a relic in the Moscow Museum of the Revolution. He wrote to his sister: "To-morrow they are going to take me and Joseph Dshugashvili (Stalin) to solitary confinement further up into the northern solitude. I will be taken to Turukhansk, Stalin some miles beyond the Arctic Circle to Kureika.' Turukhansk was a place for particularly dangerous exiles. It lies 800 miles north of the railway—twice the distance from London to Glasgow. At that time a monthly boat provided the only means of communication with the outside world (correspondence with relatives took three months).

'Our Trotskyists are better off now,' a local inhabitant assures me. He had started talking to me, while I looked at Sverdloff's hut. Now I recalled my surprise at finding a few men with pince-nez and felt hats staring at me from the shore when we landed. I had asked who these short-sighted solicitors were and what they were doing among the fishermen in this forlorn place. 'They are teachers in the school and economists on the collective farm', I had been told. Now I learned that they were political exiles.

Curious creatures, I thought, as I watched them going about their business in Turukhansk. Permanent revolutionaries; they have got conspiracy and rebellion in their blood. Could not leave it even when they found their own Party in power. Another young man who joined me insisted on explaining the political background of these exiles to me, who, according to him, formed 44 per cent of the local population. 'They are theorists only. When they found that the psychology of the peasantry did not develop exactly on the lines of the programme that they had themselves worked out on paper before the War, and when they saw Stalin shaping his policy in harmony with practical possibilities, they called him a Bonaparte and an opportunist traitor and decided that they had to smash him to save the revolution. But, by overstraining the development, they would certainly have ruined the country. They wanted the working class of Russia to dissolve the small peasantry within a few years; they insisted on a foreign policy in conflict with capitalist powers. That put them into the same boat with *provocateurs:* they were jeopardizing success at home and courting a Fascist attack on us at a time when we had not even established ourselves firmly at home. We had to bring them here where they can do no harm. They are victims of history. Pitiable perhaps as individuals. But we had to sacrifice them to save the country. Some became real criminals in their blind hatred, like Kamenev and Zinoviev, for instance. These two were quite near here before they were taken to the Moscow trial. And even here they tried to organize cells and opposition groups within their own small community. It was a real scandal.'

The short-sighted lawyers stood again at the shore when I left. Their glances at me were anything but friendly. Did they consider that the mere fact of my presence in this part of Russia was evidence that Stalin was again becoming too friendly with Capitalism abroad?

From Igarka onwards I had a bigger machine. The

N 150 had been a single-engined 750 h.p. wooden aeroplane. It had a cruising speed of little over 100 miles an hour, and could carry a ton of mail, or cargo, or four passengers. Its wooden structure made it unsuitable over the Arctic Sea, for the smallest ice-floe could smash its walls in taking off or landing. From Igarka, therefore, we had a large Dornier Wal, entirely of steel, bought from Germany six years ago. Its two engines developed 1500 h.p. and gave it a carrying capacity of 2 tons of cargo or up to fifteen passengers. It was certainly not a luxury liner; no country cottage with a veranda; and Sadkov, our new pilot, did not think so either. There were no seats in the cabin and no windows from which to enjoy the view. The celluloid of the small bull's eyes had lost its transparence under the influence of low temperatures and the frequent salt water showers it got each time the machine came down on the sea.

I sit in the front cockpit as we fly further north across the Taimir Peninsula. The service on this route will be opened for regular schedules only next year. My fellow-passengers are new people, scientists, prospectors and pioneers, who are going on to Nordvyk where a new Arctic town is to be built. I am to be present at the laying of its foundations. Although the temperature is not below freezing point the onslaught of the wind and the additional draught from the airscrew behind makes me feel chilly. The pilot has at least a screen in front of him; but I am carried across the northernmost tip of Asia in an open saucepan. I draw the collar of my pullover up to my nose, tie the ear-flaps under my chin, and bandage my face with a shawl quickly improvised out of a towel and the leather straps of my camera. Goggles shield my eyes, and at last—looking, I fancy, more like a gangster than an airman—I can breathe, as I certainly could not in the full pressure of the wind. Nor do I sit comfortably. The small floor space of the pan is covered with a spaghetti-like labyrinth of ropes for use in tying the aeroplane to the landing stages at night. The sharp fangs of a steel anchor make it impossible to stretch my legs. I have tried thirteen different positions; it really would not work. I recognize now I have to pay for my privileged seat by folding myself like a penknife—again not an easy process in my heavy leather coat and fur.

But all is forgotten as soon as the dramatic change of scenery sets in below.

The sky is mostly clouded at a height of 600 feet, so Sadkov keeps within 50 and 300 feet above the ground. Soon we are at the front where forest and Arctic desert make war on each other. The trees embark on a battle of conquest and try to expand their territory. But the North uses strong weapons to force the invaders into retreat. They have no business beyond the Arctic circle. The tundra whips them with winds; sends slashing cyclones against them. It starves them of light, attacks their food supply by freezing the soil underneath their roots into a mass as hard as glass. The sun is no longer an ally; it has not enough time to soften the ground; its rays are too short. The tree army finds it increasingly difficult to raise a reserve of youngsters who could fill up its ranks. The front line grows rapidly thinner. Many have to give in and accept the low standard of life which is the rule of the locality. I can see how struggle and gradual subjection tears at their health. Starvation reduces them to dwarfish, degenerated, ill-looking little fellows. It would have been better for them to stay at home. They present such a pitiful picture of defeat, caricatures of once free and noble trees.

Larger become the patches under the occupation of the Arctic. More numerous are the stretches of land under the colours of the North. The green flag of the Southern forest is torn and battered. The grey and yellow banner of the Arctic moss expands triumphantly over the plains. What was a rich and thick fur for the earth in its prime has become a mangy old skin. Holes of water and swamp shine through. The last outposts of the taiga disappear; the tundra expands from horizon to horizon. The Arctic has won the battle.

Wild reindeer herds are frightened out of their grazing complacency and disperse in all directions as our steel bird flies over them. They had never seen or heard anything like it. The barking of the wolves and the threatening grumble of the bear are angels' music by comparison. Here and there a score of grey fur tents stand up from the ground, and natives engaged in fishing look up to us in their skin clothes. They are obviously less impressed than the stupid animals, who were not yet told by the Comsomols that aeroplanes are by no means wild beasts.

It took three days to get to Nordvyk from Dudinka, over Norilsk, the mining centre and the trading factories of Volotchianka and Khatanga. Before the last hop we had to spend twenty-four hours in the log cabin of the air base. Sadkov lay on the reindeer skin which covered the plank bed. He glanced through a Russian translation of *Pickwick*, which he found on the book-shelf next to Jack London and Lenin. Tassya Markova, the girl radio operator, went out to send off a message asking for a weather report. We were impatient and wanted to get away. But the forecasts had bidden caution. Ivan Alexandrovitch, our talkative navigator, put some more iceberry jam on his black bread and asked when the fish would be ready. We got the most delicious sturgeon on that journey, or river salmon or ossitrina, the delight of gourmets in Northern Siberia. Half an hour after our arrival the dinner was usually caught in the river near the anchorage of the machine. By the time we had finished with an *apéritif*, consisting of either tea and jam or biscuit and cream, a plate the size of a car wheel would be brought steaming into the room with heaps of fish steak piled on it. Some of the dishes I ate on that part of my journey tasted like turkey or pheasant; I had never known such exquisite fish fare in my life.

While Sadkov battled with sleep over his book, Ivan Alexandrovitch put the globe on the table next to his plate and did as many of his colleagues had done before. He covered the blue of the oceans and the yellow of the lands on this miniature of the world with finger-prints. From the back of the room Sadkov grinned. 'Pity this Dickens fellow is dead. Would have preferred to pilot him across the Arctic rather than you, Petr Albertovitch. Sure he would have written a better book about it all than you will!' Sadkov was not impressed with the way I looked at things and collected my information.

'Shut up, and sleep,' Ivan Alexandrovitch hurried to my defence. 'Otherwise you won't even be able to get us safely through, let alone Dickens.'

Then he gave me some well-meant advice. 'Don't tell your readers too much about how primitive this air base is. In ten years' time some of them will spend a night here themselves. And then they will think you have been lying. Because by then this will no longer be a rough timber cabin. There will be a beautiful hotel, with soft beds and central heating. Out there, where the sledges are stored in the open, will be signposts: "To San Francisco, left staircase. To Tokyo, central staircase. To London, right staircase." And a nicely polished chromium plate, lit with neon tubes throughout the winter months, will say: "Trans-Polar passengers, any staircase." The path down to the airport will be cemented and railed, and no one will tumble on slippery mud.' (He was tactful enough not to add, 'Like you, Petr Albertovitch.')

'All that is really important in the world, politically and economically, lies on the northern hemisphere,' he continued with his fingers on the globe. 'Russia, Europe, America. Quite naturally, therefore, the shortest air lines are over the Arctic and not east-west round the waist of the earth.'

He unbuckled his leather belt and measured the comparative distances on the globe.

'Londoners will fly to Tokyo *via* Novaya Zemlya, Cape Chelyuskin, Khatanga, Yakutsk and Khabarovsk. New Yorkers to Shanghai over Canada across the Pole and again *via* Arctic Siberia. We ourselves will have alternative routes to America along the north coast of Asia or across the Pole, with a base at Franz Josef Land, and near the Atabaska River. English people and Scandinavians who want to get to America quickly will perhaps fly across Greenland and the Western Arctic.'

Ivan Alexandrovitch was day-dreaming. But his fancies were not quite unfounded. The Soviet Government are convinced that their part of the Arctic will be one of the main highways for future air traffic. They have declared all territory from their northern coast to the Pole—whether explored or not—to be under their sovereignty. Wrangell Island, for instance, which was unclaimed by the United States or Canada and refused by Ramsay MacDonald's Labour Government when offered to them by the Arctic explorer Steffansson—was settled with Eskimos and Russian Polar workers by the Soviet Government. For the last six years the Red Flag has been kept flying over it continuously, and a colony of about sixty people live there at present. This island is to be one of the most important air bases and, lying above the Bering Straits, will also have some strategical importance with the growth of traffic along the Northern Sea Route. As Ivan Alexandrovitch put it in his richly imaginative language: 'Tokyo-New York passengers will breakfast there, together with people flying from Moscow to San Francisco.'

All this is, of course, music for the future. But one important development is to be made soon: the line to America along the northern coast of Asia, across Bering Straits, down Alaska and the eastern shores of Canada and the United States is to be opened this year.

For the present the importance of Russia's Arctic air lines lies in their strategical value and the support they provide to the opening up of the northern region. Without aviation the whole scheme of industrial development, settlement, geological and geographical exploration, and of navigation along the Northern Sea Route would be unthinkable. The aeroplanes serve as scouts for the ice-breakers, which they keep informed of the floes at distances not visible from the crow's nest. When Bleriot flew across the Channel in 1910 Fridtjof Nansen—with other Scandinavians who were even then keen on the commercial development of Arctic navigation as a trade route to Siberia—said: 'Now the road for shipping in the ice-bound Arctic Ocean is open.' Until Bleriot's time—and for long after—navigation in ships in those altitudes had always remained an experiment; success or failure depended on chance more than on skill. This is how it was described at the time: 'Days and days passed by. The danger of being caught for the winter increased while we tried to find a clear passage among the ice. The view from the observer's highest mast did not reach further than about twenty miles. Hours were spent in desperate effort to cut through a field behind which we hoped to find clear water. Cursing and swearing was at its worst when we found after all the labour of crew and ship that everything had been in vain. There was more ice ahead.'

When I was on board the ice-breaker *Yermak*, watching its strategical operations against the white enemy of shipping, the treachery and power of our foe was no less than it had been thirty years ago. But we were better armed. As soon as we set out to fight for a passage we sent a radio message for the dispatch of an aeroplane from the shore base. Within half an hour the ice watch pilot was circling over our bridge. He left us and surveyed hundreds of square miles, rising high above the sea. His observer watched the slowly drifting fields and floes below. He drew a map of their constellation. His first advice reached us by wireless.

After two hours the ice watch returned and dropped a parcel with a small parachute. It contained the map of our route ahead. The captain and his staff laid out their plans of attack. A strategic line of approach was fixed; the course decided by the thickness of ice on the one hand and by the time factor on the other. Choice of weapons was made. Explosives against the heaviest massives; full steam through the thin floes. I could understand what Arctic aviation means much better after this experience than now when Ivan Alexandrovitch was simply praising its manifold blessings.

At Krasnoyarsk I had seen a woman doctor start in an air ambulance on her round to native tribes and trading outposts. At a time when Russia suffers most of all from a shortage of scientifically trained people it is of the greatest value to save her doctors months of travelling on river boats and with dog teams. The radius of action for each medical base in the North is widened. I also saw aeroplanes engaged in forest observation. Before any new saw-mill is built wood experts of the Northern Sea Route Administration fly over large areas near the projected industrial centre and assess the potential yield of the woods around. A regular supply of logs is essential to keep a mill working according to plan. The taiga is as difficult to penetrate as the tropical jungle. Millions of acres of valuable woods have never been entered by men.

Experience has taught the aerial observer much in the last few years. At the beginning they could only just estimate the expansion of the forest. Then they learnt to determine the height of the trees from above by measuring the shadow they cast at given times of day and month. Now they are able to tell the kind and quality of wood, and even analyse its state of health. They also advise on its accessibility. A decree was issued forbidding the Timber Commissariat to build a factory unless they provided evidence that it would pay, evidence based on the report of aerial reconnaissance. Last year experiments were also made in fighting forest fires with aerial bombardment. The range of the fire is to be dammed and isolated by smoke-bombs dropped around the outbreak.

The seal fishermen also have to thank the Arctic airman for improvements in their working conditions. Until quite recently they had sometimes to spend days and weeks of useless search for their catch. Now they wait for their spies to tell them by radio where a herd of seals was seen basking unsuspectingly on a sunny ice-floe.

Fur traders in Leipzig used to tell me what losses in capital and human energy their Russian suppliers often sustained because the agents who buy the skins from the natives had their precious cargo held up in the wilderness of the Siberian forest through a premature spring. Reindeer and dog sledges cannot transport the goods once the thaw has set in, and the parcels have to be left in the woods until the following winter. It took two years for furs to reach the auction houses in Nijhny Novgorod and St. Petersburg. Now the fur people at Khatanga station tell me that foxes and sables caught in Northern Siberia in December are skinned and parcelled for ready dispatch early in April. Arctic flyers call and take the Siberian soft gold to the annual sales in Leningrad within a few days.

At every landing-place on my flight the local inhabitants crowded impatiently on the landing-stage. When we taxied our machine ashore Sadkov was greeted with cheers. On more outlying posts he was immediately surrounded by hand-shakers and back-slappers. Occasional kisses on his sometimes unshaven cheeks would reveal the gratitude of the people for his gifts: newspapers, letters, little parcels from home. Of the greatest psychological importance is the feeling that they are no longer cut off from civilization for months, that communications with families are possible at regular intervals, and the assurance that—should they fall ill or need return for other reasons urgently—an aeroplane will come and collect them.

Land travel across the roadless forests and swamps of the North is restricted to reindeer and dog driving, and even this is possible only in the winter and at a slow speed. But every Polar station can now be reached by air all the year round in a few days. I saw an expectant mother, looking forward to her confinement in October, who was still doing regular scientific work on an island in the Arctic Ocean at the end of August. She told me cheerfully that she would be flown to the nearest hospital, should the station doctor decide during the last month that her confinement might prove complicated.

Regular air services are now in operation throughout the greater part of the year along the main Siberian rivers. Bases are on the railway line at Omsk (for the Obi and Irtish) at Krasnoyarsk (for the Yenisei), Irkutsk and Yakutsk (for the Lena). Passengers buy their tickets from any normal air company. Nice blue and white designs underlying the print show an aeroplane above icebergs and Arctic seas. They give you a last suggestion of where you are going before you start with Avyo Arctica. Fares are not abnormally high. From Krasnoyarsk to Dickson Island, for instance, costs 1000 roubles, equal to £40 or $200. Including two or three nights' sleeping accommodation in intermittent stations, it is not much more than the fare on any line outside Russia, for the distance is 1400 miles. When my fellow-passengers bought their tickets at Krasnoyarsk they took their money out of sealed envelopes containing the fare exact to the kopek. They are provided with these envelopes by the factory Trust or State organization on whose behalf they travel. Russian tourists can only afford these prices if they belong to the higher paid members of the population, such as doctors, university professors, writers and artists, inventors, factory managers, Stakhanovist workers. I saw some of them in Igarka. They wanted to be among the first pleasure travellers of Soviet Russia in their country's newly opened Northern Empire.

CHAPTER VII

'NORTH POLE—ALL CHANGE FOR SAN FRANCISCO!'

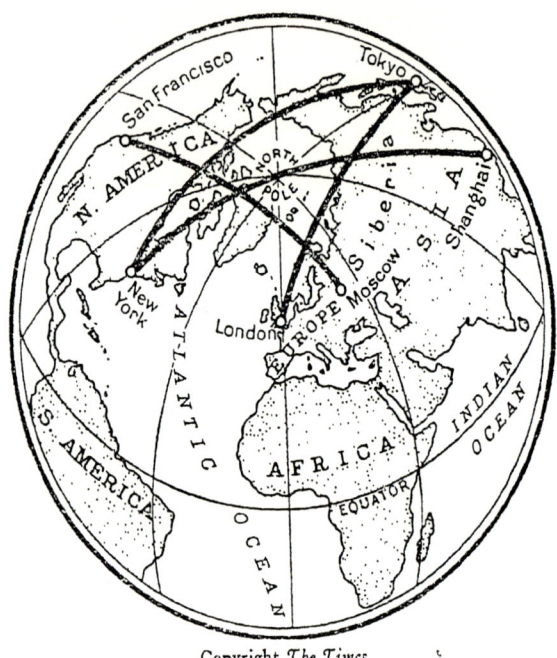

Copyright *The Times.*

FOR two of the passengers the trip was their honeymoon.
Smirnov, the geologist at Nordvyk, had been on leave and
fallen in love with a girl student in the Leningrad Arctic
Institute; and now he will no longer be alone in the long
and dark months of the Polar winter. They spend the days
of waiting at Khatanga in happily picking black-currants
and those pretty red iceberries of which all jam is made in
these parts of Siberia.

I myself was glad to set out alone for a while. I saw that

I had made a mistake in calling the earth mangy and ugly while we flew above it. The tundra has a beauty of its own. Vegetation is sparse, but is still a miniature copy of our own plant life. There are no trees, but each tiny moss represents a more or less true replica of one, with branches only a fraction of an inch in length and thickness. There were also most of our Alpine plants, only edelweiss, which grow abundantly in the plains of Southern Siberia, were missing. The bluebells, marsh marigolds and forget-me-nots made up in intensity of colour and harmony of shape what they had lost in size by emigrating to these rough-tempered regions.

Rummaging in the undergrowth the first morning I found an elephant's tusk. It was only for a split second that I wondered how it had got to this steep bank of the Khatanga river in the Arctic. Even a very clever elephant would not have climbed over the Himalaya and trotted across the Kara Kum deserts all the way through Siberia. And a clever elephant would have known that the Arctic was no place for him. The one whose tusk I found had lived here sixty thousand years ago. A mammoth !

'The tusk will be taken away soon,' the station chief assured me later. 'We have sent a wireless message, and as soon as a boat can be spared they will collect this one, with many others, and send it to the ivory market in London. It'll be good enough for billiard balls or piano keyboards. Cheaper qualities though, because, after all, it is a little out of date!'

Towards the evening of the second day we got a telegram from Nordvyk. 'Come,' it said.

'The weather's all right now,' Sadkov assured us as we started. We left at about 11 p.m. Ten minutes after the start I slept firmly, wrapped up in a dogskin sleeping-bag stretched out between newspaper bundles, bags and petrol cans behind the pilot's seat. Natasha Alexandrovna dozed with her head leaning against the shoulder of Comrade

Smirnov. Bass wrote notes indefatigably about the advance which his young missionaries had made in the tundra during the last twelve months. The propeller roared, but we had all got used to that during the past few days. Only when the engine stopped and the 'plane was down on the water once more did everybody wake up. This time I was sure that I could not have slept more than half an hour when, with a few swings of the machine right and left, the engine throttled down, and we suddenly sat on the river with a heavy bump. I crawled out to see what had happened. Sadkov and the navigator sat on the edge of their cockpit, feet dangling overboard.

'Fog', said Sadkov. 'Can't go on.'

'So what?'

'Wait. Can't do anything else.'

I sat down next to him. We were wrapped in floating white mist and could not see more than a dim outline of the river shore to our right. Nothing to the left.

This is the worst thing about Arctic aviation in summer. Only when the territory will be fully mapped and a greater number of radio stations established to give reliable bearings to the pilot will it be possible to disregard the lack of visibility, rise above the blanket and continue the flight unconcerned. So far, Sadkov tells me, he has to keep above the river and cannot risk losing it out of sight. As long as he sticks to its course he knows where he is going to and is assured of the continuous company of an emergency landing-field. Sadkov, who had shown his interest for literature before, when he reached for Dickens at the station library at Khatanga, now surprised me with more questions about English writers. His pet was Shakespeare (who is the pet of many others in Russia to-day). Sadkov, however, was not quite satisfied with the treatment his plays were afforded at the hands of Moscow's producers.

'I'd give a month's wages to see *King Lear* in London or Stratford. *Pravda* had an excellent review about it from its London Correspondent. It would be great fun to compare our productions with the interpretation Shakespeare is now given in England. By the way, are your workers very interested in classic literature? They ought to be, you know. They are in a much more fortunate position than we. Our people have so little background. It takes time to make them really cultured. The Government is doing all it can. Lenin said: "The proletariat is the rightful heir for all that's good in the cultural values of the past."'

He went very thoroughly into his analysis of the qualities of literature. After about three-quarters of an hour the curtain had been blown away from the river by a fresh breeze. Sadkov packed me into my cabin once more and we flew on.

We were strangely unfortunate. Within the next two hours we had to make three more forced landings. There were about 45 minutes of waiting to every ten minutes of flight. Early in the morning we came down again in the estuary of the river. It was difficult to say whether it was not already the Nordenskioeld Sea where we floated. We threw no anchor; the current was negligible. One shore could just be seen dimly in the mist; dark blue, looking like the end of the world. Softly the sea rocked our cradle on her tired waves. Eight human beings carried by a steel bird of their own make, we waited there at the fringe of the earth. Everybody listened to the silence that surrounded us. Trusting only to the skill of the pilot and the reliability of aircraft constructors, we felt sure that time would restore us to more familiar surroundings.

I was probably the only one to feel for a moment that perhaps men had no business at all in these last reservations of nature. One of the outstanding beliefs of Soviet Russia is a spirit of crusading against all forces not yet conquered by men. Their conception of the future of humanity is that of a highly organized, entirely disciplined, heroic army to subject the universe. Wars and revolutions are to them only intermediate cleansing processes in the forging of that final phalanx. Marx's assertion that the history of mankind will only start after that of class struggles is ended has become a religion. It is little discussed nowadays. But this dogma underlies all the optimism with which they tackle the problem of building up their country.

Sadkov fetched some tins of salmon in tomato sauce from the depth of his cockpit. He opened them with his knife and served breakfast.

'How long will the fog last?' I asked, judging the size of his provisions anxiously in relation to the number of passengers.

'Half an hour, half a day, half a week,' he replied.

'And . . .?' I pointed to his tin provisions.

He grinned and showed me a collapsible fishing-rod and a small net which he had tucked away in his suitcase.

'There are hundreds of breakfasts and dinners swimming around down there in the water. Don't worry.'

'And how do you manage in winter time?'

'Winter flying is a different thing, and we have only just completed our experiments. We have constructed heating equipment that keeps up a good temperature in the cabin. Radiators circulate air round the walls, which is previously warmed up by the heat of the exhaustion gases. We have also experimented with different methods to reduce the danger of ice formation on wings and propeller, seeking means of heating the surface of the 'plane electrically, and also testing the new American method of using continuously inflating and deflating rubber tubes to prevent ice forming on the rigid parts of the 'plane. We shall also have more fuel on board and a larger food reserve. But this question which seems to concern you most, Petr Albertovitch, is really the least. The Arctic is well populated with animals even in the winter. We can hack a hole in the ice and get fish, or shoot hare and wild reindeer.'

At that moment, sitting on the board cover of the 'plane

and gulping cold tinned salmon and rather wet biscuits, I had in fact only thought of food at first. But Sadkov had started a lecture on Arctic flying. And as it is with these young Russian enthusiasts, they are so keen on showing foreign visitors that they go thoroughly into every question, Sadkov once on the run would not finish so soon. He liked talking about his job because he liked the job.

The whole country watches the work of its Arctic pilots with intense interest. Their services are richly rewarded with money and, what seems much more important to them, with great public honours. Each of the twenty-seven pilots and board mechanics I met during my flights in the Soviet north had received the Order of the Red Star or the Banner of Work; a few even had the Order of Lenin, the highest decoration in Red Russia, which even the popular Foreign Minister, M. Litvinov, only got after he had been in office continuously for ten years. Molokov, Levanevsky, Lyapidevsky, Vodopyanov, Chkalov, Belyakov, Baybukov, Chukhnovsky are all 'Heroes of the Soviet Union'—a title more jealously guarded and coveted than an Earldom in England. All this helps to attract ambitious and intelligent as well as skilful and courageous men, to this profession. A Russian schoolboy will dream of them as a French child dreams of Napoleon or an Australian boy of Bradman. A recent Russian film dealt exclusively with the adventures of a gang of little toddlers who set out from their kindergarten to kidnap Molokov and bring him to their school as an honorary chairman of their Pioneer Group.

Russia's 'Knights of the Northern Skies' are blazing a new road over the roof of the world which their fellow-citizens regard as most important. Their successes may have consequences not less direct and far-reaching to us than to them.

I consulted three people who are outstanding authorities on Russia's Arctic air lines before I left Moscow.

The first was a non-Bolshevik: General Umberto Nobile. The unfortunate chief of the ill-fated Italian airship expedition to the Arctic was courtmartialed in Milan after the Russian ice-breaker *Krassin* saved him and the greater part of his companions. Because he had allowed himself to be rescued before all his crew were in safety he was found guilty and went abroad as an exile. He is now employed by the Soviet Government as a specialist and builds dirigibles for them. But he has not given up his pet idea of exploring ice-bound regions round the North Pole by Zeppelins instead of steamships.

The Fascist General received me in a nice little apartment which I found after some hopeless wanderings through gloomy backyards in the centre of the Red capital.

Over a cup of Russian tea he told me first that he had a very high opinion of Russian airmen.

'I believe in their efficiency in peace as well as war time. As regards their achievements in the Arctic, I do not doubt that they have a great economic and strategical importance. The possibility of air traffic along the shores of the Arctic Ocean between the settlements in Northern Siberia and to the islands in the Polar Sea is proved. But flights across the Pole? Well, I think such ideas are a little premature. The difficulty is not so much one of suitable machines. Any modern powerful engine can get the better even of the strongest head winds in the Arctic. Clear weather at the start and arrival are of course essential. The distance of 3000 miles between their northernmost base on Franz Josef Land and the nearest landing-place contemplated at the other side on the Atabaska river would have to be flown non-stop. Even that is feasible. After all, the Red Army has bombers with a radius of action up to 6000 miles now. What is still to be done and could not be dispensed with is the establishment of a sufficient number of radio stations in the innermost circle round the Pole and emergency landing-grounds. For that purpose exploration of this area has to be carried some steps further. I doubt that it would be safe to build on the pack ice. The drift is not yet fully explored. One would have to see whether there are not some more islands nearer to the Pole so that these could be used for stations. Since dog expeditions in this circle are rather risky and not even the strongest ice-breaker can penetrate so far, the airship is certainly the given means by which that region can be surveyed fairly comfortably. It can carry a larger scientific staff and equipment than the 'planes. Also it allows the observer to descend lower towards the ground. After some more experiments I should think that even the dropping and picking up of landing parties should present no unsurmountable difficulty. This should be done before one thinks of taking passengers over the top of the world.'

Mark Ivanovitch Shevelyov, whom I met in Krasnoyarsk and who was the chief of the air arm of the Northern Sea Route Administration, at the age of thirty is keener on trans-Polar flights than Nobile. He has been everywhere from Murmansk to Vladivostok, including Spitzbergen, Franz Josef Land, North Land, Wrangel Island and the Chukotka Peninsula. He was at least as serious as jestful when he told me he hoped to fly to another planet within our lifetime. 'Why should we?' I had asked him that evening. 'Why should we not?' was his reply, a key to his character and that of his contemporaries. He had learnt his English while lying with a broken spine in hospital at Rostov on Don. Amundsen's works and the poems of Longfellow were his textbooks. He said the motto of his life was Nansen's admonition: 'If you succeed—go on. If you do not succeed—go on.'

Probably very much under the spell of this conviction, he said to me: 'What we need for flights across the Pole is a meteorological station on it. This should be constructed as soon as possible. If Schmidt would only let me I would go to-morrow. A plane would get me there. I would descend by parachute and take a tent, a wireless set, some provisions and tools with me. I would always guide the pilot back to the spot by radio signals. He could bring me a wooden house in parts which I would put together. There is nothing to prevent me having one or two assistants. For a while we would explore meteorological conditions and see whether it is possible to find food locally by cutting holes into the ice and get animals from the sea. This would make the experiment easier because we would be independent on regular food supplies by 'plane and parachute. We would send very valuable reports on the weather conditions, winds, air currents, etc. etc., by radio. After a year or two we would have some facts about the centre of the Arctic which we could never get so reliably by occasional expeditions, test flights or synoptic conclusions by synthesis of meteorological data from stations around a radius of at least 500 miles from the Pole.' *

Vodopyanov, who was the first airman to fly to Franz Josef Land from Moscow, is ready to try the hop across the Pole in 1937. Levanevsky had given up his attempt in June, 1935, because his machine had a defect shortly after he left Moscow. Vodopyanov is still comparatively young. His biography is very typical; most men whom one meets in responsible positions all over the country tell a similar tale. As the old guard of pre-War Bolshevik revolutionaries dies out this type of man comes more to the foreground. A peasant boy at the time of the revolution, too young to fight in the Great War, Mikhail Vasilievitch Vodopyanov had never seen other means of transports than horse-carts up to his nineteenth birthday. His first encounter with self-moving vehicles like railways, motor-cars, aeroplanes, took place in 1918. He joined the Red Army. It was the best school he had ever known. A student of law, who was the commander of his battalion during the civil war, taught him to read and write. There also he learnt to drive an automobile and later became a mechanic on aeroplanes. When

* Attempted March 23, 1937.

95

the Red Army returned home he settled as a chauffeur. In 1926 he got a chance to perfect his knowledge of aviation and qualified as a pilot. First he flew between Khabarovsk and Sakhalien, then he carried mail between Moscow and Kiev. Finally to Tashkent and to Tcheran. In 1929 he flew across Siberia, in 1931 to the Chukotka Peninsula. In 1934 he took part in the saving of the Chelyuskinites and was 'knighted' by the President of Tsik, Kalinin, who on behalf of the All Union Government made Vodopyanov 'Hero of the Soviet Union.' When I asked for his opinion on trans-Polar aviation he said he would give me a written statement. Mikhail Vasilievitch, the one-time peasant boy, has got used to being interviewed. When we met first in the room of Glavsevmorput in Moscow, which accommodates three typists, two secretaries and any number of people waiting to talk to the chief, Vodopyanov had just flown up from Odessa. He had given some advice to the constructors at the hydroplane wharf. While we talked five reporters from Moscow papers came in to get a story from him. He would only give written statements for publication. His experiences compelled him to do so, was his explanation. This is what he wrote for *Forty Thousand against the Arctic:* 'Regular trans-Polar passenger lines will be possible only when we have 'planes able to fly in the stratosphere. In such altitudes above the Arctic the temperature is stationary, no clouds obstruct the flight, no ice formation on wings and propellers ever occurs. Seasons will not influence flying conditions. All we shall have to care about is clear weather for start and finish. We shall have to build multi-engined strato planes with motors developing 1000 h.p. each. Once that is achieved the whole problem of trans-Polar aviation will be solved and a new stage reached in world air traffic. Meanwhile we shall build aerial lighthouses sending out radio beams on most of the Arctic islands. Aerodromes for intermediate landings will be prepared by the station crews. I myself have much contact with the masses. They regard

me as their comrade. I depend on the support of the workers as much as they on my work as an Arctic pilot. They have shown their confidence in me by electing me as a deputy to the Tsik. (Under the pre-1936 Constitution, Soviet equivalent of our parliaments.) I get hundreds of letters by young people asking me for advice, and I have to give lectures and reports to the factory workers on all my flights.'

On the basis of these statements it appears that Transpolar passenger traffic from Europe and Asia to America will still be a matter of some years.

The strategical importance of the Soviet Arctic air routes, however, is a reality of the present day. The world must count with it as a newly-gained military asset of the Soviet Union.

On July 20th, 1936, three test pilots of the aircraft construction section at the Commissariat of heavy industries started on a non-stop flight from Moscow to the Far East via the Arctic. Chkalov, Belyakov and Baybukov took off from Moscow military aerodrome under utmost secrecy. Not until their 'plane had covered 1700 miles did the world hear the news. Within 56 hours and 21 minutes they had reached the Northern Pacific. Their 'plane was specially built for this flight. It was a wide-winged monoplane. The engine was constructed by A. Mikulin and named after him A.M. 4, the plane by A. N. Tupolev and typed ANT 25. Throughout the flight the authorities in Moscow had reports from the airmen at regular intervals of thirty minutes. They established an unofficial world record for non-stop long-distance flights: 9374 kilometres, 5860 miles, was the distance which the ANT 25 bridged in one hop; 270 kilometres, 175 miles, more than the official world record.

The constructors claim that the 'plane has a radius of action of 12,000 km.

This means that the ANT 25, instead of landing at Nikolayevsk on Amur, as it did, could have flown to Tokyo straight away.

Considering the route chosen, this flight must have given the Japanese a lot to think about.

Chkalov and his companions had breakfast in Moscow. By dinner-time they were flying above Franz Josef Land, only 450 miles from the Pole.

Their message at midnight read: 'ALL CORRECT OVER-FLYING FRANZ JOSEF LAND. SEEING ISLANDS. GREETINGS TO HIBERNATORS AT TIKHAYA BAY.' (An air base is at present being constructed on that spot.)

Next morning the flyers were over North Land, as high up as Northern Greenland, as far east as Bangkok.

At ten o'clock they looked down on Nordvyk, at lunch-time on the mouth of the Lena, after tea they crossed the mountain ranges of Yakutsk in dense fog.

They spent an anxious night flying over the windy crests.

When the Red Army and Navy garrison at Petropavlovsk on Kamtchatka, Russia's outpost on the Northern Pacific, got up at the bugle call to rush to their breakfast the ANT 25 was 12,000 feet above their town.

At midday the powerful radio station of Khabarovsk, headquarters of the 'special and autonomous Far Eastern Red Army', helped Baybukov to find his bearings. At two o'clock in the afternoon the ANT 25 landed at Nikolayevsk on Amur.

Up to the last six hours of the flight the 'plane had been entirely out of the range of Japanese aircraft. These last six hours were above the Sea of Okhotsk, which is notorious for its fogs and storms.

The route was 200 miles shorter than the air line above the trans-Siberian railway, which we are used to regard as the shortest link between European Russia and the Far East. The short cut is due to the 'Arctic detour' of ANT 25, which brought it as near to the Pole as Madrid is to Paris. Flying along the railway line would mean being almost within continuous reach of Japanese planes for the last third of the journey.

Up there in the Arctic the Russians can build refuelling and landing bases unassailable by anyone.

There is oil on the spot, and since the navigation along the coast has been made possible for the summer season any quantity of reserves can be brought there safely.

What ANT 25 achieved as an experiment other 'planes built from the same blue prints can do as well. The Menshinsky plant is there for it.

And then: there is no need—in case Russia is actually attacked by Japan—for her airmen to fly non-stop from Moscow to the Far East. They can rise from Tiski Bay on the mouth of the Lena, swoop down to Tokyo and return without a single landing (unless they are shot down).

Chkalov and his two companions were received in Moscow when they returned like Lindbergh in New York after his trans-Atlantic flight. The Government, including Stalin as head of the Party, were at the aerodrome. They drove through eight continuous miles of cheering crowds to the Kremlin. Flowers showered down from the windows, streets were beflagged, Russia went as wild over them as America over Lindy.

Three weeks later Levanevsky and Levchenko, another 'Hero of the Soviet Union', with his navigator bought an American Vultee plane in California. On August 6th they started from Los Angeles harbour on a 10,000 miles trip to Moscow. Up to the American west coast they went, crossed the Pacific at Bering Straits, its Gibraltar, then followed the northern shores of Asia and got home down through Siberia and over the Urals. They made many stops. Theirs was a different task than Chkalov's. They were checking the organization of a safe route from the United States to Russia. But perhaps there was also more than that to their flight.

Suppose Russia is attacked by Germany and Japan simultaneously? Leningrad and Vladivostok harbours are blockaded. No munitions, no arms, no food supplies can be brought from Europe or America across normal sea routes. Russia may want to buy aeroplanes from the U.S.A. How can these reach the battlefields in the Far East and the Ukraine if no ships can get through the cordon drawn along Russia's Pacific coast, none through the Baltic and the Bay of Finland.

In such an emergency Russia could send one hundred pilots on board of an airship to America via the Arctic. Each of them could pick up and bring back one plane. Each of them might fly with provisions and war materials on the route which Levanevsky has tested.

Of course it is a risky thing. Of course it is expensive and only a drop in an ocean. But if conditions do actually develop as they are depicted above—and no one doubts that they will should the Soviet Union be attacked—there would be one more communication line between Russia and the New World. Its scope may be limited. At any rate it is better than nothing.

No one discussed this in Russia when I asked for the military background of Arctic flying. But I do not doubt for a moment that millions of Russians, ever conscious of the danger of war, have not overlooked what I and many other observers recognized as the strategical importance of these last flights. Nobody, however, seemed keen to make practical use of the experiences gained through them. I have seen how much there is still to be built and done in Russia to let all people partake of the comforts and achievements of our technical age. I am ready to believe that from year to year the Russian people will be more anxious to avoid conflicts and keep away from war. Every citizen will have more to lose—in improvements gained and hoped for. The last few years have brought small luxuries and better clothes and, above all, sufficient food for the larger masses. They are increasingly conscious, that perhaps at last the time has come for them to reap the reward for the period of sacrifice and self-deprivation which is behind them. Since the riches of earth are still untapped for the greater part, and land available for three or four times as large a population, it could take generations before they would ever turn their eyes toward the property of other nations.

We waited for several hours. Sadkov had long exhausted his urgent desire to tell me all he knew about Arctic flying. He charged Ivan Alexandrovitch to keep watch while he would go under deck and sleep for a while. At the first spell of clear weather, was his command, Ivan Alexandrovitch was to wake him up. We would then fly back a little up-stream to be nearer the shore of the river and stay there until the weather would change definitely. 'I am sick of going up and coming down every ten minutes', he said.

When the sun came through, Sadkov got up and we started. A curtain of rain was hanging down from the sky. A rainbow stood before us supporting himself on legs firmly pressed against the surface of the water. Sadkov swung our course a little to the right and left as if he wanted to scratch the supports of the rainbow with our wings. Then he handed me his white celluloid pad. He had scratched the words 'Arc de Triomphe' on it in French. 'Getting romantic, comrade pilot', I wrote back after erasing his writing from the glossy surface of the tablet with my glove. I could feel the plane tremble as he took one hand off the steering to write one more reply and was damned glad when I had it in front of me, knowing that now at last he would again attend to his job. 'Dickens would have understood me', he had scribbled. And unconcerned with my lack of poetic sympathy he flew majestically through the centre of the rainbow.

CHAPTER VIII

MECHANIZED NOMADS

'Is anybody hurt, citizens? Can we save you?'

A young man in skin clothes was shouting up to us from a boat. We had had to come down owing to the fog, and had alighted in a kind of harbour at a bend of the river. A canoe had put out from the shore, and Sadkov, his feet dangling overboard as usual, answered the friendly offer. 'But do you know anything about a seaplane?'

'Our heads do not contain the picture of its life', the young man replied in slow Russian. 'But we wanted to offer our arms and hands to help you bring it to reason.'

We told him that there had been no accident and we were only waiting for the sun to warm the fog away. I said that I should like to go ashore with the natives and wait in their tent. The young man said some guttural words to his companion, who looked like his elder brother. The latter passed the question on to an old man, their father. Father nodded consent, elder brother nodded consent and the spokesman in turn shouted an invitation up to me.

I promised Sadkov to return within two hours and jumped down into the boat. It leaked in several places. The young interpreter had to make a half-time job of emptying the water out with a shovel while helping father with the rowing. As we slowly approached the banks of the river I watched the party. They wore tight trousers of reindeer skin, with stockings and moccasins in one piece. Strings were tied round the legs underneath the knees and above the ankles. The material looked like dirty wet docskin. Father was the proud possessor of a woollen jacket; the sons were content with reindeer blouses. Their ears were hidden by tight-fitting fur-lined caps. At first glance, they all looked

THEY ROWED ME ASHORE

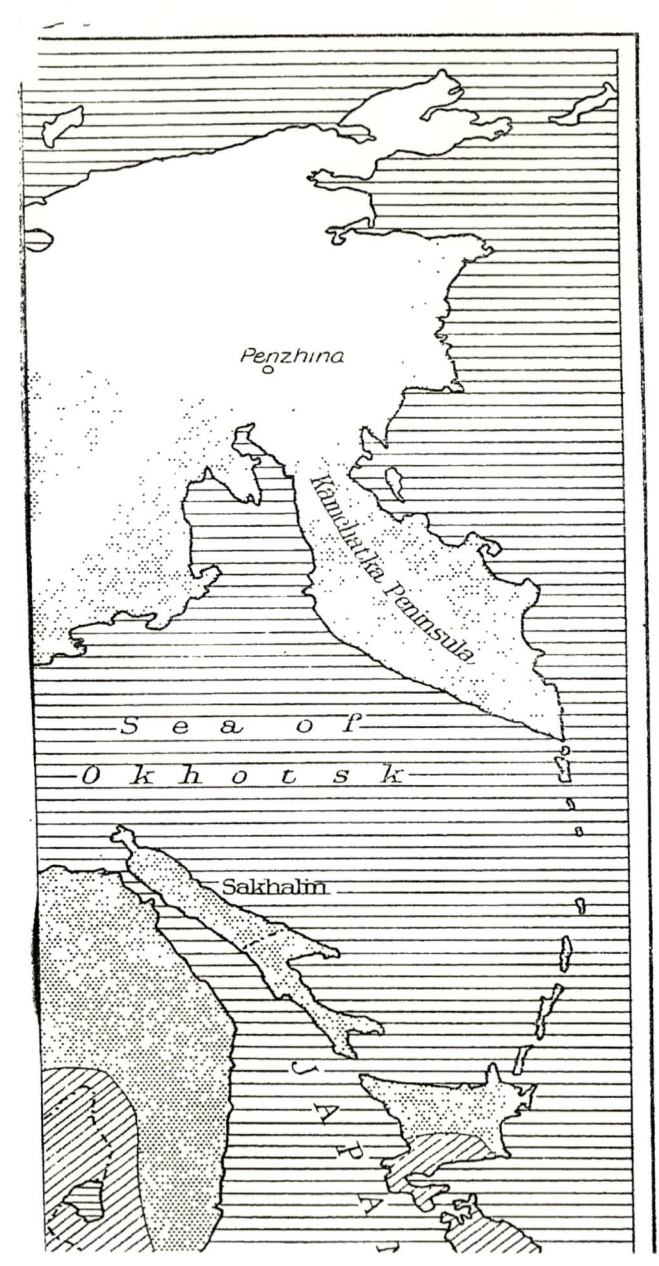

like Chinese coolies; a relation to the Mongols was quite evident. Father's skin was dark and leathery, scarred into a thousand wrinkles.

There was still some snow in the hollows of the river's bank. We climbed up the slimy clay ridge and made for the tents, which were made of reindeer skin, with the fur outside. Wooden poles rammed into the ground supported them against the wind; the ends stuck out on top, where they left open a hole, the size of a large frying-pan, to let the smoke out.

There was plenty of it inside, nevertheless, as I found as soon as I stooped to enter the first tent. The smouldering charcoal underneath the suspended tea-kettle filled the 'room' with thick clouds. They drew tears from my smarting eyes. The place was occupied by seven people, all sitting on piles of fur blankets and cushions. As a matter of fact everything was made from reindeer. It is the basis of existence for these peoples of the Arctic. They eat the animal's flesh, dress in its skin, build their *yurts* with its winter coat and make needles of its bones and knife handles of its antlers. It draws their sledges in the winter towards the trading centres, where they sell the fox and ermine and buy provisions.

In my tent an old and a younger woman attended the fire; a little girl stared at me with a mixture of curiosity and fright in her eyes; a baby cried underneath a heap of cushions. Three boys between six and twelve huddled together in a corner of the *yurt*. I was offered some tea in a dirty mug; it tasted like dish-water. The grown-up members of the family, including the women, were all smoking Makhorka in long pipes.

'When will the boat come on the river and bring us new provisions?' the young boy interpreter asked me on behalf of his father. 'It has saved us many days of travelling since it started coming two summers ago.'

He was referring to the swimming grocery shop which the

Soviets have introduced into the Arctic. Its purpose is to spare the natives their long journeys to the trading centres. Reindeer have to be sent north during the summer to escape the stings of mosquitoes that come out as soon as the ground is thawed in June; so men have no efficient means of transport in this so-called warm season. Often the provisions bought and carried home on sledges during the winter perish or do not suffice for a whole year. And so a large 'Stop Me and Buy One' motor boat, loaded with flour, tea, biscuits and some tools, comes down the rivers as soon as the ice is gone, and the natives have only got to perch their tents upon the banks to wait and wave it ashore. Meanwhile they can repair their sledges, and sew clothes. In the coming winter fewer will need to travel to the factories if they lay in sufficient stocks now. Instead of spending a lot of time with travelling they can devote themselves longer to fishing and hunting. It is all-round economy. The fur output of the native trappers is increased, their reserves of dried or frozen fish are swollen. The general standard of life is raised as insecurity and the continuous threat of starvation recede.

There are still twenty-six different native tribes in the north of Asia. Very little was known about them until quite recently. True, Samoyeds were already brought to the Court of Peter the Great, like Abyssinians to Louis XIV. With the Yakuts, who suffered exploitation from the Russian fur dealers and with the Tungus, the aristocrats of taiga and tundra, they were the only people whose existence was familiar to more than a few ethnologists. But there are also Ostyaks, Gellyaks, Goldis, Lamuts, Yuraks, Yukagirs and Chukchee besides some Eskimo, who form a link with the indigenous tribes of Alaska, Northern Canada and Greenland. My hosts were Dolgans, relatives of the Yakuts. Their name meant very little to me until I met them. To be frank, I had never heard of them at all before I made this journey. And yet these nations are some of the most interesting and last unsolved puzzles of ethnologists and linguists.

All except the Ostyaks have a clear Mongol streak in their faces and the shape of their skulls and cheekbones. Yet blood tests have revealed a closer affinity to the American Red Indians than to their southern neighbours. The Ostyak has unmistakably the eagle nose, the high forehead, the piercing eyes and the long head of the Redskin. Where have all these people come from? Are they original inhabitants of the North, have they never known a higher standard of culture and economy than reindeer breeding, fur trapping, fishing? Or are they weak nations from Central Asia driven up North by the Turkish first and the Russian expansion afterwards? Did they degenerate in their long struggle against the inhospitable climate or have they never advanced much further than the Stone Age until the Russians gave them plenty of liquor and very few tools in exchange for their sables and foxes? Are they the legendary races whom antiquity knew as dog-heads because the ear flaps of their fur caps look like dogs' ears? Are they the happy hybrids, 'who, live in the country that knows only day during the summer and only night during the winter', as Greek geographers describe them? What is there in the story of the monk, who told Castren, the Finnish scientist, that they were a stray stem of one of the lost Jewish tribes because they knew the Ten Commandments (a story, by the way, which Jewish merchants in Amsterdam used in order to get the local community to put up some money for an expedition in the seventeenth century, allegedly to rescue this tribe, in fact to get precious furs)?

Their languages, at any rate, vary greatly. Some have Finnish Ugrian traces—Hungarians in the Arctic. Others have Mongol grammar but a Turkish vocabulary. Many do not possess a word of their own for 'sea'—a clue to the theory that they wandered north and were introduced to the Arctic Ocean only by tribes who had lived on its shores before them. I have to leave all those problems to scientists. Nansen had ideas of his own on the subject; so had Castren and Kay Donner. Professor Koshkin, of the Institute of the Northern Peoples in Leningrad, is evolving new theories based on the latest and most thorough investigations of the Russians.

The facts of practical importance are clear: Here are 150,000 men and women, left over from nations who might have numbered millions in the past. They know how to live in the North. They are the natural human element that can develop the resources of this new continent. On these facts the Soviet Government bases its policy towards them. Quite apart from the principle which the new state has adopted after Lenin's rule—that each nation within Russia should be the trustee of the territory in which it lives and be regarded as its primary owner—Russia expects much of its Arctic population. They are the only race that can stand the climate permanently. However enthusiastic and happy to sacrifice themselves the young Comsomols may be, their health and temperament is not suited for life-long work in the North. Only a few, a mere handful, ever learn to hunt and trap like the natives. Seldom can they drive a dog-team so efficiently. Almost never are they able to wander across the tundra without compass, map or even stars, as the original landlords of the North have done. About 40 per cent of Russia's export in raw materials in the first Five-Year Plan had been fur. It is the natural product, most easily gained without machinery or capital investment. Raising the cultural level of these nations, who were dying out rapidly during the last century, means enlarging the human basis for economic production in the Arctic.

My Dolgan hosts that morning on the Khatanga river were not yet drawn fully into the orbit of this civilizing campaign. I asked the mother what she thought of the new schools which I had been told were now springing up in the tundra.

'We have decided to risk one of our little boys', she told me. 'A young Russian joined our herd last year and travelled with us for many months. He was a good companion and helped nicely with our animals, and with the hunting and fishing. But all the time he pestered us to give him our children so that he could educate them as he did his own. I thought there was no need for my kids to follow the ways of the Russians. I do not see that the Russians are so very much happier in their manner of life than we in ours. We were able to live very, very long without living as they do. Why should we suddenly change? But then he told my husband that all the new things that they had brought—such as the boats that go without men having to row them, and are faster than ours, the metal traps that can endure more winters than our wooden ones, and the other things which we found quite useful—were possible only because children went to school to learn how to build and use them. Of course he knew he had chosen the right man in my husband; anything that saves work will catch on with him. So he also got me to agree finally to an experiment. We gave him Tychta to see whether he could live through the experiences of Russian children. We accompanied him to Khatanga with Nikolay Alexandrovitch, the teacher, and left him there in the wooden house. Twice during the winter we returned to look him up, and found that he was not yet unhappy.'

I had been told before that the nomads of the Arctic have a deep mistrust of settlements and houses. They associate them with memories of their fathers who were made drunk by Russian traders and cheated of their valuable furs. They also noticed that frequently their women, when they slept with Russians, fell ill. Their children catch colds from the Europeans, who carry influenza and cold germs to the pure and germ-free air of the Arctic. The natives actually call some settlements the Valley of Death, the Turmoil, the Pond of Tears, the Whirlpool, the Hills of Misfortune, or the Ford of Unhappiness. At the beginning the fervour of the Soviets to convert the aborigines to civilization was too hasty. They took young boys and girls away to far off towns, made them live in houses and eat cooked meats. They who slept in tents throughout the Arctic winter and had been brought up on raw meat and frozen fish, caught pneumonia in Leningrad or died of indigestion because their stomachs had never known cabbage soup and bœuf stroganoff. Others languished miserably and died of tuberculosis and other infectious diseases; their bodies contained no anti-toxins against bacteria. A brake was put on the process a few years ago. Children are no longer taken away for education in Europe. Schools are brought to them.

The figures which the Culture Department of the Northern Sea Route gave me were: 13 cultural bases administered from Murmansk, Archangel, Omsk, Krasnoyarsk, Yakutsk and Vladivostok, controlling in their turn 466 schools and 300 medical centres. Over 2,000 teachers for the North. Schools comprise at present four classes with thirty children to each class; 15,500 children altogether. There are also courses for the liquidation of illiteracy among the old. Nearly 30 per cent adult illiterates have already been taught the alphabet; 65 to 70 per cent of the children are able to read and write. I should add that, among my hosts, the father and the old woman, the girl and the three little boys, had no idea of writing. The young women, the young man and the boy who had come with his father to look at our machine, could draw some Russian and some Latin letters on a piece of paper which I gave them. They also knew the inscription on a five-rouble note, which I left when I departed.

The method of education now adopted is gradual. After passing through the tundra school, the most intelligent children are sent on to some larger Siberian settlement for further instruction: to Igarka, to Dudinka, to Yeniseisk or even Krasnoyarsk. There they learn history and geography; they begin using their newly acquired knowledge of the alphabet to read books in their own language and in Russian. The curriculum of the elementary school, which contains technical instruction in the use of the rifle, fishing net and rowing boat, is continued and carried to a higher level of efficiency. Everything is done to preserve the talents of the tundra for hunting and fishing, while they become more acquainted with Soviet civilization and technical equipment. They are taught scientific means of reindeer breeding and veterinary care; they learn to handle motor boats and build timber houses. In order to preserve and help them to develop their own culture, as much time is devoted to the proper use of their own language as to Russian, which is regarded only as a kind of esperanto. The best students are finally sent to the Institute of the Northern Peoples in Leningrad. My Dolgan hosts had heard of the 'Tent of Miracles'. The eldest son had listened to the recital of some poems which a student there had written in their own language. The Arctic natives never knew how to put words on paper and pass them on. Russian scientists have created alphabets for them, as missionaries in Africa have done for some of the negro tribes. All these alphabets are based on the Latin not the Russian script.

The Soviets are very anxious to avoid being charged with Russifying even the smallest national minority. Native newspapers in Samoyed and Yakut language are now appearing in the northern settlements, and some of the Russian dailies in those localities have one or two vernacular pages.

The Northern Institute in Leningrad is anxious for its students to produce literature and urges them to write down their legends and sagas, describe their own lives, tell of their impressions of town life and their first reaction

La urḍ.
Our luḍ.
Our-luḍ urḍ.
Laq urḍ.

larq

laqr

Our luḍ. larq

From the text book for children of the Gellyak tribes published by the State
Publishing House for educational books Moscow, 1936.

zaq

z | a | q

zaq

Zz

Oɦlagu p'suɖra.

Maʈki-oɦla	ŋəŋk-zuɖra.
Umgu-oɦla	ŋəɦs-ʈuɖra.
Utku-oɦla	təmk-zuɖra.

Oɦla-men imŋ-əri p'suinəɖ.
Oɦlagu plakat-rajuɖ.

Tət ozr, təmk-zuja,

ŋəɦs-ʈuja, ŋəŋk-zuja!

Z Z Z zom zaq

From the text book for children of the Gellyak tribes published by the State
Publishing House for educational books Moscow, 1936.

towards civilization. Work in rhyme and prose produced by these students is printed and sent to the North for the children in the Arctic schools to read. Translations of Pushkin, Tolstoy, Gorki and Turgenyev are also made at the Institute by the students representing their tribes. Of course there are also pamphlets containing the fundamental ideas underlying the Soviet conception of State, society and economy, and others with useful hints for the improvement of their economic life. My hostess, who was quite a staunch reactionary, said: 'She would certainly not be taught by Russians what to do with her reindeer', but her son dared to contradict her and said that, so far as he was concerned, he would not mind learning to drive a motor boat if all one has to do is to stand behind a wheel and look out instead of having to sweat at the oars.

At the cultural bases, special educational films are shown to the natives, dealing with their own methods of production. They are invited to see them when they come in the winter to sell their furs. To make it more pleasant, they are also shown short pictures dealing with national life and Arctic expeditions, and some which teach them how other nations live within the Soviet Union.

My host, who kept mostly silent, being the eldest in the tent and apparently rather piqued because he had to use his son as interpreter to talk to me, once remarked casually: 'I know probably more about the life of the Russians far away than they do about ours.'

To check how far he was actually acquainted with modern life I chanced a question. 'What do you think about motor cars?'

'Good', he nodded, full of dignity.

'Ever seen one', I went on.

'No, but I know all about it.'

'How would you describe it?'

'Describe it, describe it . . .' he got a little sore at my unrespectful interviewing. 'Simply a seaplane like

yours outside. But no wings, and it runs on the ground only.'

The people of the Arctic are getting to know modern technical instruments in a curiously inverted order. The territories in which they hunt for precious fur, and roam about with their reindeer herds, are rapidly being penetrated by Soviet aviation. River steamers follow later; and for cars it is still too early, as there are no roads. Motor sledges, however, are already putting in an appearance in some places and give rise to new superstition among the old and admiration among the young drivers of reindeer sledges.

After I had taken the tea which was offered me as breakfast, my hosts took me to a neighbouring family. They seemed to be relatives of some sort. Their tent looked cleaner and the landlady there was just cheerily using a sewing machine. It stood on the floor in front of her, while she, with her legs tucked under her like a Turk, drove the wheel with her hand.

'What a beautiful machine', I greeted her.

From the baby's shirt which she was just manufacturing, she looked up and grinned broadly. 'Where did you buy it?'

It was a stupid question. Of course she had not bought it.

'I got it as a premium', she said, 'on March 8th this year, International Women's Day.' Premiums are very much in vogue in Russia to-day. Goods of which there is still some scarcity, such as bicycles, gramophones, cameras and motor cars, are given to good workers and to 'cultural leaders'. Apart from their actual value the goods have also a social importance as a sign of honour and privilege. 'I am a cult Stakhanovist', the woman went on. I had heard of Stakhanovist workers before; here apparently the term was also used in connection with special merits in the field of cultural progress. 'Don't you see how clean my tent is?' she challenged me. 'And I wash my children every week, as the doctor told me. They will live twice as long as Natya's.' She pointed to my reactionary hostess, who had introduced me but was now leaving furiously at being insulted by her cousin. As she did not understand Russian herself, the cultural champion had repeated her remark in Dolgan, lest there was any misunderstanding. With this good woman culture and progress were obviously supreme. She had picture books which she took out to show to me; they are printed for illiterate natives and describe scenes from their lives and also give propaganda for the leaders of the State, including the native chairmen of the district Soviet. Pictures were given of native children marching in a row with Russian, Georgian, Chinese and Turkoman boys and girls from other Republics in the Soviet Union, all carrying Red flags demonstrating their solidarity.

This spirit is propagated everywhere in Russia. The sentimental love towards the national minorities is remarkable among the Russians of the younger generation. Wherever the Russian workers come into contact with the native population, agitators are at work continuously telling them that it is their first duty to behave like brothers, like elder brothers, towards them, to help them on and to respect their peculiarities. The idea of the white man's burden is very prevalent among the Red missionaries. The Russian girls at the club in Port Igarka—who were never slow in asking the boys to dance with them—were careful to give the Tungus and Samoyed boys at least an equal chance with the Russians. It has become more than a political dogma for the large masses in Russia to regard the different races in the Union as brothers. A kind of pride and joy at the variety of colours and nationalities of the country has been established. The feeling of being rich in different national cultures, languages, arts and customs, from Arctic to sub-tropical, from Far Eastern to European, is imbued into the youth. 'We have all the

(LEFT) SHE WASHES HER CHILDREN

varieties of men that exist in the world within our own country', a worker boasted to me at Igarka, when I discussed this question with him. And he had an almost snobbish liking for the negro stokers on the British ships that called at the port. 'There are no blacks in Russia', I teased him. 'But they would like to live here', he replied. 'A black comrade from New York said so only the other day when he was interviewed before the microphone in Moscow.'

The main principle applied in the campaign to 'raise the Arctic natives' is to get it done as far as possible by the natives themselves. They are asked to form nomadic Soviets, a form of government which is presented to them as only a short step away from their own tribal councils. Nor is the revolution halting at the fringe of the Arctic. The tribes are encouraged by Red missionaries to collectivize their reindeer herds, and the resistance of the *shamans*, their medicine men, is broken by young Communists who expose them to ridicule. They do it by giving them a taste of their own medicine. As soon as the tribes find out that doctors and veterinary surgeons can drive away just as effectively as the *shaman* the evil spirits that have crept into the bodies of men and reindeer, they give their confidence to the new doctors. And soon they believe what their new friends tell them: that the *shaman* is a parasite who tries to live on their ignorance and superstition.

My little progressive Dolgan hostess No. 2 on the Khatanga river told me how she herself was convinced that the young Comsomol girl who visited her was right and not the *shaman*. 'He said that the aeroplanes were flying devils, with whom the Russians had made a pact to destroy us. But last year I saw one and touched it myself. Then I saw that it was really made of the same material as my tea-pot. And when the pilot invited us to fly with him, my grandfather decided that, being the oldest, he would risk least if he exposed himself to the danger. When he came back he reported that he had been in heaven and seen no gods there at all. Then we knew that the *shaman* had been lying when he told us that the birds had told him that they would always bring him messages from the gods, which we would have to obey.'

There are rich and poor in the tundra as well as anywhere else in the world. Some men have herds up to 3000 reindeer, others only 25. Those with the many reindeer are likely to get richer because they can afford to take the sons of poor men into their services and augment their herds. The poorer are likely to lose the few animals they have as soon as one or two fall ill. Once they are reindeerless they and their families offer their services to the rich, receiving as payment their food and shelter in the colder parts of the rich man's tent, and five or six reindeer a year. This number is so small that it is hardly worth while trying to breed more; also they have not the time to look after them properly, having to devote all their energies towards watching their employers' herd. They usually slaughter them, therefore, and keep their frozen meat as a reserve from which they augment the daily food wages.

The system adopted by the Russians is not simple or dictated expropriation. They try to persuade the poorer people in the tribe to decide that the richer have to give a number of reindeer for communal service. A resolution is taken in the tribal council that the rich man has to supply all the reindeer needed to carry the fur of the trappers to the trading centre and to carry back again the food for the whole tribe. If he refuses he can be taken to court, but this has not happened so far. Then a Comsomol girl or boy, specially educated, is sent out to help the small reindeer owners to organize themselves as a collective community. Ten families are taken together. In winter they pitch their tents near each other. Some women wash and watch all the children. Others go out and collect firewood for the whole unit. The men go out and put their traps collectively and inspect them every fifth day according to a rota. In the second half of April all tribes in the Arctic move north. The ten families collectively move together. They stop at the great rivers, where the old people and children remain. One tent with a few young men as reindeer-shepherds follow the animals still further north in their search for food, while the rest devote themselves to fishing. Instead of each family laying out a small net, they are persuaded to try out the larger nets, some a mile long, which the Russians give them. Just as there are motor tractor stations in agricultural regions of Russia from which machinery is lent to the collective farms, so centres for mechanization and rationalization of fishing and trapping are now being established in the Arctic. Motor boats, metal traps and large nets can be hired there. There were three such stations open last summer; there are to be 13 by 1937, if the plan is fulfilled, and 18 in 1938. These stations are at the same time equipped as cultural bases with a staff of forty-eight employees: including doctors, veterinary surgeons, nurses, teachers, technical advisers, experts in cattle breeding, and others.

The experiment is, I think, extraordinarily interesting. What one aims at is the raising of the native methods of production in order to increase their output and give them more security and freedom to develop their cultural life. If the Russians have their way, the natives will leave their children at the cultural bases at least during the winter months and they will transform the life in the tundra within one generation. There is no intention to make them settle on a permanent basis. This would be inconsistent with the natural economic requirements of the Arctic. But they could—as the Soviets hope they will— become half settled in so far as they will recognize the cultural bases as their political, educational and economic centre, and also improve their living conditions with the help of modern technical equipment. Mechanized semi-

nomads would be the right definition of this future state of
the Arctic population.

The law protects them against exploitation. Trade
with them is only permitted to the State or to co-operative
organizations. They are exempt from all taxes and con-
scription. Minimum prices are fixed for their products,
and the prices of commodities supplied to them by the
trading stations are determined by the State so that they
can afford all necessities of life. It is regarded of lesser
importance whether the scheme is a paying proposition
immediately. The Government hope that it will prove
very profitable on a national scale in the future, and the
primary object is to preserve them and, if possible, help
them to grow once more into larger communities. Autonomous national districts are established—at least on the
map—according to the usual area travelled by each tribe,
and a comprehensive right to the soil and its content is
given to them on paper as a guarantee for the future.
Native chairmen of such autonomous districts are already
officiating in some regions.

I met the chairman for Taimyr in Khatanga. He wore
European clothes and owned a gramophone. Special
broadcasts for the natives from the cultural bases, and the
distribution of wireless sets to all tent-collectives is a programme for the next few years. The minimal plan of
achievement for 1937 is the general acceptance and use by
the tribes of soap and toothbrushes, and the persuasion of
the largest possible number of mothers to bring their
children for regular medical examination. Hygiene is a very
essential point in the scheme, as only through it will it be
possible to arrest the decline in the native birth rate and
the spread of the trachoma.

New names are given or, as the Soviet insist, the true
names recognized for those tribes. The Tungus, for instance,
never called themselves by that name. Their answer,
when you asked them who and what they were, was, Evyenki.

The Samoyeds called themselves Nyentse, the Eskimo Innuits, the Ostyaks Keti, the Dolgans Sakho. These words were always the equivalents in their respective language for our word 'men', 'humans', or 'people'. They had no consciousness of national entity. The names under which they were known to the Russians had often a root in despising and ridiculing descriptions which Russian traders gave them after first meetings. They called some of these native tribes 'dirty ones'; and the Samoyeds, for instance, owe their name to a Russian phrase meaning 'self-eaters'. The main purpose of the Institute of the Northern Peoples in Leningrad is to educate cadres of teachers, political leaders and organizers and technical instructors for the Arctic population.

'I shall go to the Institute myself next year and take all my children with me', my culture championess declared. 'And my husband can stay behind and remain like an ignorant bear, if he does not want to come with me.'

There are three faculties at the Institute: a Soviet section which comprises history, law, political education and economics; a business section (agriculture, fishing, hunting with modern technical instruments, trade, fur breeding and elements of zoology and botany generally, industrialization etc.); and a pedagogical section.

From No. 1 faculty come the future organizers of nomad Soviets, political agitators and instructors; from No. 2 the chiefs of trading stations, organizers of collectivization; from No. 3 the teachers for the native colleges and schools.

This education is free—and more than free, for each student gets a stipend, including clothes, food, quarters, books, sports, theatres, cinemas, excursions and twenty-five roubles pocket money a month. When they write or translate for publication, the royalties are paid to them according to general standard. The same applies for works of art, painting and sculpture. A small number come with their wives and some even with children, who are educated at the Institute from the outset. Some get married during their school period. In such cases they are given separate rooms. Marriage to Russians is discouraged, because it is hoped that they will go back to the North after their studies are completed. Two cases of inter-marriage have occurred, and the couples were asked to live outside the Institute. The general instruction is given in Russian, since the native languages represented by the three hundred students are so different that some common language has to be used. But, each race or tribe has also its own class in their mother tongue. There they are taught the proper use of their own language and encouraged to make it richer and develop it with the help of the new alphabet.

The Institute fulfills a twofold purpose. Practical scientific work, (ethnography and philology) and the education of native cadres. One of the students of the Institute, a Yukagir from the Kolyma region, Tacki Odulok, who has meanwhile qualified for a professorship, has written several books, one of which is even published in English.

When I visited the summer camp of the Institute at Luga, near the Estonian border, I had an opportunity to get more closely acquainted with the students. In one room I saw about thirty of them, boys and girls, round a circle, two by two, and practising steps at the command of a Russian teacher who stood in the centre and shouted continuously, 'one, two, three', 'one, two, three', 'one, two, three'. They were learning the elements of the foxtrot. Once they would be familiar with them, the dance-master told me, they would proceed one step further and try it with piano music. I could not see the reason why it was necessary for them to partake even of that blessing of our civilization, when they had pretty dances of their own. The dance-master, however, explained it. "They live here for four years, and of course they are going out frequently. We want them to get used to mixing freely with Europeans.

Also in the Northern towns that exist or will be built within
a few years they will move among Russians and other nations
from all over the Union. Everybody wants to dance nowadays. We would not like our students, who should become
selfconscious leaders of their tribes, to feel shy or inferior
in the company of Europeans merely because they cannot
share in their social amusements. There is no need for
them to carry the foxtrot into the tundra, and we tell them
so. But why should they feel at a disadvantage in company
with Europeans? All our efforts are directed towards
making them self-assured. We must do away with the old
idea of their national inferiority, prevalent among themselves as well as among their Russian fellow citizens.'

They showed more skill at their native dances which
I asked them to produce for me later on. But first they
introduced me to their own sport. From six stools they
improvised a row of sledges, such as usually stand outside
a tent camp in the winter. Then they jumped over them—
a distance of six feet—without taking a run. That was one
sport.

Then they tied a boy with a cord. He crept on all
fours and, acting the part of a young bear caught by Tungus
hunters, he moaned and groaned and tried to bite his
friends' legs who held him at a short leash. The idea
of this game is that a bear wins his freedom if he succeeds
in catching the leg of a hunter who in turn is then tied
up as the bear.

Their native songs sounded rather monotonous to my
European ear, yet there was a distinct note of cheerfulness
in them and they were quite free of the melancholy of many
Russian melodies. Their round dances were definitely
expressions of a serene joy of life and gaiety, a trend of
temperament common to all people of the Far North.

Among the students was one who is by way of becoming a
famous star, for he has appeared in a circus in Moscow as
an imitator of the cries and movements of birds. He has

composed short rhymes in the form of stories such as the birds would tell. Between each line he gives typical birds' cries and reproduces the fluttering of their wings and their hopping over the moss in a manner that is both deliciously funny and true to life.

'I am the Cuckoo, I am the Cuckoo', he cried, and with knees bent, jumped round our circle, 'I am the Cuckoo, I am in the South, but although it is warm here—Cuckoo! Cuckoo! I long for the quiet and freedom of the North. I am the Cuckoo! Cuckoo! I shall come back to you, my friends in the North, I shall lay my eggs in the safety of your Northern tundra. . . .'

He then sang similar songs for the hazelgrouse, the heathwild, the ptarmigan. The cries of all these birds may differ little to our ears; but Vilka, who as a boy has known and loved the birds as perhaps other children know and love Mickey Mouse, could characterize each of them distinctly by some slight change of tune or voice. He also showed how they fly over the water with wings extended, how they dive for fish—he contorted his neck and swung his head—and how they snap for insects, which he acted by throwing his mouth forward and clicking with his tongue.

A few students wrote down some lines of their biography for me when I asked them for it. Here they are:

'Dunya: My mother was Chinese, my father a Goldi. 5000 Goldi live in Russia, 15,000 in Manchukuo. But they are suppressed by the Japanese and the Chinese as well. I lived in a native village north of Vladivostok. When I was thirteen my parents decided to wed me to a boy in the village according to local custom. This I would not do and in my grief I went to a Comsomol girl who led a pioneer group in our village. She helped me to run away and come here to this Institute. I have now been here for four years, have learned to read and write, can speak Russian fluently and have read much literature, Tolstoy and Pushkin and, of course, Gorki. I have also been to Moscow and seen

the new underground railway. Soon I shall go back to my
people and teach them how to become free from their old
superstitions and the whip of the *shaman*.'

Alexander Konstantinovitch Tychta: 'I am a Gellyak.
The Gellyaks are now called Nivkhy, as they really should be
called. I was born in 1909. In 1920 I came to the region
of the Amur River and worked there in a small village for
four years. It was nearer the world than the village where
I had been born. That was far out in the taiga. But my
parents were so poor that I had to go and work for others.
Now they are collectivized and better off together with
other families. I had to go south and work for a rich
peasant. I helped him for three years. All I had to do was
to fish. I could not read nor write. His wife was a *shaman*.
I had to help her to beat the drum and boil the water for her
medicines and catch dogs, which she needed to brew
medicines. I did all the two asked from me, because my
head was empty and my stomach too. Once I said I wanted
to go to a school and learn to read. That day the peasant
beat me and forbade me ever to talk of it again. In 1927
I finally ran away from this *kulak* and soon joined the Young
Communist League. I learnt something about agriculture,
became an instructor on Sakhalien and helped to organize
collective fisheries. The Comsomol built up my personality.
My sight got clearer. I was soon out in charge of a collective
formed by forty-six family units. But I wanted to learn
more. And so I took a preparatory course for this Institute
and after five months showed such great efficiency that
I was given a money premium and sent to Nikolayevsk
on Amur, where I taught children in the school to read
and at the same time perfected my own knowledge further,
until finally I got here where I shall study to be a real
pedagogue. Please tell the world that I have been born
in darkness, but that now that I have seen the light, I
regard it as my duty to go on further and further.'

Maremjamin: 'I am twenty years old and come from the

upper Obi. I can kill a bear as quickly as any man in my tribe. Now I am a Voroshilov sniper. I love Stalin. His picture is tattooed on my chest. I had this done when I was still at home. But here they have told me that this was an uncultured way of showing my loyalty. I should have worn his picture, which is to me the symbol of my liberation, inside my chest and not outside on my skin. I long to go back to my people. I am happy here. But I want them to become quite as happy there, all of them. I shall take everything that made me happy here to them in my chest and my head. I shall show that I have been worthy of the education I was given here. There is much to be done. Do you know how my people lived before? Russian traders came and gave a man vodka, then they said: "For this vodka you owe me ten squirrel furs". The man replied: "No, no, this is too much hunting for so little vodka". So the trader gave him a few more glasses and then said: "Now you owe me twenty squirrel furs. I shall come for them next year". The Ostyak was quite drunk meanwhile and so he said: "Yes, I owe you twenty squirrel furs", and he sang that dirtiest of all songs which Russians taught my countrymen: "I thank thee, elder brother, for thou hast stilled my thirst, I bow to thee, elder brother, for I am a scoundrel anyway". Once he had contracted such a debt he would stick to it and his sons would have to pay for him, should he die, or become ill, and be unable to shoot enough squirrels through their forehead. It was a sacred debt. When someone said: "But you have been cheated by the Russian trader", the man from my tribe would reply: "I know, but if he is a crook, that is no reason at all why I should follow his dirty example and break my word". That is all different now. I, for instance, am given a good education. I have learnt to fly on a glider. I can drive a motor car. Our Institute has an automobile and six gliders, on which we all practice.'

The library of the Institute had a record of what the

students read.   In 1935 the following numbers of books
had been issued: 960 'Poems of Pushkin', 950 'Tales by
Tolstoy', 950 'the Stories of Jules Verne', 815 novels and
plays by Gorki, 700 Swift (*Gulliver's Travels*), 600 Kipling
(the *Jungle Book*), 450 different fiction by Jack London.

The students I interviewed in some of the colleges actually
in the North were much less advanced in their knowledge
of Soviet theories and the world in general.   One boy at the
native school of Igarka—his age was twenty-three—could
show me America, England, France on a map when I
asked him where these countries were.   Yet about life there
he could say little more than: 'They are all very unhappy.
They have still got capitalism.   And their workers and
peasants have to work for people who are as cruel and bad
to them as our rich reindeer owner was to my father and
mother before the revolution.'

Great efforts are made to stimulate artistic activity
among the Northern races.   The Institute in Leningrad
has produced some theatrical plays, written and acted by
students, depicting scenes from their national life.
Uspienski, a famous painter in the Soviet Union, has
arranged classes in graphic art and sculpture for them and
achieved results some of which I saw and which were
really astounding in their originality and genuineness of
subjects and treatment.   Of their literature I have taken
some examples home with me.   Here they are:

TUNGUS RIDDLES

1. An old woman stands, holding up the sky.   (Smoke.)
2. I go and go, but leave no trace; I cut and cut, but shed no
   blood.   (A boat floating on the water.)
3. An elk walking in a birch grove.   (The tongue and teeth.)
4. Five peasants in one hut.   (A glove.)
5. One peasant, walking, has dropped a lasso.   (The road.)
6. Two brothers cannot see each other.   (The eyes.)

SONGS OF THE TUNDRA

THE MIGHTY VICTOR

A Nenietz (Samoyed) Song (New)

And death in the North
Migrated to live
The day the herd of preying beasts arrived
The heads of Nenietz's from the Gidayansk tundra
Lay everywhere. With every year there
Were more of them on the earth.
Death conquered the nomad life,
Until there arrived at the white island
  A mighty,
   Good,
    Wise
     Man.
He was the great leader of the peoples of the earth
The wisest man in the world,
The great Stalin,
With an ancient thing of a pipe!
We buried death in a cave
And sowed life in the tundras of Gidayam.
Now everything is good with us in the bands.
We have a bath house,
It is lighter than the sun in our tents,
Fiery bubbles
Splash with light.
And the skull of our ancestor
Washed with snowstorms
And the blood of grandsons, said:
'Drink to the man
Who has conquered the nomad existence.'
And we drink a song to the leader and friend:
'We have a collective farm, factory and town.
Large, handsome, unusual,
Like the blossoming life of the snows,
Is he, the great victor of death,
Wisest under moon and sun,
As great as the world,
Man and leader as great as Lenin,
Great friend of the peoples of the world—Stalin.'

(Written down by F. Duborov.)

126

ABOUT MYSELF

My father and my mother I have lost,
An orphan child, I walked among the deer
For days and nights . . .
No human words I heard,
I only knew the lowing of young deer,
I never washed myself with water, for
It was the rain that washed me of itself.
   An orphan, then,
   I worked and slaved
   For other people, a drudge.
   I wore fur-jackets (not my own),
   I carried wood and ice
   And was a Son of Frost.
I never came to see fat meat,
For all I ate were scraps.
I never tasted proper food,
Berries alone I ate.
   I never saw things fair and light,
   Except the Sunshine fair . . .
   I fought the mighty Frost, I was
   In sore need, and to sleep
   I often went half-starved.
But, like a bird's white young, out of dark night
I rose at daybreak, orphan that I was,
And I became a Son of Splendid Day.
I am no more a shepherd for the deer,
A teacher I will be for many a man.
I left off carrying wood and ice, I now
Keep studying hard, a writer I will be
And I will put smooth speech into men's lips
And open many eyes on many a thing.
   Like a blind egg, I lived in darkness, and
   I had no knowledge in me and no wit,
   But Lenin showed all men a new, bright life.
   When I knew that, I took the Lenin way,
   I took the way of Lenin, straight and fair.
I strive to make the life of Ewens bright,
I want them all to know who Lenin was.

(Translated from Lamut into Russian by B. Levin. English
version by Lydia Averianova.)

THE GLIDER

A fine, swift-running deer they caught for me,
One fit to trod the clouds . . .
On that fine deer
They put me
They said:
"'Tis well to hold the bridle with all thy might.'
I grasped and held the bridle with all my might.
At last they caused the mighty deer to move --
A mighty deer that jumped up and soared high,
Thundering, whistling, buzzing
In my ears.
The wind swept boldly off my paltry hat:
It would have shot, falcon-like, down and down,
But for my holding it back with my palm. . . .
Where I look down,
The earth was fair to see:
Enormous houses looked like tiny beads,
Green fields --
The size of little blankets, spread below, ·
The railroad stretched itself as thin as thread.
Bird-like I face the wind,
In noise I fly,
And while I flew, I gave a thought
To my deer Kotatchan, who would have stopped
And been behind, had he but tried to run. . . .
Space trodden in a year
By him, I leave behind
In one short day.
He's left behind, pasturing. . . .
While I love
And do enjoy a deer that treads
The air.
If that deer could be taught the proper way,
It would get to the Indigirka river in three days.
Eagle-like I soar: the deer that treads the air
Is mine.
I have become a Son
Of Clouds.

(Translated from Lamut into Russian by B. Lewin. English
version by Lydia Averianova.)

Planer

Min nonon həl dəgi nudun modu dətlə!kəndu
dəgsidu hupkucəku

Mindu ajiŋu tugsə ucikkon
              həpkəmkēn,
Minu ajiŋna ucikla uwur.
Gun: — Ņogi ajmakaņ ʒawli!
Ņogdi kiŋkimakaņ həpkənəm.
Ucikanʒaw ilʙəsnə.
Ucikanʒacakan tusaŋcin,
Dəgəlrən ugəsjēki
Kurərgəkən, dirərgəkən.

The first bars of the Lamut original.

THE IRON BIRD (New)

A reindeer runs through the tundra, runs, runs. . . .
Many dreams we dream in the snow. . . .
Oi, long is the road to Kheti-River. . . .
Oi, Oi!

But now has flown to us in the tundra
A new bird, swift as a bullet,
A Soviet bird,
Oi, Oi!

This iron bird knows no dreams,
Swift as the wind,
A fine bird,
Oi, Oi!

(Written down by A. Klimov. A song sung in the Avamo-Khatansk tundra about the aeroplanes of the pilots Molokov, Alexeev, Makhotkin, Golovin, Orlov, etc., by a young native girl, Agasha Aksenova, April, 1935, at Dudinka.)

THE STORY OF KOLYA NOYANOV

Spring. The sun was warming the tundra. Along all the coast of Kamchatka the people were beginning to come out of their dark dug-outs to warm themselves in the sun.

One day I awoke early. I was lying in our summer tent—the tundra was all singing like a bird. I listened and heard a cow crying out. Four times it cried. When it cried out a fifth time I went out of my tent and saw an enormous floating house. I went to look at it. The people were all still asleep. The house was as white as a swan which floats on the river. My heart beat. They had arrived to fetch me, and I wasn't ready.

Soon the boys arrived. I began to collect my things in my reindeer-skin sack.

Then I went to the shore with the lads. I began to pick flowers. 'Good-bye, my dear flowers', I said. All the tundra was beautiful with flowers.

In the evening the floating house came close to the shore, and I began to say good-bye to my friends. Those who had come to fetch me explained that the floating house was a steamer as they took me on to it up a wooden hill. And I wondered what I had got on to. When this steamer moved I looked in front. There was nobody pulling it along, yet behind it the water was running away in waves. Afterwards I guessed what it was: there was a *shaman* on the steamer, and evidently evil spirits were drawing it along.

The steamer seemed very big to me. My head swam round. I felt sad. Then I saw one of the Russians I had met going into a little cabin. I went in too, and it didn't smell at all nice. It was a lavatory, as he explained. I began to laugh at myself. He took me along to his comrades. But I didn't start talking at once, because I was looking at the little lamp. I was wondering how it kept alight without reindeer fat.

And I wondered again how the steamer was moving. If we had to row with oars, it would be difficult for me ; the steamer was heavy. I longed for my home.

When I awoke next morning the steamer was at a standstill. I saw the settlement of Uka, which I knew. I thought it over. It took two days to get to Uka by dogs, and only a night by the steamer. The steamer was large and heavy, but it moved swiftly. We move swiftly with dogs, too, but it was a couple of days' travelling to Uka. I didn't know then what makes a steamer go along.

A few days later we arrived at Petropavlovsk. It is the chief town of Kamchatka. I was glad. Now I would see a town! I hardly had time enough to look around me, there were so many steamers and boats. Then something glittered in my eyes, some kind of red ladder. I thought it must be a *shaman's* ladder: it was so tall. Only a *shaman* could go up it. Afterwards I was told it was a wireless station.

Then we went on shore. I walked as though in a dream. I was very astonished. In the evening the steamer went on to Vladivostok. The town of Petropavlovsk was all burning with lights. I thought: that's where people live like people. Only I didn't know where the light came from. They told me it was 'electricity'. I didn't understand what 'electricity' was.

We arrived at Vladivostok early in the morning of the eighth day. And only when the others began to get off the boat did I come to myself. I stared at the shore, and there I saw some kind of animals running with round legs and great icy eyes. When they came close to anyone they cried like a bear: 'Boo, boo!' There were lots of these running animals. When I went into the town with my comrades, I stumbled, because I wasn't looking where I was going. I walked along as though on my head, and my head didn't understand a thing. I was very afraid that a strong wind might blow and the walls would fall on me. They were very high; I had never seen such walls before. We walked along. Suddenly I saw a house running, and people sitting inside it, and on the ground was a stout wire rope. And the house went along the rope. They told me it was a tramway. Then came some more running things with great eyes. They stared at the road all the time, and didn't look at anybody, and ran along so.

Then I was sent for to go to Leningrad, to the Institute of Peoples of the North.

In Leningrad I didn't like the houses, they were so tall they hid everything. I wanted to see something farther away. But afterwards I saw a good deal in Leningrad.

When I was at home, I didn't know that there was anybody living anywhere else besides in Kamchatka.

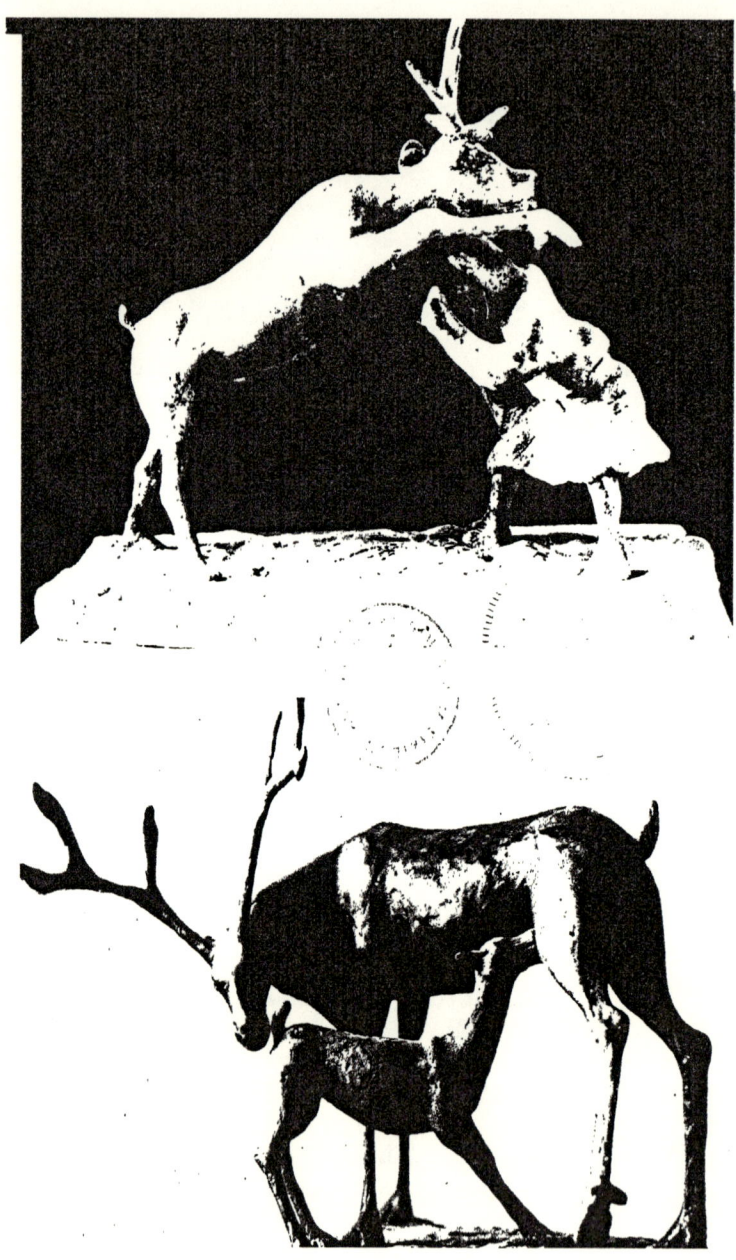

When I was sent to study by the district Executive Committee, I wondered what could be made of such an ignorant youngster. I didn't know anything then. I was very ignorant.

Now I am studying in the Institute of Peoples of the North.

Now I have learnt what moves a steamer and what radio is.

Now I laugh at my former incorrect understanding of everything.

(From: *The Tent of Miracles.*)

CHAPTER IX

SHIP-LOADS OF TOWNS

A TOWN, a whole town with population, houses, motor boats, library and livestock, was dispatched in July, 1936, on five steamers—four from Archangel and one from Vladivostok—to the point on the north-eastern coast of Siberia where the longitude of Hong Kong crosses the latitude of Central Greenland. Everything had been packed into boxes and parcels. The houses, of Karelian timber, had been so constructed that they could be taken to pieces for the journey and reassembled later.

Behind these strange ship-loads is a long story of exploration and venture. Four years ago, Emilianzov, geologist of a dog-team expedition in Eastern Taimyr and the Republic of Yakutia, was told by natives of salt deposits at the Bay of Nordvyk, on the Nordenskioeld Sea. Samples were taken home, and during the next year a Polar station was built in a favourable position on a fairly well sheltered spot near 74th degree Northern latitude and 112th Eastern longitude. As in other Polar stations, the staff watched the weather, sent meteorological reports by wireless to Moscow, and explored the surrounding country. Smirnov, the chief geologist on the station, continued Emilianzov's investigations; and in the next spring a radio message was sent to Moscow:

LARGE SALT DEPOSITS DISCOVERED IN DISTRICT ROUND CAPE NORDVYK STOP GEOLOGICAL ANALYSIS SHOWED TRACES OF MINERAL OIL STOP THEORY JUSTIFIED OIL NEXT TO SALT LIKE AT BAKU STOP 16 MILES INLAND ALSO OPEN COALFIELDS STOP CONTINUING EXPLORATION AND CALCULATION STOP WILL ADVISE PRESENTLY WHETHER TRIAL BORINGS FOR ESTABLISHMENT ECONOMIC VALUE FINDINGS JUSTIFIED.

Since then the staff of the Polar station has been gradually increased. When I arrived at Nordvyk on August 18th, 1936, after my somewhat hazardous journey in Sadkov's plane, 108 men and 8 women, the whole population, welcomed us on the beach. Within two minutes after we had come down on the water, the machine was pulled ashore and tied to wooden poles. I got hold of my rucksack and suitcase and we walked up a small hill softly rising from the beach. The ground was muddy, and I stuck almost at every step. Once I had to extract my foot first and my boot afterwards to free myself.

In a wide depression behind the hill stood four timber houses. In the forest parts of Siberia, the houses had all been made entirely of logs. Here beams were used only to carry the structure, which was of isolating material of treble thickness, covered on the outside by wooden boards. It was curious to notice how the buildings, so near to each other, were yet connected by telephone wires—for there are times in winter when the fierce Arctic cyclone makes even those small distances a fearful hazard. The telephone saves much time and risk. A motor-car engine, driving a dynamo, is the power station for this settlement, providing current for light, telephones, and the radio transmitter.

'From next year onwards we shall use our own coal for heating and electric power. This will be cheaper than transporting petrol all the way from Baku up to the Arctic, and we shall then have a larger reserve tank for our air base' the station chief told me.

Alexander Alexandrovitch Deviatkin, a man in his forties, with white hair, and a very human smile, had taken charge of Nordvyk Polar station three years ago. He had had previous Arctic experience on Novaya Zemlya and is a trained geologist. His wife, who stays at Nordvyk with him, works as a geodesist. On the day of my arrival he was to hand over his reign to Boris Vassilyevitch Lavrov. From that day Nordvyk was no longer to be called Polyarnaya

Stantsia Nordvyk, but Nordvykstroi in other words, Nordvyk construction job. I found that everyone spoke in the future tense. 'Next week the boat will arrive.' 'In two months we shall have six hundred people here and ten houses.' 'In the winter, a newspaper will appear twice weekly.' 'Next summer we shall dispatch the first big load of salt, and in two years the boring towers for Nordvyk oil will be working at full speed.'

My party had been the first outsiders to reach Nordvyk that year. The bay had only cleared itself of ice in the middle of July. A change of wind brought in some flocs even in August—and in September they were already expecting winter to set in afresh. Nordvykers know two seasons only: winter and August. But that seems to concern them very little. I had expected to see nothing but ice and snow in the Arctic, and had even been a little disappointed to find such comparatively high temperature throughout my flight. At Nordvyk itself it was never colder than 36° F. while I was there. The local people said that the finest time was May and June, when the snow was still covering the hilly 'suburbs' of their four-house town and there was full sunlight the clock round. The weather that year had not been too good, the thermometer stayed around zero, but the sun had been so good and so strong that they were all tanned like Palm Beach bathing belles.

'What a romantic life you are leading up here,' I exclaimed while we were talking over our boiling hot fish soup. Deviatkin's wife looked across at me eagerly. 'Romantic, not at all! You don't think that we came here because we wanted thrilling adventures, do you? We are just soldiers on one section of the front of Socialist construction. This town is not a newspaper stunt, and we are not crazy to come up here just for fun. We came because of the industrial importance of the place. We are here to build and to enrich our country—for no other purpose.'

I had insisted on going to Nordvyk because I had read an

article by Boris Lavrov, its founder-to-be, in the *Sovyetski Polyarnik*. He wrote:

'The valley of the river Khatanga is among the least explored regions of the Far North. It is very sparsely populated, chiefly by nomads. The lower part of the river belongs to Yakutia, the upper to the administrative district of Krasnoyarsk. The tremendous distances from the administrative centre are responsible for the fact that it is very poorly served. At the same time this region is of great importance. Investigations have established that there are enormous deposits of coal, oil and rock salt, and it is quite possible that there are also various metals. The growing industry of catching and canning fish in the Far East and in Murmansk has raised the very serious question of its supply with salt. Hitherto the Far East received its salt from Odessa, whence it has had to travel through the Mediterranean, the Red Sea, the Indian Ocean and the Yellow Sea to the Northern Pacific or across the Atlantic and through the Panama Canal right across the Great Ocean. Pavlodar salt, also had to be brought over 5500 miles of railway to Vladivostok and loaded on ships for Sakhalien, Kamchatka and the Chukotka Peninsula.

'Khatanga river salt, as it is found near Nordvyk, lies half-way on the Northern Sea Route and can be sent both east and west by vessels arriving with loads for the rivers Lena and Kolyma. It would not only allow a fuller use of the boats and greatly cheapen the transport. The quantities expected from the salt valley would be sufficient to supply all the eastern sector of the Arctic and the Far East for 150 to 200 years of intense and industrialized fisheries. About 20,000,000 roubles of capital investment, to be sunk in this enterprise in 1936, can safely be regarded as a sound proposition.'

Hence the decision of the Council of Labour and Defence to build Nordvyk as a new industrial centre. Hence the explorations and boring work in the salt valley, the search for coal, the plans for borings for oil and the preparation for a port. Hence, also, the five ship-loads of town from Archangel and Vladivostok.

It was proposed to end the research work by January 1st, 1937, and then to open the first mine. Boring for oil would probably not have begun before March, 1937. It was hoped, however, to have begun the coal mining before then, for the coal was needed for the town itself. During 1936, about six hundred people came to Nordvyk. A large number of them settled in the district round Koshevnikov Bay, some remained on the Peninsula of Urung Tumus, some went higher up to Sindasko Bay in the estuary of the Khatanga, and about forty began work on drawing the coal and hewing the timber on the river Kotui. In addition the organization has certain secondary tasks—the development of fisheries and trapping, the capture of wild reindeer, the development of cattle rearing and vegetable planting.

According to plan, Lavrov told me, Nordvyk will produce 150,000 tons of salt in 1938. Two tons were all they had got out by the time I got there in August, 1936. But this was mined with most primitive methods. Heavy equipment was only just on the way. With 150,000 tons of salt one may preserve quite a few million barrels full of salmon and sturgeon. From that point of view it sounded not at all unreasonable to build a town even under the very difficult conditions of the Arctic. How far Nordvyk's oil will be usable for ships and aeroplanes will only be proved when the first year's boring is over. They will still have to find out whether they can build refineries on the spot. But the chief idea is, of course, that there should be an independent fuel base on the Northern Sea Route. Once the boats can take only so much oil as will take them to Nordvyk from Vladivostok or Murmansk, knowing that they will find sufficient fuel half-way through their journey, their cargo capacity will be almost doubled. The big ice-breakers in Soviet service are all of pre-War make and burn coal which they

138

get from Spitzbergen. A bunker station on Dickson Island will store some of the coal from Norilsk, the new mining centre on Taimyr. The new ice-breakers, however, will be driven with Diesel-electric power, and they also will benefit enormously from the oil to be had on the Northern Sea Route itself. Last, but not least, is the great importance of oil on the spot for Arctic aviation.

Madame Deviatkina was, of course, quite right in her emphasis of the economic importance of Nordvyk. Nevertheless I am sure that the idea of fighting in the Polar regions for new wealth—just because it is wealth that enriches a whole nation—brings a great element of romance for the people (almost all very young) who go up there. Nordvyk, when I visited it, was still a place run entirely by pioneer enthusiasts, fully conscious of the value of their work and proud of it. Friends at the dinner table talked of Nordvyk as if it was already an accomplished fact. 'Of course, you cannot understand this attitude of ours', Deviatkin said, when I interjected one of my rather sceptical remarks. 'You come from the world of capitalism that knows nothing but decline and restriction. Nothing grows with you. Your economic system is on the down grade. Therefore you have the psychology of the old. It does not matter that I have grey hair and you are only a young boy. I live in a country which changes continually. What was a dream for us five years ago, when you called our plans of construction only lies and Bolshevik propaganda, is reality to-day. What you will publish about Nordvyk as it is to-day will no longer be true when the pages of your book have come out of the printing press. When we look at a bulb we can already see the colours and enjoy the perfume of a future flower while all you see is a dirty brown onion. Our optimism is not a matter of temperament and national character as you pretend. On the contrary, the old Russian was a melancholy nihilist. Our optimism is the logical consequence of our experience. We have seen that what our leaders, and what we ourselves, laid down as our plans has come true. And therefore we can now claim your credibility and understanding for our further plans.'

He had started these remarks in a low voice between two spoonfuls of soup; he ended up in rhetoric voice and I noticed, as he finished, that the whole long table in the dining-room had overheard his speech. They applauded him loudly before they helped themselves to a second plate.

I admit that I am only a product of my surroundings. And therefore I hope that Comrade Deviatkin, who is very proud of his Marxist philosophy, will forgive me and understand if I only describe what I have actually seen and relate plans as intentions and not as achievements.

The boats that were bringing the town and its inhabitants to Nordvyk did not arrive while I was there. I could not risk having to spend the winter on the Arctic Ocean in case they arrived too late for me to catch an aeroplane back to Europe. Perhaps I ought to have done so, in order to give an authentic account of the developments I set out to investigate. As, however, I am not in the employ of any Government and have to earn my living with economic conditions of our world I had to stick to my time schedule.

But I was not to miss the ships after all. Duty brings its rewards. I saw them in the Kara Sea a fortnight after I had left Nordvyk. At that time the four of them—the *Molotov*, *Kossior*, *Vishinski* and *Soviet*—were waiting in Dickson Harbour while the ice-breaker *Yermak* and the cutter *Litke* were battling with the ice in the Vilkitski Straits; this is the most difficult point of the Northern Sea Route, between Cape Chelyuskin and the island group of North Land, and it provided greater obstacles to navigation in this last season than at any time in the last ten years. The ice conditions in the Arctic were said to be worse than at any time since the North-east Passage was opened by the Russians. I went on board the ships and talked to the people. There were 200 skilled workers, some of them from the Donbas coal area and the others from the underground construction plant in Moscow. There were 150 timber workers from Archangel, 85 skilled mechanics, 15 engineers (graduated from technical high schools), 4 doctors (one of them a woman), 1 woman dentist and 2 journalists who will edit the local newspaper (which is to appear regularly from the first day of the town's existence) and also do 'cultural work'—that is, lecture on history and politics, organize study circles for languages, art, science, etc. There were also 5 printers, 5 cooks (two of them from the Intourist Hotel 'Novo Moskovskaya' in Moscow), 2 club organizers who had been trained for this job in other new Russian towns and told me they knew exactly what was needed to keep pioneers in good spirits. The passengers also included 2 wireless operators, 1 chemist, 1 hairdresser, 1 bootmaker and 10 peasant boys who would be trained for any trade which would turn out to be too thinly provided with 'cadres'. There were also 15 hunters from the Kola Penin-sula, their job was to hunt in winter and fish in summer to provide Nordvyk with fresh food. One agricultural expert will organize the first vegetable plantations, with subter-ranean hothouses if necessary.

Altogether there were 517 men and 83 women. The women were meteorologists, hydrologists, scientific appren-tices, cooks, waitresses, for the communal restaurant, geologists, geodesists and one dressmaker. There was not one 'simple housewife'; the men's families may only follow them next year. By then, according to the plan, the town will have reached a stage when accommodation will be available for 'non-producing members of the community'. There was a remarkable confidence in all the people that everything will turn out all right. They trusted their organizers, they said and one challenged me: 'You ask us about our feelings as we go to an unknown and solitary place in the Polar region. Did not workers go to Alaska in the Klondyke rush? And they were only driven by motives of private profit to enrich themselves, nobody else, in the company of ruffians; they were ready to kill each other for a piece of gold or a better prospecting spot. Read Jack London and compare the conditions under which we are going to work. All of us are cultured men and women, sons and daughters of a free proletariat, disciplined, working on an ordered plan and safeguarded by every modern amenity. There are doctors with us; we shall have a hospital, a radio station, aeroplanes and social centres like civilized human beings. We shall not be conquered by the wilderness. We are carrying our human standards of civilization with us into the wilderness.' This man said that he was a tractor driver, 'able to repair, not only to drive, a tractor'. He was twenty-three years old and a member of seven organizations the names of which I cannot remember for they were all compositions of abbreviated words.

The cargo list, which must have been worked out by the most pedantic employees of the planning commission, contained: 6 transportable two-story houses with accommodation for 9 persons each; 10 caterpillar tractors to serve as transport lorries as well as passenger buses (with sledges in tow); and 7 small motor boats and a 200 h.p. river steamship to keep up communications between Nordvyk and Sindasko, Khatanga, etc. I also saw a complete radio transmitter, an X-ray equipment, carefully wrapped up in one of the ship's holds side by side with 35 tons of butter, 150 tons of flour, 30 tons of dried vegetables, 15 tons of fresh potatoes, 10,000 lemons, innumerable boxes of chocolate, sacks of lentils, peas and beans, barrels of sunflower oil, condensed milk, 10,000 boxes of cigarettes and 95 lb. of *makhorka* (peasant tobacco). The ships also carried 28 horses, 30 cows, 1 bull, 50 pigs, 120 chickens and 15 cocks.

It was the Soviet version of the Ark. Comrade Noah, that is Boris Lavrov, was particularly proud of the piano and the library. The library contained 3000 volumes, and I was told it had been compiled by a special committee

of cultural, political and technical experts. It found its place in the Ark next to the furs, the boots of felt leather and rubber, the 2000 packets of razor blades, and the 3 boxes full of soap and toothbrushes. Every member of the 'army' had been told what he should take with him. But Noah was taking no risks. And since it is the rule for these Arctic pioneer towns that every necessity of life should be shared out free to the pioneers, the doctor could even show me a tin drum full of birth-control appliances. 'Abortion is prohibited under the new family law. I shall therefore make it my duty to advise the men and women in Nordvyk on methods of voluntary prevention of conception.'

Each member was also entitled to 25 cigarettes a day and the rations had already been given out daily from the day of departure. One of the journalists, who was a non-smoker, gave me six boxes which he had stored under his bed. 'There are some girls who smoke furiously', he said. 'It makes me sort of popular with them if I can present one or other of them a box from time to time. But a journalistic colleague, of course, ought to be given precedence.'

All whom I asked about the problems that could arise in such a small and isolated community owing to the striking disproportion of the sexes, ruled out such problems as incompatible with cultured and disciplined people. Now that is a thing which I do not believe, even of people who (as they say) can see a hyacinth when it is still a bulb. If they do look upon each other—as everyone of them professed with stereotyped unanimity—simply as 'brothers and sisters, and nothing else', then there must be a lot of repression underneath their demonstrative self-control. A geodesist, who went to Nordvyk to advise on the lay-out of mining plants, took me into his confidence regarding this question. 'It must be hell to live on a Polar station where there are twelve men and three women', he said, 'but that I should perhaps accept as unavoidable and should concede that the people who go there are exceptional personalities of a very high courage and moral integrity—others of weaker calibre would not lock themselves up on an island in the Polar Sea for two or three years. But a place with six hundred people, and with hardly more than 10 per cent of them women, is ridiculous nonsense. Let them have no women at all the first year. I could understand that. But I would not go about a place starving and see pastries lying about here and there.'

'So what have you done about it? You are here after all', I said.

'Well, since you are not going to live there and make a scandal of me, I don't mind telling you. I picked out the prettiest girl of the lot on the first day I came on board in Archangel. We were in harbour for over a week. On the fifth day I took her to Zags, and we inscribed ourselves.' (He meant they got married at the register office.) 'So I for one am married.'

'And do you think that this is a sound basis of matrimony?'

'Don't be silly. She is pretty and a clever girl. We have two years ahead of us to get used to each other. I like her quite well already. If it does not work, we can still separate afterwards. It is the most sensible thing I could do at any rate.'

I reported the case hypothetically—changing the conditions and the places—to a number of workers, men and women in a different Arctic settlement later. There was nothing but indignation and strong condemnation for such 'irresponsible action'. The younger people, by the way, were the most severe in the judgment of the case. The majority of them have accepted the new Soviet's code of social morality completely. And this new Soviet morality demands the greatest possible self-discipline, holds marriage in high honour, condemns repeated divorce as a sign of instability and of lack of social conscience. The promiscuity of which Soviet youth was often accused abroad five years ago had already been most severely condemned by Lenin.

And the words of the deified leader of the Russian revolution have since been made the basis for widespread criticism of all offences against the correct attitude demanded of the young towards sexual problems. I raised the problem on later stages of my journey, particularly with regard to conditions on Polar stations, and everywhere I found the same almost puritanical conception of what is right and wrong in this respect.

I left Nordvyk very soon. I had seen all there was up to that time and listened to all the plans for an early development of this settlement into an Arctic town of 40,000. In saying good-bye I made this little speech: 'I wish the courageous pioneers and town-builders of Nordvykstroi success and happiness. I hope keenly to return one day. Then I shall stand on this very spot of mud which will by then have been turned into the main street—the Ulitsa Lenina—by you. Looking down towards the plain over there I shall see the Stalin Square, where unconcerned by the darkness of Arctic winters, you will hold your November parade under powerful searchlights. On the right I expect to see the great power station, and behind it the "Prospect Otto Yulievitch Schmidt" on which motor cars, aerosledges and tractors will drive out towards the "North Light" oil wells, the "Polar Star" salt mines and the coalfields "Conqueror of the Arctic". At dinner in the "Ice Bear" restaurant I shall be able to tell my friends that I was the first newspaperman in the world to have flown to this town when it consisted of nothing but your hopes and your will.'

I was thanked most cordially for this appreciation. One young man replied: 'You have proved that you have almost as much power of imagination as we. We on our side will follow it up with constructive work.'

CHAPTER X

THE CRIMINALS LIVE NEXT DOOR

'OF course, you will not be allowed into any of the criminals' and exiles' camps in Siberia,' friends prophesied before I left London.

I did succeed in getting into one of the G.P.U. camps high up in the North. Newspapermen in Moscow said that it was one of the most dreaded, probably worse than the White Sea Canal or the Moscow–Volga Canal, and something like the concentration camp on Solovyetski Island in the White Sea, whither most hardened fighters against the Soviet régime have been dispatched since the revolution. What I saw was the railway construction which is to link Dudinka, on the lower Yenisei, with Norilsk, the mining centre on the Taimyr Peninsula. Only at first I did not know that I was in the camp.

Flying back from Nordvyk we had alighted on the river at Dudinka at 6 p.m. I climbed out of the machine, thinking that we would continue the journey after dinner. We had to walk for a quarter of an hour from the beach until we reached the first timber house. The mud was worse than anywhere else on the journey. Sinking into the knees had been an occasional accident of sight-seeing in Nordvyk. Here it was the rule.

The landscape was fantastic. The other shore of the Yenisei was ten miles away. The sky was grey and full of clouds; the water dirty and drab. The shore rose steeply up from it; and there was no vegetation to be seen. Up on the bank barrels of petrol for the planes, were lying about somehow together with rails and sleepers for the new railways, parts of heavy mining machinery, huge cases containing Heaven knows what. Men in black quilt jackets and high boots could be seen laying rails, away across the tundra. Some were driving about on propeller tractors that had wooden sledges trailing behind. Near the air base, where the staff lived, a dining-room and dormitory were kept for passengers, and round the base stood long wooden barracks and large military tents. From these smoke rose up through primitive tin chimneys. By the side of the narrow wooden foot-walks were huge boards bearing printed slogans and coloured banners. Graphic statistics displayed a list of names with figures against each of them:

Arosvey (Ivan Yefimovitch)	96½%
Rosenzweig (Moses Lazarovitch)	111%
Nikolayev (Maksim Gavrilovitch)	134%
Sterlikov (Nikolay Vladimirovitch)	78%

and so on. I was interested to see groups of men staring at these figures, spelling the names out precariously, joking and quarrelling among each other. I was told that this display was an effective means of raising the efficiency of the pioneers. Those who had fulfilled only 78 per cent of the monthly plan for rail-laying or for transport by tractor felt ashamed (I was told) when others were announced as having done 111 per cent or even 130 per cent of the allotted work. The banners carried inscriptions such as 'We are building the northernmost railway in the world', 'Stakhanovism is the Socialist method of raising production', 'The Arctic will be conquered by us, Comrades.'

During dinner two men in khaki uniforms sat at the next table, both very tall and well shaven. They had coats reaching to their ankles and cut *en taille*, with wide skirts from the belt downwards. I overheard one saying: 'My brigade will finish the No. 2 shaft by the first of September. I promised to get them five balalaikas and to arrange a dance on the night we complete the job.' The other replied: 'My boys say they will beat yours if I promise them a vodka night.' 'Fine crowd you have got', retorted the first.

I talked to Shevelyov. He had left me with the 'Nordvyk-party' when I changed machines the previous week. Here in Dudinka we had met again; he was inspecting the transport service between Dudinka and Norilsk, for which a number of aeroplanes had been hired from his fleet. Norilsk lies seventy miles east of Dudinka in hilly tundra. The district is being opened up because of its nickel deposits. Nickel is one of the few metals, if not the only one, in which the U.S.S.R. is comparatively poor. Up here, a little further north than the northernmost tip of Alaska, they found so much of it in the mountains that they are now talking of becoming independent of Canadian nickel within a few years. There is nickel next to the coal at Norilsk, and also copper, platinum and gold. To reach Norilsk by water from the Yenisei, one has to go down the river by steamer, then along the coast of the Kara Sea with the help of ice-breakers and eastwards to the mouth of the Piasina. The Piasina, being shallow, will not carry large vessels. Barges have to be used up all its course to the Piasina Lake and Norilka Lake and then along the Norilka river as far as Valiok, which is a few miles away from the Norilsk mountains. This is a journey of 1600 miles, and it is only possible during two and a half months of summer. For the rest of the year, anyone who attempts the journey has to use reindeer sledges.

Yet Dudinka offers good harbour facilities on the Yenisei — which is about to become the central South-North highway, the spine of Siberia. That is why a railway is being built from Dudinka to Norilsk. It will run on Norilsk coal and carry Norilsk nickel. It will bring fuel to the river which will no longer be used by steamships that burn only timber, and so have to stop every day to take logs on board to heat the boilers. Norilsk coal will also be taken by the vessels of the Kara Sea expedition. They come from Europe now to fetch Siberian pine. But they must load enough coal at Murmansk to carry them there and back—which not only wastes time but takes up loading space. The Russians hope that fuel on the spot will help them in their plans for importing large quantities of goods into Northern Asia *via* the Arctic Sea Route. Such are the reasons that have inspired the building of the little railway from Dudinka to Norilsk.

The mines of Norilsk cut through the frozen soil, through eternal ice, no railway has ever been built so far north before—these arguments do not impress Shevelyov. He was glad to think that I believed all these enterprises to be a little daring and complicated. 'Never been done before', 'terribly difficult', 'great sacrifices', 'tremendous amount of energy',—so much the better. The Bolshevist super-lativists like that kind of thing. It appeals to their imagination. They love calling themselves large-scale business magnates and sound economists, but a daring scheme is more tempting to them than one which is only profitable. At least, that is how I always found them.

Meanwhile the people building the line and the mines at Norilsk have to be provisioned with food, building material and machinery. All bulky stuff—preserved food, timber, and heavy steel—are brought to them once a year by water with the 'Piasina Expedition'. But everyday needs—bread, butter, vegetables, and light metal products, such as electrical machinery, pneumatic drills and hammers, spare parts, transmission wheels, newspapers, letters and of course the people themselves—are flown there. The organization of this transport service was Shevelyov's share of the job. There are already over 3000 people living and working in the mines and on the railway.

'It is believed', said Shevelyov, 'that Norilsk will employ 10,000 men in the mines and the metal combine, and 5000 on the railway and in the port. That means that within five years we shall have townships at Norilsk and Dudinka with an aggregate population of 35,000. A fine job to build this up here in the Arctic, don't you think? Only one industrial settlement in the world was built by air transport—Salamaua, in New Guinea, where the rich gold fields could not be reached from the coast because there is a jungle between, infested with wild animals and cannibals.'

Eight aeroplanes were flying between Dudinka and Norilsk, when I was there. One of their pilots, Nikolayev, whose wife was the pretty Ukrainian girl who complained about the lack of flowers at the air base during the women's meeting at Krasnoyarsk, told me how they worked. 'We make between four and eight flights a day, according to the weather. It takes half an hour each way in normal times and I usually carry 1.5 tons of cargo. Stradinin can only take 800 kilos on his small machine; Sadkov's N 8 will take as much as two tons, perhaps a little more. He works with us whenever he is not needed on the Yenisei passenger lines with his big machine.

'We are paid a kind of piece wage; 57 roubles per ton, which brings an average 37 roubles per flight; 200 roubles per day and, if you allow for longer stretches of bad weather, which may take as much as 13 to 15 days out of a month, I make roughly 3000 roubles a month. My mechanic is paid less and gets usually 2000. Then we get premiums for treating the engines carefully, saving petrol and over fulfilling the plan. And we can have up to three months paid holiday each year, with free sanatorium vouchers'.

These are excellent wages. A university professor in Moscow gets rarely more than 2000; a doctor less; and only opera stars, scenario writers, and very successful inventors reach figures above 5000. But it is hard work in rough surroundings; and the pilots do not earn this money as easily as their wives spend it in Krasnoyarsk and Moscow.

After dinner Sadkov said he would rather not go on any further. We had covered the return journey from

Nordvyk in one continuous hop of almost twenty-four hours, whereas going there had taken us three days. I was annoyed that he had not told me so at once, because I had left all my luggage in the 'plane and dreaded the way back in the mud to get my things for the night. 'You can buy a toothbrush in the shop, if you like', said Sadkov 'and I shall lend you my razor in the morning.' He carried a little outfit with him. The blade was rather blunt, and he used ordinary soap instead of shaving cream, but the powder he offered me after I had gashed my face was strongly perfumed and even contained disinfectant, according to the announcement of the box. We went to buy the toothbrush. There were caps and warm quilt jackets in the shop, the jackets were marked 25 roubles a piece. Thermos bottles cost 10; goloshes, 18.50; stuffed fruit salad in tins, 5.60 and 8.72. A hunting rifle was 256 roubles. On the shelves of the store was a display of cigarettes, dried fruit, matches, coffee, soap, needles, warm trousers, clothes, brushes, candles, kerosene, pictures of Lenin, Stalin and Schmidt, notebooks and pencils. I paid 1.75 for my toothbrush, and remembered that a similar brush would cost 3 roubles in Moscow—a difference which seemed odd in view of the long and costly transport of goods to this outlying region. 'The country is not profiteering on its pioneers', said Sadkov emphatically, glad of his chance to hit out against my capitalistic outlook.

'Where are we going to sleep?' I asked.

'We are going to find a place, don't worry.'

August was drawing to a close and so it was becoming a little dark from shortly before midnight until two in the morning. In the dusk we followed a girl from the air base, who promised to lead us to our quarters. On the way we got to a barbed wire fence and had to walk through a turnstile. A man in a long uniform coat with a thick cloth helmet and a tall rifle with bayonet, demanded a *propusk.* I said that I had no pass and that all my documents were in the machine. The girl guaranteed my good faith.

'Why must we suddenly produce documents', I asked her.

'Because this is a prison camp of the G.P.U.', she said.

'What, are we going to sleep in jail?'

'No!' She roared with laughter, and Sadkov grinned like a Chinese god of mirth.

'We have just come out of the camp. Now we are in the town of Dudinka.'

'So we have been in the camp all the time?'

'Of course, what did you think?'

'But are the prisoners on holiday during the summer, or what?'

'Why should they be on holiday? Did not you see them? There were plenty about on the way till we got to the barbed wire.'

She could hardly control her amusement at my ignorance, and Sadkov began to tease me: 'Did not you see the heavy chains they carried, and the guards with the knouts, beating the slow ones on the railway track?'

I reserved judgment until next morning, fully determined to look at the place more carefully in daylight if I got a chance. We were given sleeping quarters in the house of the local Party secretary. He had two bedrooms, a sitting-room and a 'bathroom'. There was no tub and of course, no running water. He had the usual washbasins, with a small tank, suspended on the wall above, and an unusual kind of tap. One had to hold up a lever with one hand to keep the water running and pop the other hand in the stream. Being used to washing with both hands I was rather clumsy. Sadkov picked the mattress that was laid out on the floor of the sitting-room, and left the plank bed to me. Hundreds of beetles were crawling around the room, and I tried desperately to find a place for my clothes where they would be safe from these little beasts. But it was hopeless.

They were everywhere—on tables, stools, window-sills. Even the books were not spared. I saw Sadkov beating a copy of the luxury edition of *A Thousand and One Nights* to chase two beetles from one of the five-colour prints with which the edition is illustrated. I found a little volume, *English for Beginners*, standing between a *Short Encyclopedia of Agriculture* and *Stalin's Speeches*. Cuddling up on my couch, well wrapped up in my leather and fur coat, with my head on a pillow which I covered with my pullover, I read under the light of the sparkling kerosene lamp.

'Lesson 16.

'Are you a comrade?

'Yes, I am a comrade!

'I am glad you are a comrade.

'Yes, we shall fight together for the liberation of the world proletariat.

'We in Russia are building socialism already.

'How is industrialization proceeding?

'Very well, thank you. Our pig iron output has increased tenfold since the Revolution. How many members has the Communist Party in your country?

'I do not know the exact figures, but we are making good progress.'

The wind was blowing through countless fissures in the wooden wall at my bedside. I put the book down, and drew the fur collar over my ears. Across the room a teacher from the Khatanga cultural base who had flown back with us, and a workman from an outlying factory who had come here to see the dentist were unpacking their feet. Under their wide heavy boots they had a wrapping of cotton rags, like true Siberians. It is a very sensible habit, both useful and comfortable. The rags keep the feet warm and, by skilful arrangement, they can be shaped so as to fill and soften all bends of the boots which are often too large or too wide for the person who wears them. I could not take to it and wore four pairs of socks instead. These two men were making conversation, the worker interviewing the teacher on Dudinka, which he had not visited before:

'How many inhabitants?'

'Three thousand.'

'Good! And last year?'

'Two thousand two hundred.'

'Oh, excellent. Plan?'

'Five thousand by 1938.'

'Hm, Hm. How many bureaucrats?'

'Too many!'

'Of course.'

'How many workers?'

'Four thousand.'

'Comrade teacher, you are an idiot. Did not you say just now there were only three thousand inhabitants altogether?'

'You are an idiot yourself, comrade. Don't you realize that plenty of people do the job of two in a place like this?'

'Hoho, hoho, comrade teacher, you are a scream. If that is your kind of arithmetic, I shall have to ask you to leave the room. It is too small for five people.'

'I count only three, we two and the Correspondent over there.'

'Yes, but I do the work of three men, if you don't mind. Good night, schoolmaster.'

'Quiet in there', Sadkov shouted from his floor in the next room. 'Mister, do you know who wrote *A Thousand and One Nights?*'

'Sadkov, I am ashamed for you. Don't you know?'

'Of course I do, it says it on the flap. I only wanted to examine you. Good night.'

'Good night, Sadkov.'

I woke up with a stiff neck the next morning. It had been very hot in the room, and I had thrown off the fur during the night, but the draught through the walls had kept

on blowing against my head. I was glad that the beetles had
not eaten me up overnight. I had not felt a single bite;
there were no bugs or fleas; but, while getting up, I pondered
over the dirt I had seen in the 'streets', and the shabbiness
of the house. The teacher greeted me with a hearty good
morning, and the worker, who hurried to keep his appointment with the dentist, said, as if reading my thoughts:
'Plenty of work to do still in this place—better houses, and
log parquets over the mud. Plenty of work. But it will be
done, *Budyet, budyet.* It will be done.' This *budyet* is
Russia's Open Sesame. Some day all these things will
really have been done. They believe it firmly.

'In about ten years' time Norilsk will be a town of free
men and women. We shall have reclaimed most of these
scoundrels for society, and they will be proud colonisers.'
One of the 'administrators' was giving me his *credo* over
breakfast. I had told him of my surprise of the previous
night when I heard that all the men I had seen working
round the air base were convicts. He bent across to me and
whispered: 'Say something nice about them aloud once
more. The fellow who sits at the table over there, making
entries in the big ledger, is also one of our boys. He was
chief cashier in the electrical plant at Voronesh, and has
embezzled 100,000 roubles. Now he will keep the books
for the provision department of the camp, for five years. It
will have a good psychological effect on him when you, as a
foreigner, say that you thought all these men were free
people. We want them to forget that they are criminals and
to feel they are an ordinary community of working people
on a pioneer outpost in the Arctic.'

'You seem to have good and keen workers up here', I
bellowed, and the 'administrator' rewarded me with a
grateful wink from his left eye, while his right squinted
across the room to see whether his pet-embezzler was cheered
up by my expert judgment.

After we had finished our last round of fried eggs with

caviare, I asked the 'administrator' whether he would be good enough to take me round the place.

'Sorry, Mister, it can't be done.'

I had thought so. . . .

'I have no time, but you need not be afraid. They won't hurt you. Just go and talk to them politely, without asking too many questions about their past. Only don't take any photographs. It is against the regulations.'

I started with the long wooden barrack opposite. There were almost no people on the ground floor dormitory. An old man was sitting on his bed scratching his hairy chest and mumbling something into his beard.

'Good morning, father', I said.

'God be with you, my son', he replied, and grinned.

'Nobody in?'

'I am in, can't you see?'

'Oh yes, you are; I did not mean to call you nobody. I really meant to say: 'Are you the only one at home?'

He grinned again.

'Oh no, I am not the only one in. By no means the only one, my son. There are many young doves in the dovecote. Why don't you climb up to bid them a good day, since you have Sunday?'

I thought I had landed in the camp's asylum. The old man looked more like a mental case to me than one who was about to be 'reclaimed for society'.

'Of course I will bid the little doves a fair day, father. Where are they?'

'Can't you see the ladder. It is right before you, and you ask me to show you the way.'

There was a ladder on my right. It led up into a kind of attic. Up I went. Little doves, indeed! There were twenty-six men between thirty and forty in that attic, which covered the whole length of the barracks under the triangle-shaped roof.

156

'Good morning, citizens', I greeted them. 'Nice morning!'

'Nice morning, nice morning', one aped me. 'One morning is no different from the other. They last from breakfast water-soup to luncheon water-soup. And then it is afternoon until the evening water-soup, and night until the breakfast water-soup. If you have some vodka, then you can say nice morning and it would be a nice morning. Am I right, boys?'

'Quite right, Grishka, quite right, Grishka', they cried from all sides.

The little doves were obviously not in the best of spirits. They looked like real jailbirds. They were dirty and uncombed, and had beards of a few weeks' growth. Their laughter was shrill and grim. A few were lying on their bedsteads and whistling tunes. Some sat together with feet tucked under and seemed to hide something under their blankets quickly as I approached them. I think that they had been playing cards.

Rallying my courage, I said: 'Well, boys, how long have you been in this place?'

'Six weeks', said one of them, and began to give me a particularly juicy example of Russian swearing.

'How is work?'

'What do we care?' said a fair-haired youngster. 'Do you think we are idiots to work in such a —— of a place. We are not as foolish as those babes out there who let themselves be exploited by the bloody G.P.U. Building a railway in this bog! My eye! We are staying right here. As long as they are not beating us up they will not get us to take a shovel and dig up mud for them, not me, anyway. And they can't beat us, because their bosses don't allow them to. Not nowadays. So we are simply striking. Aren't we?'

A few clapped their hands in applause for this fine speech. Obviously cheered by his success as a speaker, he went on. 'What can they do to us? Nothing. They can do nothing,

I say. They can reduce the daily rations, if they want to, but then we shall simply sleep a little more and be hungry. They cannot starve us to death because that is against their regulations. So all they can bloody well do is to lick our arses. Nice morning!'

At that moment a man came up the ladder; he was besmeared with mud up to his hips and had sweat pouring down his cheeks. He sat down on a bed in a corner and ate an apple which he took from his pocket. The gang started abusing him. The fair-haired youngster turned to me. 'See that milkface, over there? He is yellow. He has given in and is playing the goody-goody boy now, that's why they give him apples, you can —— your apple, do you hear me? I don't care tuppence for your rotten apple. Mud digger, a fine fellow you are, you crawling mole. Shovelling mud for them with your hands.'

'Shut up, or I'll smash you against the wall, so that they have to scrape you off with a spoon, you ass. And let me inform you, you cock-eyed scoundrel, I am not digging mud with my hands, but with a machine, and I am getting ordinary wages for it, not gifts or presents like a beggar, like you, and I am doing work, a socially valuable work, that means something, that we shall all get something out of—but I don't believe that either, so you need not grin, only it is more amusing to play about with the machines out there and get money for it than sit about with you here for weeks, getting bored with hearing you tell the same damned old yarns all over.'

I thought it was time for a tactful retreat. They would better have it out among themselves.

Near the tents a row of men were queueing up alongside a field kitchen, tin plates in their hands, waiting to get hot soup. I met the 'administrator' again. He waved to me across the pathway, but did not stop to talk. Shevelyov came out of the air base and rushed by. I went in to get some cigarettes. The girl who had led us to our sleeping quarters last night was busy in the kitchen. I asked her what the camp administration would do about the men, who refused to work and stayed up in the 'dovecote'. 'Nothing', she said; 'They'll get bored sooner or later. They always do. Some after a week, others after a month. Very few hold out over a year. It is a matter of temperament. Those who stay longest become the best workers afterwards in most of the cases. You ought to see them when they come to ask for work the first time; they are terribly proud and at the beginning they all think that work is degrading—those who strike of course—there are some who work from the first day. But those others only give in when they are bored, and then they say they work simply to amuse themselves, not to help the job. They might only do an hour or two the first day. Then, when they are given wages for it, they are surprised, because they had said they were only working to amuse themselves. But once it has started, they cannot stop. They buy tobacco and extra food—the free rations are, of course, only soup and bread —just enough to keep them alive. So when they start earning, they soon get the taste of it and then the administrators begin working on their vanity: tell one he is particularly gifted, the other that he is a disappointment, that one had expected to see him do more and better work in view of his athletic build. So they get the sporting spirit. And it is a contagious thing. Once three or four of a gang have fallen for it, the rest follow. It's a good system. It works. And the railway grows. In five months it will. . . .'

When she started telling me about the future, I left. I walked up to a party of men working on the railway and offered them a smoke. They accepted it gladly and I asked whether any of them had been to the mines yet. 'I have worked there myself', one of them said. 'But then I was transferred because I am a very skilful mechanic and can fix the sleepers better than any other boy around.' (I learnt later that this man was an ex-cracksman.)

'What is it like there?'

'Does not look too good', he said. 'Place is full of mud now in the summer. When you climb up the hill to get to the pithead you slip back three steps in every four. But of course that will be better next year. We are building huts on the hilltops now to save the workers going up and down every day. They are on the 'phone, and need only come down once a week for the *vikhodnoi* (free day) to attend a meeting or a sing-song. The mines are all right. No gas—you can smoke a cigarette inside. And in winter they are warmer than out in the open. But in the coal walls you can see dull white fissures here and there, contrasting curiously with the glossy black coal and the glassy icicles that hang from the ceiling. That reminds you that you are working under permanent ice.'

The foreman of the party approached us and asked my friend whether he did not think it better to stop talking and to go on with the work. He apologized to me '. . . but you see we have to get on because in three weeks this part of the line must be ready, and in five months it will be . . .'

'I know, I know, don't bother to give me the whole plan. I know it by heart now. Are you also one of the boys?' I asked him with little tact.

'Oh, no. I am a free man. I am here voluntarily, as an engineer. I served my sentence on the Baltic–White Sea Canal three years ago. But I was so skilful that the rest of my sentence was quashed and I was even decorated for my good work.'

Seeing some doubts in my glance, he got very insistent. 'My dear friend, I will prove to you that what I say is true. Let me tell you: I was the king of the pickpockets in Leningrad seven years ago. No man in Russia could slash a fur coat in a tramcar as efficiently as I. But when I went to Moscow on holiday last year—I am now an employee of the Construction Section of the Commissariat of the Interior (the new name for the G.P.U.)—I was robbed of 1500 roubles myself in the underground. Do you believe me now, when I say that I am a free man?'

I did.

Returning to the air base in the belief that we should be leaving soon, I was met by a tall fellow with watery blue eyes and a red beard. He lifted his cap, and said: 'Health to you, *Tovarich Natchalnik!*' (This means Comrade Chief, and is the usual way in which workers address their factory managers.)

'*Tovarich Natchalnik*', he went on, 'please give me some bread or cheese.'

'I am sorry', I replied, 'I am only a guest here, and I have nothing to give you.'

'I am hungry, *Tovarich Natchalnik*. Please give me something to eat.'

'Who are you? A *kulak?*' He looked like a peasant.

'Yes, yes, a *kulak*, a poor peasant. I have been sent here, I don't know why or what for.'

'And don't you work, so that you can earn money to buy food?'

'Oh, but I can't work every day, *Tovarich Natchalnik*. I must rest a little too, mustn't I?'

At that an administrator, who had overheard our conversation, approached us and said to my red-bearded *kulak*: 'Why do you lie to this citizen, Vladimir Stepanovitch? Are you ashamed to have been a robber? Don't you realize that criminals are really victims of the old capitalistic society, whereas *kulaks* were its exponents?'

Vladimir Stepanovitch disappeared quickly.

An hour later I left. We circled over Dudinka and saw the narrow track of the railway winding its way into the tundra which it will open to the world. Will the work also open the world once more to the convicts who are sent here in order to be cured of crime, a social disease? Will this prisoners' colony really become an Arctic port, with the northernmost railway in the world and the greatest nickel mines of Asia, as the 'administrators' hope? The G.P.U. promise all 'good' murderers, thieves, speculators and procurers who behave well at Norilsk that their families may follow them if they behave well. Convict colonies have been known to become prosperous new countries before. There is nothing unique in this Arctic convict camp. What I found new was the great and sincere belief of the young 'administrators' that they were really pioneers of the soul in the wilderness of these ruffians' minds.

CHAPTER XI

IGARKA—POLAR CAPITAL

THE Russians love figures nowadays; many figures, large figures, glowing statistics.

When I asked a worker in Igarka what was the importance of the town, apart from its being the largest Polar city in the world, he instantly replied: 'Five hundred thousand trees cut up for export last winter.'

I worked out that 500,000 would be sufficient to line both sides of a road from London to Cairo and let the motorists drive in continuous shade.

'But', the worker went on, 'that is only one per cent of what we could cut in Siberia each year. Our natural annual growth is fifty million trees. How much is that?'

I wrote the number in figures, and at each added o, his delight visibly increased.

'If you were to lay these fifty million trees out in a straight line two by two, you could build a footbridge from the earth to the moon.'

'And to think we could do that each year!'

He gaped at the implication of his own words.

'That gives you an idea how rich we are.'

Russia's timber wealth is indeed enormous. Her forests cover a larger area than the whole of Europe. Siberia's woods alone are as big as France and Great Britain together. And Siberian timber is the finest of its kind in the world. Its red pines are so straight and so high that one can make a ship's mast out of a single trunk. Its white pines are the best available for cellulose, paper and artificial silk. While the reserves of Canada in that particular quality will probably be exhausted within another ten years, Siberia could supply the world for a few more centuries. The timber

163

coming from Igarka is so precious that London merchants are supplied with it only if they buy a quantity of other Russian wood together with it. Millions of houses can be built and furnished out of Siberia's trees ; hundreds of thousands of ships constructed and equipped; many hundreds of square miles of artificial silk manufactured from its pulp; and all the books and newspapers in the world could be printed on them for several hundred years to come.

I admit that when I saw those forests—beautiful, thick and green—I did not think that the stockings we see on pretty legs, and the pages of this book, and the turpentine with which our parquet floors are cleaned, and the spirit with which I heat my coffee machine, and the many kinds of explosives with which we blast roads when we are sensible and kill each other by the million when we are not, could all be made from these trees.

There is one snag. Siberia's timber becomes useful only if it can be transported on water. And all the main Siberian rivers flow northward into the ice-bound Arctic Sea. The logs must be taken down in rafts in the summer: cut up in Arctic sawmills in the winter, and shipped off to the world in the following year. That is the cheapest way. Railways would not pay.

Igarka was the first port and town for sawmills in Arctic Siberia. It is now six years old and has twelve thousand inhabitants in the winter and fifteen thousand in the summer. The Russians see in it the vindication of their claim that industries in the Polar regions are both possible and profitable. After having been to Nordvyk, the salt and oil town of the future, and to Norilsk and Dudinka, the coal, nickel and railway centres (of the nearer future), I visited Igarka to see what the finished product in the line of Russian Polar cities looked like.

I arrived at 11 p.m. My curiosity was great. But my fatigue was greater. I had many hours of flying in bad weather behind me. As I climbed out of the machine, I

asked: 'Where is the bath house, and how soon can I go to bed, please?'

The man who clipped my ticket at the airport looked at me with astonishment. 'What, you want to go to bed at seven o'clock, citizen? That is a bit early for a grown-up person, don't you think?'

'Seven o'clock?' I replied indignantly. 'My good man, your clock must be four hours slow. It's eleven. Surely my watch is right. Look at the sky. It's getting twilight already. I have been up since five this morning. I have a right to be tired.'

A sudden understanding lit his face. It took some explanation to make me share it.

'Don't you know, we do not live local time in Igarka. It's eleven o'clock, East Siberian time, all right. But this town lives like Moscow.'

'Why, that is crazy. It means a difference of four hours between your clocks and the sun.'

'Never mind the sun, *tovarich*. If we took any notice of him, we should not be living here at all. Or we should have to sleep three months in the winter and keep awake three months in the summer. We cannot accept all the moods of the arctic. It's we who are the bosses. And, besides, our workers want to listen to the Moscow broadcasts every day. They would not tune in to the Children's Hour after supper, or stay up until two in the morning to hear Operas from the Bolshoi.'

So that was the law in Igarka! Men decided to live here and they are bending Nature to their command. They do not even abide by the mills of time.

Half an hour after my arrival it got very dark in the wooden streets. Searchlights lit up the town. It was now the end of August. The twenty-four-hour day of the Arctic summer was getting shorter. It finished at half-past seven (Igarka time, Moscow time, violated time). I went into the Turkish bath, had dinner in the restaurant, and was then pressed into a stall at the theatre. As a visitor from a far off country, I had to sit in the first row. I fell asleep as the curtain rose and woke up when it fell over the melodramatic finale. The actors resented it until my departure twelve days later—indeed, they probably resent it still.

When I travelled home from the theatre on a horse-drawn open Siberian cart, the sky lit-up and by the time I stumbled up the wooden staircase to my sleeping quarters it was broad daylight. The clock on the tower of the fire station struck half-past eleven. A night of four hours, starting at dinner time and cut off by sunrise at the end of a theatre performance—that is the ridiculous state of affairs which the Soviet have created in their Polar city by disregarding the most primitive laws of the earth.

Two seconds after lying down, I was fast asleep. But a companion who shared the room with me, a doctor from the Kremlin hospital who had come from Moscow to spend his holiday in the Arctic, woke me a quarter of an hour later. 'Forgive me, citizen', he apologized, standing at my bedside in his pyjamas, 'I must ask you to help me with this rug. I have got to curtain that window with something dark. Heaven knows how you manage to sleep with the sun shining right into your face.'

Next morning I went on my first sightseeing tour. As the town lacked hotels I had been put up in the suburbs at the flat of a small clerk employed by the 'Port of Igarka Authority.' A duck-walk led me down from the house to the bank of the river. Asters were planted by the side of the walk, and Soviet optimism had also lined it with young fir trees in the hope that they would grow as well as the wild birch which surround the city. Man has drawn a strict line round the world at 66.50 and called the line the Arctic Circle; but Nature does not obey this regulation strictly. At some points there is vegetation far beyond the line; at others plant life stops a long way to the south of it. Igarka lies 67° 27′ 37″

north, and round it taiga and tundra, jungle and bush, intermingle.

I asked whether I could drive up to town in the little open Ford car (made in Russia) which I had seen driving to and fro under my window. It had been flying a cheerful red pennant, indicating that it was doing public service.

'No', said a bearded old fellow. 'It will not come back here before lunch. It's needed in the port now. We have only got that one. You must either walk or take a motor boat.'

I chose the latter. Down at the landing-stage of the air-port, one was just taking in passengers, and soon, sputtering, we were passing along the quay. Five steamers were lying alongside; four British and a Norwegian; all loading timber.

A small loop of the Yenisei offers good docking here. A sausage-shaped island about two miles long protects harbour and town from the main force of the river, which is over five miles wide at this point. In June, when the ice is a-move and floods tear roaring down the river-bed, the Yenisei can be highly menacing, but Igarka is safe behind its shelter.

The port extends for roughly a mile between the mainland and Bear's Island. I got off at the main loading pier, from which wooden bridges led up in dignified curves to the steep bank—like the impressionist stairs in Tairoff's sets in Moscow. Horse-drawn carts and automatic timber carries were trundling up and down, bringing the naked pink boards to the ships. Red bunting was hanging out; a huge portrait of Stalin, executed by a workman-artist, smiled cheerfully at the busy people below. Huge letters under his bushy moustache proclaimed in Russian and English, 'Workers Of The World Unite'. Banners appealed in flaming words for good and efficient work. A girl and a man, as I passed, were painting slogans in English on high hoardings; slogans designed to introduce foreign sailors to the problems and achievements under socialism. Statistics demonstrated the progress of industrialization, the growth of collective farming, the liquidation of illiteracy, and the spreading of evening classes, university study and village kindergartens. Most prominent of all, framed by red flags and golden bushels of wheat, the coat of arms of the Soviet Government shone above a huge white hoarding. On the hoarding were displayed—as impressively and grandly as (I fancied) the Mosaic laws on their twelve tables—the salient paragraphs of the new Constitution.

I walked resoundingly along the main road—resoundingly, because the streets of Igarka, as everything else in it, are built of timber and are, in fact, little else than bridges of well-polished beams over ground that is caked in ice for most of the year and dissolves into swamp during the short intensive summer of ninety days of almost continuous sunshine. Motor cars, lorries, trucks, watercarts and little bogies that carry timber in hidden claws between their wheels; all boom and throb cheerfully along these floating parquets. Some of the timber houses at the sides of the road had tilted and half-collapsed, I noticed; and I was told that these were the houses first built. Five to eight feet below the surface the ground is perpetually frozen. In the first winter of human habitation—when the huge brick-stoves were blazing furiously to keep the citizens of Igarka warm— this age old ice started melting on the surface. Structural pillars sank in, walls sagged. A different method is adopted now. The ground floor is raised by ten inches or so above the surface of the ground so that air can circulate freely underneath. That isolates the earth of the Arctic against the warmth of human comfort. Most of the houses in Igarka are built in the style of Swiss chalets. But the public buildings, the theatre and club, the cinema, the fire station, the Port Authority building, and the Town Hall are fine experiments in modern functionalist architecture. The

coldness and impersonality which sometimes make buildings in this style look like prisons or barracks disappear entirely when the material applied is timber, as here.

My first concern in arriving at a place is to see how I can get away again. There is no regular passenger boat from Igarka further down the river into the sea. I had to arrange for some means of getting out into the Arctic Ocean by cargo boat, Russian or foreign, of boarding an ice-breaker there, and of picking my way to the Polar stations and to Murmansk. Up to now my happy-go-lucky arrangements had not worked badly. With comparatively little delays—and those unavoidable on the new and still sparse network of Avyo Arctica lines—I had been able to fly whither I wanted. At Igarka my difficulties started.

'None of the foreign ships stop on their way homewards between Igarka and their home ports', said the harbour master. 'The Norwegian trampship *Matilda* will bunker at Dickson Island. She leaves to-night', said one of the guards in the harbour. 'Our motor ship *Andreyev* will be here in a week and, after five days' loading, she will go back and let you transfer to the ice-breaker *Yermak* in the Kara Sea', a stevedore on the quay assured me. 'You have come too late', was the opinion of the waitress in the restaurant. 'A week ago', she added, 'you could have flown on to the coast with the new ice-patrol aeroplanes, when they went on duty. They would have taken you to any ship or ice-breaker *en route*. But now—you had better give up the idea of sailing further north.'

It was all a little disturbing. I had it in black and white in my pocket, that I was to be given all assistance possible by local stations of Glavsevmorput. But I could not ask the impossible. I sent a wireless message to Schmidt who at that time was on board the ice-cutter *Litke*, battling against the drift ice in Vilkitski Straits. But he had probably more urgent things to attend to.

'The best you can do, whenever you are in difficulty, is to

address yourself to the G.P.U. or the Politotdel', was the recipe which a diplomatist in Moscow had given me. I was not quite sure what the 'Politotdel' was, but I asked for it as soon as I got to the Town Hall at Igarka. And the reply was: 'Oh, you should see Comrade Ostroumova. That's the most sensible thing. She can do anything up here. Only she is out in the sawmills just now. Ask her secretary on the first floor when she will be back.'

On the first floor a very friendly little girl, young, anæmic-looking, obliging, and resolved to try her English out on me, went through Comrade Ostroumova's diary. 'She will be at the factory until 10.15. At half-past she has to see the managers of the timber yard. . . . But, wait a minute, I can hear her car out there just now.' She ran to the window, opened it and shouted down to the chauffeur.

'Vladimir Stepanovitch, I say, when will Valeria Petrovna come up for lunch. This foreign writer chap wants a talk with her.'

'No hope.' Vladimir Stepanovitch cried back. 'She won't have lunch at all to-day. Too busy, she says. I talked to her all I could. She won't obey, crazy woman. One day she'll break down, I told her. . . .'

'All right, all right, where is she now?'

'Looking at the apartment of a kitchenmaid at the *stolovaya*, who complained that her room was smaller than that of an exiled *kulak* woman.'

The little secretary rang through to the *stolovaya*.

'Is Valeria Petrovna still with you?'

'Just left a minute ago for the foreign captains' room', she said to me, sighing deeply as she replaced the receiver.

'Is that the foreign captains' room? Blast you, idiots, I did not ask for the North-Construction Office—Exchange! Exchange! *Tovarich*, what kind of a service is this? I want Valeria Petrovna at the foreign captains' room, and you give me the Building Trust. The foreign captains' room, do you hear?'

But Valeria Petrovna had not arrived there yet. It seemed hopeless.

'It would be best for you to wait a little. I shall try to catch her somewhere. Meanwhile—I am not too busy this morning—tell me all you want, maybe I can arrange a few things myself before Comrade Ostroumova gets back. She is ruining herself with all that work. What a pity! She is the most energetic person in the whole Arctic.'

There is one Russian verb which will stand out in my memory more clearly than any other: *Ya zhdu*—I wait. I heard it and I said it in all its forms. Will you wait, please? Cannot you wait? I shall wait until he comes. I won't wait any longer. If you keep me waiting another minute, I shall write to *Pravda* about it. . . . Usually it ended up with me saying to myself. . . . Nothing doing, you'll have to wait after all.

But this time I would not. I asked the little girl secretary to give my compliments to *Tovarich* Ostroumova and tell her that I would ring up in the afternoon to get an appointment.

What was there to do but to spend the morning hanging around, trying to 'get the flair of the place', breathing the sweetly smell of slaughtered wood that soon established itself in my subconscious as the odorous symbol of Igarka? I found myself outside a *Parikmakherskaya*, a barber's shop, after a while. That's an idea. I went in and sat down in the chair. While I looked suspiciously at the wash basin before me, only to find that it was not so bad as I had expected, someone tied an apron round my neck from behind and a soft voice asked me to lean back. I found myself in the arms of a woman. She was high-cheeked, full-lipped, and had great blue eyes. She washed her hands like a surgeon, then tackled my face with tender fingers. The shaving cream was strongly perfumed. So was she. I waited for her to hand me over to a man who would finish the job. But no! She herself brandished the razor! All the tact and caution required by the strategic position, I asked:

'No men working as barbers here, eh?'

'There's heavier work for them to do', she replied icily, and bent my head back. My life was in her hands. She seemed fully conscious of that heavy responsibility. Careful to the point of pedantry, she worked her way up and down my cheeks and round my chin. Twice more she applied the cream, twice more I felt the razor on my skin. It was a close shave, to use the term in its professional sense. No word was spoken. She was too closely concentrated on her work to tell jokes or discuss the weather. I was offered no toilet waters, no brilliantine, no preparation against my incipient baldness. Then came a hot towel, and afterwards witchhazel, cream, and powder. It was a thorough job and I cheered up at the thought that it would last me for at least two days. That is one of the advantages of a country suffering from underproduction and lack of labour. The barber is glad to see you out of the shop as long as possible. When it was all over and I was about to get up from my chair, she bent my head forward again without a word, and began to lather the back of my neck. I was to go out of the place like a real Russian. They wear their necks as smoothly shaved as their upper lips.

I paid forty kopecks and got an official receipt from the State Hairdressing Trust. No tip was accepted. To show my gratitude somehow, I asked, with a strong undertone of appreciation: 'How long have you been a barber?'

'Five days; since I left the saw-mill.'

I was grateful she had left this revelation until the end of our acquaintance. While my coat was being brushed I read a crudely illustrated poster hung next to the mirror. Seeing my interest, she took it down, folded it and presented it to me as a souvenir. A new one was fetched from the cashier's drawer and put up with drawing-pins. The poster read:

FOR CULTURED CONDITIONS IN SOVIET HAIRDRESSING SHOPS
(Drawn up by the District Committee of Sanitary Culture)

Barbers!

(1) Shave carefully. Do not cut the visitors. If they bleed do not use alum. Carefully anoint the wound with iodine.
(2) Wash your hands thoroughly before attending each person.
(3) Do not talk while working.
(4) Use only sterilized brushes.
(5) Disinfect your instruments after each person. Metal, in boiling water or a weak solution of carbolic acid; combs and rubber instruments, in hot water with soap.
(6) Wear clean working kits.
(7) Give a clean towel and napkin to each new visitor.

Visitor!

(1) Insist on having your face washed after shaving, with warm water or eau de cologne.
(2) Insist on having your hair combed after you have it cut.
(3) Wash your hair with hot water and soap at home afterwards.
(4) Don't soil the shop. Refrain from smoking.
(5) Stay away if you are suffering from an infectious disease.
(6) Write about any anti-sanitary state of the shop in the book of complaints and inform the Sanitary Inspector, Dr. Kagan, Ulitsa Lenina 23, Apt. 19, immediately.
(7) A dirty barber's shop is the source of infectious diseases of the skin, hair and eyes.

WE MUST PUT THE WORK OF OUR HAIRDRESSERS UNDER STRICT SOCIAL CONTROL AND SUBJECT THEM TO THE TASKS OF CULTURAL SERVICE FOR THE TOILERS.

(*Editor:* Lebedev. *Artist:* Nemirovski.)

I turned to the girl and asked her: 'Well, how do you like this job after the saw-mills?'

'All right. But it does not satisfy me. I am taking evening classes now to become a trained nurse. Later I shall study medicine. I want a cultured career.'

I left with a torturing vision of Russia 1950: No hairdressers, only beard specialists.

CHAPTER XII

'A GENERATION OF GOOD FATHERS'

Two days of waiting (yes, waiting, *Ya zdhu, Ya zhdal*) brought me finally into the sanctuary of *Tovarich* Ostroumova's office. Meanwhile, I had heard her name more often than Stalin's and in connection with simply every sphere of life and work in the town. She was the virtual dictator of the place.

Fifteen minutes after the appointed time the door opened and a tiny woman, fragile, but as active as a trapeze artist, rushed through the door with a bulky attaché case under her arm. A swarm of men and women, holding documents, letters and posters followed her. 'Comrades, you must wait five minutes for me', she said, and closed the door in front of their noses. The first impression I had of her was a large workman's cap of heavy tweed, which she wore over the left ear like Jackie Coogan. A large coat of military cut emphasized her boyish demeanour, which was emphasized further as she threw the cap on the table to uncover her sharply cropped hair.

'Your papers, please.' She stretched out her arm to take Schmidt's letter from me, without shaking my hand.

'Right', she said, after glancing at it for a second. Taking notes, she continued: 'What do you want from me?'

Resolving not to be beaten by this display of ultra-efficiency, I adopted her style of conversation and jotted down my requests in arithmetic sequence:

(1) Transport by boat to the sea.

(2) Introduction to local problems through an interview with you.

(3) Your own biography.

(4) Permission to go about, take photographs and see whatever I like.

(5) Organization of a meeting with exiled *kulaks* and permission to talk to them.

(6) Your own suggestions for speedy acquaintance with the town's life.

She smiled and handed me the note she had been scribbling while reading Schmidt's letter. It said 'Permission. The foreigner, Smolka, is to be admitted to all parts of the port and factories and not to be stopped from taking photographs.'

Then she shot out: 'That disposes of No. 4. As regards 1 I shall let you know in due course. Re 2. I have no time for an interview, and, besides, my idea of modern journalism is not to interview chiefs, but to talk to people. Re 3, I am a Party worker and, as such, am anonymous. Re 5, if there will be time there will be a meeting. Re 6, open your eyes and ask anybody what you want to know. Good-bye.'

'Wait a minute, wait a minute, that's all very nice. But what is your position here? What does Politotdel mean?' She tapped the inkpot nervously with her long fingers. It was a miniature aeroplane, the pen stood in the cockpit.

'Politotdel means *Politicheskaya Otdelenya*, political department. Important organizations in Russia have such departments attached to them. They look after the spirit of the workers, see to it that they understand what they are doing and why, so that they should not work for the money only but be conscious of their ownership of everything, and the importance of our work of construction. There are politotdels in railways, army, navy, air force, food industry, film industry, and Glavsevmorput. Good-bye.'

She quickly wrote out a second slip and gave it me, leading me to the door:

Economics and industry	Stukater
Port	Mamoshkin
Club	Noreiks
Agriculture	Kossianov

Walking downstairs I summed up the result. She is a rude person. It is always the same in Russia. Seeing women in positions where I am dependent on them—as the ticket inspectors on the railway, as conductors on the Metro, as passport and Customs officials at ports—I always felt that they were terribly rude and arrogant, even if they did nothing but behave as a man in the same position. It is just that a man does not like to subordinate himself to the weaker sex. The Russians react differently. I saw Ostroumova giving orders to men double her size, and they obeyed like soldiers. But when she talked to stevedores her whole manner changed. She became the most charming and soft-voiced girl, and that did the trick, again they adored her. 'Office clerks hate her—the workers love her', said the teacher of English in Igarka. 'She is the real proletarian leader.'

Ostroumova was an intellectual herself—a pre-War Russian university graduate, I found out in Moscow—and, as such, she had the highest admiration for the manual labourer and no spot in her heart for intellectuals. She is a fanatic as regards her work; devoted to the revolution body and soul; and, as regards myself, I think she took me for the greatest nuisance possible. When I left I told her so, and remarked that it was not absolutely established that my sort must be kept away from Russia at all costs.

'To me you are a bourgeois journalist. If I see that you have not lied when I read your reports, I shall think of you with respect. Lenin taught us: He is an idiot who believes in words.'

She had been a secretary to Lenin in the days of the revolution, and until a few years ago to Kalinin, the President of the Soviet Union. She loved to quote Stalin's proverb: 'American efficiency, German accurateness, Bolshevik ideology—that's what we need.' As regards the last, she probably had it. With the two first requirements she was still battling. My transport to the sea was never organized by her.

I felt a little lost during the first few days in Igarka. Until now I had travelled with small groups, as is usual by aeroplane. Wherever we arrived, my companions had friends or business acquaintances, to whom they introduced me. In one way this was a disadvantage: I could not at first rid myself of the usual prejudice that in Russia 'they show you only what they want you to see'. Actually my friends made no attempt to show me nice things only; there were not many things to pick from anyway. All they did was to interpret what we saw in their own way: full of the vision of what would be in so-and-so many years. On the other hand it made contacts easy; I felt 'one of the boys' in the end, and I was honestly convinced that I had had my ear more closely to the ground than on many previous journeys abroad. Here at Igarka it was different. Igarka is a large town. I had no business with anybody and no one had any business with me. So before I succeeded in mingling freely with the men in the street—there had been no streets in the other towns—I stuck to officials for a short time. They had to talk to me when I talked to them, because they were in official positions. Of course I had no illusions as to how much their opinions were worth.

I had better luck with Stukater (Abram Abramovitch) than with Ostroumova. His official title was 'Chief of the Glavsevmorput Territorial Administration of Krasnoyarsk', or 'Business Manager of an estate four times the size of Germany', as he put it. A kindly looking man; on the wrong side of forty. He wore horn-rimmed spectacles that were out of harmony with his military breeches, boots and dark

TO HER I WAS A BOURGEOIS

green tunic. In fact he himself harmonized little with his gold-buttoned cavalry greatcoat and officer's cap. He lectured me cheerily for quite a while on the economic and industrial development of his area. He was very proud of his large budget. His annual turnover in fur alone amounted to half a million pounds (at par). The poly-metallic combine and the coal mines at Norilsk would be his as soon as the G.P.U. had completed the construction. At Ust Port he had a fish-canning factory that turned out one and a half million tins of preserved fish each year—worth £200,000. At Potapabo, not far from Dudinka, they were breeding reindeer, the first State reindeer farm in Russia, with two thousand head of animals. Out in the Kara Sea, they had sealing and whaling. At other parts they were organizing native hunters and fishers into collectives. They have also to manage the supply of all commodities to the dwellers in the district and the building of the towns, the 38 radio stations, the 20 meteorological observation posts, the 2 State cattle ranches, the agricultural estate with 100 tractors and 50 combines. They had to control six educational areas, with hospitals at many district centres, a graphite mine and the coal mines in the huge Tunguska Basin and on the Kureika river. All these things were under Abram Abramovitch Stukater's direction. And while his chief accountant wrote out a profit of 6 per cent on every business transaction of this large enterprise, all that Abram Abramovitch got out of it was 1200 roubles a month—a third of the earnings of a pilot on his own air lines. When I pointed this disproportion out to him he laughed. 'Oh, well, if you look at it from that point of view, you'll think me a big fool. Do you know that some of the men who load the ships in the port out there, and whose wives work in the saw-mill have more than that for their family? But what should I want with money? My family live in Moscow; they get their flat at a ridiculous rental; they have the use of my official car, and have quite enough to live on. My daughter is a student of medicine and paid by the State. I get my room free up here—a very nice room, as you will see when you come to have tea with me, sometime after midnight—with bearskins on the walls and a nice polar bear rug on the floor. And my food and clothes don't cost me anything. If it were money I was looking for I could stay at home. I could easily make two thousand as an economic expert somewhere in the capital.'

'So you are probably a Party man and have been sent here on Party orders?'

'No, I have never been a member of the Party. I have never been a worker, neither was my father. Can't you understand how fascinating this work is: building up an entirely new land, organizing and directing the affairs of such a huge concern, and knowing that it is for the benefit of hundreds of millions—for the good of my country? I have never been so happy in any other job before. I could not imagine myself without it. Take any of these papers on my desk. They are full of life, full of new life just about to materialize.' He picked up the printed proof of what looked like a price list to me.

'You see—here I am bringing out a questionnaire. We are sending ten thousand of these into the tundra round here and further north. I want to know what the natives want to buy. And, at the same time, I offer them all we can already bring to them, to see how far they understand the use of our manufactured products. The replies will be more than the basis of a wholesale grocer's shop. They will be a film of the growing civilization and culture among people whom we regarded as "savages" before.'

The leaflet was headed with the following questions, to be filled in by the heads of trading factories in the tundra after inquiries among those who were illiterate:

First name, father's name and family name of hunter.
How many wives, sons and daughters, with their ages.

Number of working reindeer owned.
Number of working sledge dogs.
Number of fishing nets.
Number of sledges.
Number of tents.
Number of traps.

Average value of goods handed in last year:

Fur.
Fish.

Then followed the list of commodities offered with the request that a cross be put against, and the quantities of, each product required.

It started with textiles—cheap cotton material, various kinds of cloth, flannel, woollen shawls, and went on to—short sheepskin jackets, overcoats, shirts, men's and boys' underwear, towels, women's clothes, young Communist blouses and woollen sweaters.

Here, as I read, Stukater interrupted me and said: 'The natives stick to their own costumes on the outside. But underneath they are starting to wear European clothes more and more, and they find them both healthy and useful. It is less work for them to catch the fish or squirrels that will buy them a woollen sweater than to make a skin jacket which is not half as practical.'

Further down the list I found: beads, combs, mirrors, tooth-brushes, soap, tooth-powder, safety-razors, skates for men and women, and domestic utensils such as glasses, teapots, spoons, lamps, painted cups and saucers. Then there were sleigh-bells, primus stoves, tobacco, cigarette paper, pipes, candles, firearms, cartridges. Near the end, under the heading 'Cultural Goods', were gramophones, with needles and records, balalaikas, pencils, writing-paper, chess and domino games. The grand finale was inevitably made up of 'Portraits of Party and Government Leaders'.

The prices, as far as I could judge at the moment, were on the same scale as those paid to the natives for their furs (225 roubles for a polar fox, 20 for a squirrel, and so on).

'And now look here what we got from the natives last year.' Stukater rummaged through his pile of papers—'22,470 polar foxes, 1275 ermines, 48 polar wolves, 27 polar hares, 1000 white squirrels . . . and that is the Taimyr region only! Can't you understand what fun it is to work and build here?'

I thought of another man who had wanted to colonize Arctic Siberia as a merchant adventurer: Mr. Lied, who had looked at me so sadly as I left him in London. I was glad to have met Stukater. He confirmed what I have always believed: that the really constructive man works for work's sake and regards the money reward only as the yardstick of success, as a source of further power, or, at the worst, as a basis of security for his own life—under capitalism as well as under a Soviet régime. I like that type of man; he moves the world forward. I told Abram Abramovitch so. He did not mind the parallel. But he insisted on one difference. 'In capitalism', he said, 'the ownership of the means of production wields absolute power, and the system works in a different direction in the end. With private enterprise the driving motive can only be individual profit —this is not a moral consideration but an economic law. Here I am restricted in my personal power by the criticism of the community and by the fact that it is the people as a whole who own that which I, as their trustee, build and direct. When I lose their confidence I am deposed and another man steps into my shoes. And that is right, because everything that is created and built is due to their sweat and effort. I am only co-ordinating and directing. And the greater personal satisfaction arising from the fact that from my post I can look over the whole, while they stand only at one wheel or one section—that is ample reward.'

It is commonplace to state that one of the fundamental

problems in judging between our economic system and the Russian is whether the motive power that drives Stukater is enough for the average man; whether personal satisfaction, pride in achievement, and perhaps social respect are sufficient to stimulate initiative and hard work in the individual. Stukater was working as hard as any man could. I did visit him once after midnight to have tea with him as he had suggested. Towards two in the morning I saw him getting restive and took my leave, apologizing for having kept him awake so long. 'Not at all', he said. 'It's only that I want to put in an extra hour to-night to get through some papers so that all will be ready by the time my staff come to the office to-morrow morning.'

Another time I put to him my reflections about the psychological factor as a driving force in economics. 'Well', he said, 'you are right in pointing out that I, and not only I but almost everyone of this present generation in Russia, sows more than we will ever harvest in our own lifetime. But we know that our children will be much richer for it. You cannot measure the lucrativeness of any of our present enterprises within one generation. They are too big to pay within such a short period. That is why they could never be completed by private business, which invests only for short-time yields nowadays. We are really nothing but a generation of good fathers. My father would have done the same if he could. But, in his time, the result of hard work stood on a much more precarious basis than ours. He was a teacher of Hebrew in a Jewish school in Vilna; he fled from one pogrom to another. I remember them all, Kishinev, Odessa. He finished up as a small grocer in Rostov and died of a stroke because he had overworked himself to keep us decently. I have no worries. My work is invested in the whole nation. And I will never have sleepless nights fearing for my savings.'

A day before I left Igarka I wanted to go and say good-bye to Stukater. 'He is very ill', his secretary told me. 'No wonder, working day and night. Now he has a heart attack. To-morrow morning they will fly him to Krasnoyarsk, and there a sleeper has already been ordered to take him to Moscow into a nursing home. He would not consent to leave now, in the busy season. But they ordered him by wireless from Moscow, and so he is having to go. We cannot risk losing such a valuable man simply because he is too careless for his own health. It is a proof of too little social consciousness if he thinks he is only responsible to himself.'

The most interesting problem about pioneering in a new land seemed to me to be the motive that inspires men to do it. It was my main concern on this journey. After all, we are no longer very much impressed by technical wonders; we take them for granted. But why men do it at all, and what they think and feel about it—that is what I tried to see. There were many motives in the past. The gold rush drove people to the Klondyke, the famines in Ireland sent whole villages across the Atlantic, the pogroms in Russia made Jews emigrate to America, adventure lured Spaniards to Mexico and Scots to all parts of the world. The Russians explain most movements in history from economic reasons. But when you ask them about their own sacrifices and hardships they will always give you an explanation that can only be based on the highest idealism. The Young Communists are proud of their materialistic philosophy, to which they cling collectively, but their own individual attitude towards life at the present time is the most radically idealistic that I have found anywhere. The party itself has the closest resemblance to a medieval order. The members dispose of any counter-argument by saying that individual idealism is really nothing but social materialism.

In the Arctic I found the most divergent types of people engaged in this great colonizing enterprise. None would accept romance as his motive. The conscious pioneers and the Red missionaries explained it as the fulfilment of a social and human duty. Stukater spoke of a generation of good fathers. Ostroumova refused to discuss it with a bourgeois journalist who would only distort her statements and tell lies afterwards. The convicts in the G.P.U. camp were half-convinced of what the 'administrators' had told them about the joy of going into virgin land, half-passively resistant against all attempts to make them work properly. But there were more types in Igarka. There were the old *kulaks* and there were the 'simple' workers, who seemed to be earning their living, here as anywhere else, partly induced perhaps by the Polar bonus which doubles their normal wages.

Down in the port I made my first contacts with the workers. Having seen me talk to the British sailors, they came and asked me to interpret some of their questions: 'Why do Great Britain and America, the powerful democracies, not line up together with France and Russia to protect the peace of the world against the aggressive designs of Japan, Italy and Germany?' 'What holidays does the British Government pay to its workers?' 'For how long is a British worker sent to a nursing home when he falls ill?' 'How is it that Eden and Hoare can sit in the same Government when Hoare deviated so strongly from Eden's policy towards the League of Nations during the Abyssinian crisis?' 'How large is the British Army, the American Army, the French Air Force?' 'Have they good parachutists in Western Europe and America, and such clever girl pilots as we have in Russia?'

I passed on these questions dutifully and translated the replies as well as I could. Then a worker offered to answer my questions. We went to his house, and his wife asked me to stay for supper. They had two rooms, one for father and mother, the other for the three children. The meal consisted of some undefinable pudding, soup and meat, rice and stewed plums. 'You can't get scurvy if you eat fruit'

185

the hostess assured me, forgetting that it ought to be fresh fruit. But they looked healthy enough. As advised by the authorities, they grew some chives outside their window —a really effective preventative against scurvy. For breakfast, so the children told me, they usually had dried fish, tea and bread; for lunch soup with meat and *kasha*. Meat was not more expensive than in Moscow, although almost double the price I had seen in Southern Siberia.

As soon as dinner was over Sakhari Yegarovitch Goshkov started a speech and conversation which was as long and as rich in minute details as any in talkative Russia. Whatever he said he accompanied by searching looks from his steely grey eyes, to see whether I was following attentively and believing what he said. He was a little pompous, Sakhari Yegarovitch, which was the more funny as he was a low-built, sturdy Siberian, looking tenacious rather than strong; and when he fingered his sparse flaxen moustache I was never sure whether he did it out of vanity or embarrassment.

He started quite logically, at the beginning.

'I came here in 1930. I was one of the first. We were only 150 altogether and no women. They followed next year. We had four large barracks, wild reindeer were still grazing not far away, until our noise and some idiots among us who thought they'd catch them drove them all away. All was swampy when we arrived at the end of June. Where the club stands now one could not even tie on a horse; it would have sunk in, so deep was the mud. Very few of us believed that we should ever succeed in building a town here. Some thought the first snow would crush our huts and we would starve and freeze to death. Others refused to believe that any decent house could ever stand on this soil of water and ice. The mosquitoes were a plague; we had to wear hoods to protect ourselves. When winter came and the sun stayed away the whole twenty-four hours for the first time a few got hysterical. They dropped their heads and said that it was the end of the world. The doctor said they were melancholic. We sent them away in the spring; they were rotters, anyway.

'We organized a club, but it was too small for all of us, so we had to amuse ourselves in shifts. We worked through the whole winter. In spring, after the flood, we built the first landing pier for the foreign ships. We had to do it again every year because each June, when the ice went, everything was swept away. This year we have a permanent mooring line for the first time. The second spring brought us 1600 people of whom 40 per cent were exiled *kulaks*, the rest free workers. We had to keep up that proportion because the *kulaks* had to be watched at work, and hurried on by us class-conscious workers. Some of them were glad to be here because they got better wages than in other places where they had been before.

'Many of us could not read and write when we came. We learned it during the winter. But of course I am still not so good at it as my boy, who is only twelve years old. There you can see how the Soviets rule a country. They govern it so that parents can learn from their children. And he cheats me sometimes, the rascal, because he has already learned more at school than I ever dreamed of learning.

'In '31 we got the first cinema. It was not a real cinema because on five out of seven nights in the week the lamps went out of order. But life was getting better, I could see that. On May 1st, 1932, some of our boys had already cameras and took pictures from the roof-tops while we demonstrated in the streets at 30 degrees. Social life was rather dull, however, when work was over the best thing one could do was to go home and sleep. But now that our industry grows our cultural life grows too. Yet the requirements of the people grow more quickly than the institutions. With mechanization work becomes easier and the men and women are less tired and can think of something more than their bellies. I am one of the best workers here. They

187

always put me on the most difficult jobs because they like me. Sometime ago there was a brigade at the mill that had never fulfilled its plan. All the time their results were round about 87.3 per cent. The brigadier said that his workers were a bad lot. I looked at them and said to them: "Your brigadier is a rotter." I started working with them. On the first day we did 104 per cent, on the second 107 per cent, on the fifth 113 per cent. At the end of the week we did 130 per cent. All I did was to put each man at the job for which he was best suited. The manager liked my method and so did my brigade. They had made 20 or 30 roubles a day extra and I got a premium of 500 roubles that month.'

Here I interrupted him to ask how his material life now compared with that of ten years ago, when—as he had told me—he was still a peasant. 'Oh, then when I went to church on Sunday I had not such a good suit as I wear now when I go to work. Why, I had never had leather shoes before I came here. Only bark. Now I have got a gramophone, six shirts, four suits, two pairs of shoes and, of course, boots and *valinki* (felt boots) for the winter. Galyushka has a balalaika and Kolya, the boy, a football. Galyushka works on the loading pier and together we make about 1100 roubles each month. That's a lot of money. I don't even spend the lot. We have a savings book at the Post Office, and from the money we put aside we are going to take an extra long holiday next year to look up old friends. But I want to tell you how I work, because that's what I am proud of, and that's also what the newspaper here is writing about.

'There was a sawmill worker in Archangel. A bloke that did 230 cubic metres in one shift with his brigade, and called himself the champion of the Soviet Union. I said to myself: You can beat that. And I did beat him. We did 240 cubic metres. What do you think the manager did? Sent a wire to Archangel to annoy the fellow there and gave me an extra 600 roubles. Do you think that was the end? No, not at all. Came back to work one morning after a free day, stood down at my frame. Hardly had we done 2 cubic feet, there came the manager holding a slip of paper in his hand. Said: "Here, radiogram from Archangel for you—250!" So I said: "To hell with you." Next day we radio'd back, "255". Do you think *that* was the end? A week later I came back from lunch—there was a telegram form, pinned to my sawing frame with a rusty nail; "260" it said. And below the form the manager had stuck up an empty telegram blank and tied on a pencil. So I called my men together and said to them: "Comrades!" "Comrades," I said, "these two rags of paper will stay here until we beat him and can rub it in to him. And I swear to you, *tovarich*, the rags had not got dirty before we sent off our reply—"289". Next day the manager called a meeting, and presented me with some furniture and a document, promising me the first one-family house in Igarka. It's just getting ready over there, across the road where the water drum is just halting.'

'What happened in Archangel?' I asked.

'Don't know. A week later they sent me on a four months' tour of the Union and took me round all the timber mills of the country. Had to make speeches and tell the men how one can increase production, what good fun it is, and how it will help us all along. In Novosibirsk and in Moscow I attended Congresses, and they even took me to Archangel. But I did not meet the bloke there. Probably they did not want us to bash our heads in. And mind you, I am not doing all this simply by sweating harder than the others. That would not be much. Anybody can work himself half-dead if he wants to. It's brain work, a more cultured kind of work. Stakhanovism. Do you know what that means? Better organization of the work, higher output through more intelligent handling of your machines and material. Pity you don't know anything about sawing timber. How could you? Should not expect you to. Can't write books either, Heaven knows I can't.'

But then the temptation to teach me something was too strong after all. He took out a pencil and said that the trick consisted in altering the angle at which the sawing blade is suspended opposite the car that leads the logs against it, and in a speed-up of the transport that feeds the machine.

The evening ended with Sakhari showing me all his clothes and those of his wife, who said that, after a year's wear, she gave them away to other women who were less fortunate in the choice of their husbands and could not afford the luxury that came to her, thanks to Sakhari's skill and initiative. He told me he wanted to become a *culturny chelavyek*, a really cultured man—the term 'cultured' comprising anything from the regular use of a tooth-brush to having studied Marx and the classical works of literature.

I was reminded of Sakhari Yegarovitch when, a few days later, I met Clavira Alexeyevna Chanchikova at the club. She came from Krasnoyarsk to Igarka in 1930 to stay with her brother. The sawing mill was not yet built at that time, she said, and she worked in a brick factory. First she was a black labourer. Then she took some courses and became a skilled timber worker. 'Did 180 and 200 square yards of boards instead of 140, which was the norm', she told me. Got married and divorced again, because my husband was not interested in getting on in life.

'Now I am not happy', she went on. 'I want to have a man to talk to, to learn with, to go to meetings and to sleep with. All I have found up to now are men to sleep with. That's good, but not enough. And I don't want to start the same trouble as with my first one all over again, by giving in to one who is not really any better.'

All these people valued the feeling of doing something useful, of climbing up the ladder of culture as it was explained to them, more highly than actual material wealth. Yet a raising of their economic status was always almost identical in their eyes with becoming, or being able to become, more cultured. For it meant money for musical instruments of which they were fond, of nice clothes which were a symbol of refined position, apart from pleasing the eye. Clavira was particularly keen on the theatre. She saw each play three times when the artists from Moscow were in town on their tour through Arctic centres.

An elderly carpenter who had come to Igarka on a two years' contract told me that his economic position had not materially improved since before the revolution, because he was always a successful and skilled worker. 'But we have risen in human values in self-esteem and are given all possibilities to satisfy our spiritual needs, to study and to read, to become educated and cultured, and that after all is the only thing which lifts men above animals, is it not?'

CHAPTER XIII

PRISONERS OF THE ICE

THE pioneers of Northern Siberia are not all hewn from the same block. It is one thing to go to a cold and primitive place where you are paid double your normal wages, where you get free (or almost free) living quarters, and where you are told every minute of the day that you are doing something wonderful. It is another thing to be taken away from your house or barn together with your family, to be herded into railway trucks for days, to be sent down rivers for weeks, and then to be told you are going to stay and work there for an indefinite period—as has been the fate of many thousands of *kulaks*.

From 1929 to 1932 Russia went through the second revolution. The workers had been won over to the cause of Socialism and Communism. They saw their advantages fairly soon. They could get over hardships and difficulties in the knowledge, or belief, that they would be temporary. They were told, and they shortly experienced for themselves, that the new régime meant privileges for their class. But what about the peasants? There are 80 million peasants in Russia. When the men returned from the Great War, disillusioned and embittered against those who drove them to three years of mass slaughter, they rallied with ' the workers in hatred against a common foe, but not in support of a common ideal. They had no thought of Socialism or Communism. They wanted more land, less taxes and better prices for their products—in fact all that had been promised to them in October, 1917. But a country bled white after the War, the civil war and the inevitable upheaval which a complete change in economic organization must bring about, could not quickly raise the material

standard of life. The peasants were disappointed. During the first period of collectivization the Communists thought that they would have to fight village unrest with machine-guns and force the peasantry into acceptance of a régime which they themselves were honestly convinced would be to the benefit of all in the end. Trotsky wanted to liquidate the farmers as thoroughly as the landowners had been liquidated and as ruthlessly as the factory owners and bankers had been destroyed. Stalin, better acquainted with the popular psychology and endowed with a grim sense of realities, suggested a different course, which was adopted. It looked a compromise at first glance. In point of fact it was a step forward in the direction agreed upon by all, a step, however, only so far as a foot would span and not so wide that the country might wound its legs. The small peasants, the village poor, and the landless farm hands were told to pool their resources in land, cattle and man-power and organize their production on a collective basis. The *kolkhoz*, the collective farm, was the new economic form advocated for the Russian village. The *kolkhoz* was granted state credits, was lent agricultural machinery, was given contracts for delivery of goods to the State. The *kulaks*—the rich and wealthy farmers who had men to till their land for them—would not join in this new experiment. A red light went up. Danger! they read. Danger to their economic and social position. For a time they carried on independently as individual farmers. Soon, however, they realized that all the odds were against them. The cards had turned. The collectives were now the ones to get credits and con-tracts; they themselves had to muddle through as best they could. The others had machines, they only horses. It became increasingly difficult to keep the servants, who felt they would be better off as members of the collective farms. Prices were too low to make production profitable on the basis of primitive ploughs and hand thrashing. Their fight for a living turned into a fight for life. They drove the tax-

N   193

collectors out of the villages, stopped sowing except for their own immediate needs, slaughtered their animals rather than hand them over to the State. With increasing bitterness some of them started sabotaging the work of the collectives, burnt their haystacks, poisoned their cattle, ruined their crops. Famine came over Russia, a shortage of meat and fat, a shortage of leather.

The *kulaks* were expropriated by village Soviet decisions or by decrees. Their farms were handed over to the community. The number of those who were sufficiently open-minded and diplomatic to read the signs of the times and join the *kolkhoz* was very small. Over a million were sent away from their homes. North Russians were exiled to Central Asia, Caucasians to the Far East, Ukrainians to Northern Siberia.

Meanwhile, the *kolkhozniki* were given more privileges. Each member could retain his cottage and a little garden, a cow, a pig, a goat, some chickens—enough to feed the family, but not enough to keep them in money. They had to earn money by their work in the *kolkhoz*, in the collectivized fields. For the time being their individualist psychology is being taken into account, while simultaneously they can learn, from practical experience, that mechanized farming and division of labour reduces the burden of work and makes for richer harvests. The system apparently works well now. There is no more food shortage in Russia. Goods are cheaper, the card system abolished.

The price for the rising happiness of 80 million farmers —the greater safety and wealth of the nation—has been paid partly by the doom and misfortune of over a million people. Those who came from the vineyards and orchards of the Crimea now shiver in Arctic towns and lumber camps. Those who loved the white snow of the winter, the nip in the air, the glowing fire in their huts, the fresh and exciting smell of steaming black earth after the spring rains, now sweat in the deserts of Tajikistan.

Has anyone the right to cause such suffering? or to deal so arbitrarily in millions of lives? This is a question of principles, a moral and ethical, at best a politico-philosophical problem. It is none of my immediate business. I saw *kulaks* in Igarka. There are 4,000 of them in the town. I am here to tell you how they live, what they think and say.

A natural question to people in a pioneering town is—how long have you been here? It was usually my first question. Many a bearded old fellow with shrewd eyes and energetic, if somewhat brutal, lines round his lips would reply, 'Six summers.' It meant he came in 1930. This and his looks sufficed. There was no need for further cross-examination. The six summer people were exiled *kulaks*. They came when the town was a year old. They do not know when they will leave. Even now, when the new Constitution restores their civic rights and accepts them once more into the community, few believe that they will ever see their homes again.

One, Strelyakoff, said to me: 'I will not go home even if I were invited to. I have got used to factory work. I have strong arms and a clear head. I have changed my outlook. It is not better than being a wealthy farmer—but it is bearable to be a worker, and nowadays more honourable. I got my passport back last year, and now I can go to political meetings, attend their debates, be heard politely when I say something, and vote when decisions are taken. I have made my peace with them. But if I went home and saw my house run by my former servants and my field ploughed by Government tractors I am not sure how long I would remain at peace with them.'

I had had a wrong conception of the timber camps of the North. The picture which had been drawn for us over here when they first sprang into the news because Russia sold timber more cheaply than Finland and Canada had been a gloomy one. A tale was told of ill-clad, underfed convicts, broken families, forced labour, deaths by tens of thousands. That is not what I saw in Igarka. And after all I heard from the *kulaks* themselves, I believe that it is not what I would have seen in other places elsewhere. A woman to whom I gave an account of what we had read exclaimed: 'Why, is it not enough to be sent away from your home to a place where you freeze, have to work in a factory to make a living, and sleep in a house that is not your own? We think that is bitter enough.'

I had a surprise with the *kulaks* in Igarka similar to that with the convicts on the Norilsk-Dudinka railway. On the first day I asked Ostroumova, the little dictator of Igarka, to write out a permit for me to speak to the 'prisoners' and perhaps to arrange a meeting in the presence of some authority. As nothing of the kind was done, and as I had my suspicion about the exact meaning of her words, 'If there will be time, there will be a meeting', I set out alone on my search for the exiles. First rather furtively I asked this man or the next one where the camp was, whether it was far away from the town, and when everybody said, 'There is no camp at all', I took it that they were all in the silent conspiracy. Finally, on the fourth or fifth day, a British seaman who was supervising the loading of his steamer in the harbour remarked to me, nodding towards the Russians working on deck: 'Not bad these chaps—all exiles—always ask us for drinks.' Only then did I realize that the *kulaks* in Igarka were everywhere, intermingling with the free workers, living door to door with them, un-guarded and indistinguishable from them—except, perhaps, for a different cut and colour of beard and hair and an odd way of walking that told of southern plains rather than northern marshes.

'No need for guards', they told me later. 'We could not break out. Where could we go? Down the river into the Arctic Sea? Up the river, against the current and the rapids for 2000 miles? Or through the roadless taiga or through swamps—to please the bears and wolves? There is no escape from here so they may as well let us be free in the town. Wherever else we reached we would be arrested within twenty-four hours, as soon as they find out we have no passport.'

My first and perhaps most interesting encounter with the exiles was on the morning of the sixth day. I was still not quite sure whether I should talk freely to the *kulaks*—both for my own sake and, especially, for theirs. So I strolled about disgruntledly. My journey home was still quite in the air; there was waiting for something to turn up and little to do. I reached the outskirts of Igarka, where the parquet roads lead straight into the swampy scrub. There, with its back to the tundra and its front to the town, stood a pretty one-family house of fresh timber. A woman was sitting on the steps, looking up to the sky. She was tall, wiry, had strong arms and long hands, and a pair of grey, deep-set eyes. She looked well over forty. Bidding her a good day, I sat down.

'Well, and how is life?'

'*Nitchevo*', she said, which means literally 'nothing', but generally anything you like.

'Good or bad?' I insisted.

'Bad, if you want to know. Very bad.'

'What's wrong?'

'Everything. This is no place for me to live in. Cold, unfriendly. No mountains, no fields—and always pork in the butchers' shop.'

'What's wrong with pork?'

'It's dirty. We are Tartars, we have never eaten it.'

'Why did you come here at all?'

'I did not want to.'

'Did your husband?'

'Of course not.'

'So why are you here?'

'They did not ask us where we wanted to go to.'

'Who are they?'

'The G.P.U. One night they came, woke us up, made us dress and go with them. Then we were sent up here.'

'Why?'

'Because we are *spezperisilentsi*' (a new term meaning special exiles, sent away by administrative decree, not as a convict after a trial).

'Yes, but why are you *spezperisilentsi?*'

'Oh, I don't know. There was no need to do much, six years back, to be sent away. Maybe my husband did something. Always told him not to be an ass or to kick against the pricks. Probably got together, with some of his friends from the pub, and ran around the village at night, instead of being at home, when a fire broke out somewhere. Counter-revolutionary activity they wrote on a rag of paper that somebody read to me on the boat.'

'And you say that life's bad here? The house is nice, anyway; it looks good and clean.'

'House is all right, but it is not my own.'

'Whose is it?'

'Belongs to my son. He makes a lot of money. Boy of twenty-one with 750 roubles a month. We live in his house. His father makes a third of his wage. What's the good of a house if it is not yours?'

'What is your son doing?'

'Accountant. Just think of it, an accountant. Sits in an office and writes figures in and out of books. When he came he was fifteen and knew all about cows and horses. Now they have made him learn from books. Of course, he is no fool. Has plenty of brains. Soon saw where fortune lies nowadays. So he became a Stakhanovist worker, and did something with the books that saves them a lot of time. So they made him a present of this house. That's how they bribe our children away.'

'But are you not proud of him?'

'No need for me to be proud of him. Is proud of himself

enough, the bounder. But he forgets what a wheatfield looks like.'

'And your husband?'

'He is no good here. Can't get used to it. Works in the sawing mill—all they use him for is to carry wood and saw-blades. Probably he can't do anything else. His father was a peasant, his grandfather was, and his great-grand-father. None of them carried wood and sawing blades round a factory. We had 20 cows, 29 horses, 12 *batraki* (farm hands—journeymen) and many many acres of land in the south. What's the good of it now they have taken it away from us?'

At this point a little girl, very neatly dressed, came out of the house with the local news sheet in her hand and began reading out of the paper to her mother.

'Leave me alone, Nadeshda, I don't care for these things.'

The mother turned to me again. 'Always pesters me to listen to her reading the newspapers. What has it all got to do with me? All right for her. She can read. They tell her what it's all about in her Communist babies' club. But I—I hate to be made a fool of by my own children.'

Then she turned to the child, looked at her half grimly, half sadly, and said: 'Come here, Nadeshda, pull your skirt down. I simply can't keep that wench from running about half naked since she's been to the camp in the south. Did not do anything but bathing and playing football; now she wants to show everybody she's got brown legs. Nobody can get brown legs up here.'

'Mother is terrible', it was Nadeshda's turn to appeal to me. 'I cannot make a cultured person of her no matter how hard I try. And I told you, *matushka*, that you have all the gifts for becoming a knowing woman. It's not like father, who is definitely too much of an old element to be re-cast.'

'What about yourself, Nadeshda? What are your plans?' I asked.

199

'Oh, I shall be a doctor; there's no need to worry about me. But why should not mother do something useful too? She can't be happy only looking after the home. She is wasting her energies.'

'There you see the ingratitude of children, and that's what the schools make of them—self-confident, precocious little brats who lose all respect for their parents because they can read and learn and we don't know what they are talking about. Shouldn't I try to make the home pleasant for the man, and help him to forget his worries and the great change?'

'Well, it's hopeless, *matushka*. You won't listen. Anyway, I have to run along now. I have to finish my chapter for our book.'

'Wait a minute, Nadeshda. What book is that?'

'Oh, we are writing a book about the life of children in a Polar town. I am doing the chapter on sleigh-riding in the winter. We have to be through with the work by next spring, because we promised Gorki before he died to fulfil our plan by then. His death was a great loss to us. He had given us the original idea and actually sent suggestions after we had submitted the first two chapters. It is fortunate that a French comrade promised to carry on in Gorki's advisory capacity, because he was a close friend of his. I wonder whether you know him? Romain Rolland. Two of us are going to take the manuscript to him in Switzerland for final overhaul.'

I admitted that I had heard the name of the 'French comrade' and asked Nadeshda whether I might see the work as far as it had gone. She was only too glad to show it to me. On the way she talked a lot about her parents.

'Naturally they are unhappy because everything was taken away from them. I remember we had a fine house, and I also liked our village better than Igarka at first. But now I understand that we had no right to own all that, and I am very glad that I can be a member of the Pioneers' (the Red

Scout organization). 'The teacher at school talked very frankly to all of us and said Stalin had told the Communists that the children of the former capitalist classes must not suffer for the sins of their parents. My elder sister is even going to marry a Party member. We shall all be completely absorbed into the new society and all have reason to be grateful, because our life will be much happier and more cultured than that of our parents.'

(The teacher, I fancy, had told her that bit too.)

CHAPTER XIV

JACK FROST'S CHILDREN

NADESHDA took me to the office of the local newspaper—
Bolshevik in the Arctic. There, she said, we should find the
half-finished manuscript of the Children's Book and also
Klimov, Anatoli Klimov, whom she called their literary
expert.

The newspaper office was a neat little cottage with an
annexe in which two hand-printing presses and cases of
type comprised the 'Printing House'. Next year there would
be a linotype, they said. The newspaper is published daily
and is sold in the streets from eight o'clock in the morning.
It has four pages, with illustrations, and during the navigation season there is added a half-page supplement in English
containing the Editor's views of what is important news for
the foreign sailors—namely, short articles on Soviet work in
the Arctic, brief news of industrial and agricultural progress
in Russia and (while I was there) telegrams from the Spanish
civil war and accounts of the first Trotskyist trial. But
occasionally they would even try a little hazily to pick up
sports news from the British wireless service and print them
in a little corner to please their guests.

Nadeshda was quite at home in the editorial office. She
showed me the Board Room and the wireless cabinet, where
a girl of about nineteen was busy taking down radio news
from the Russian News Agency for publication next
morning.

As the great Klimov was not yet back from lunch
Nadeshda raided his desk and took out a large folder containing the children's correspondence with Gorki and
Romain Rolland, original manuscripts written by clumsy
children's fingers into class-room copy-books, and also two

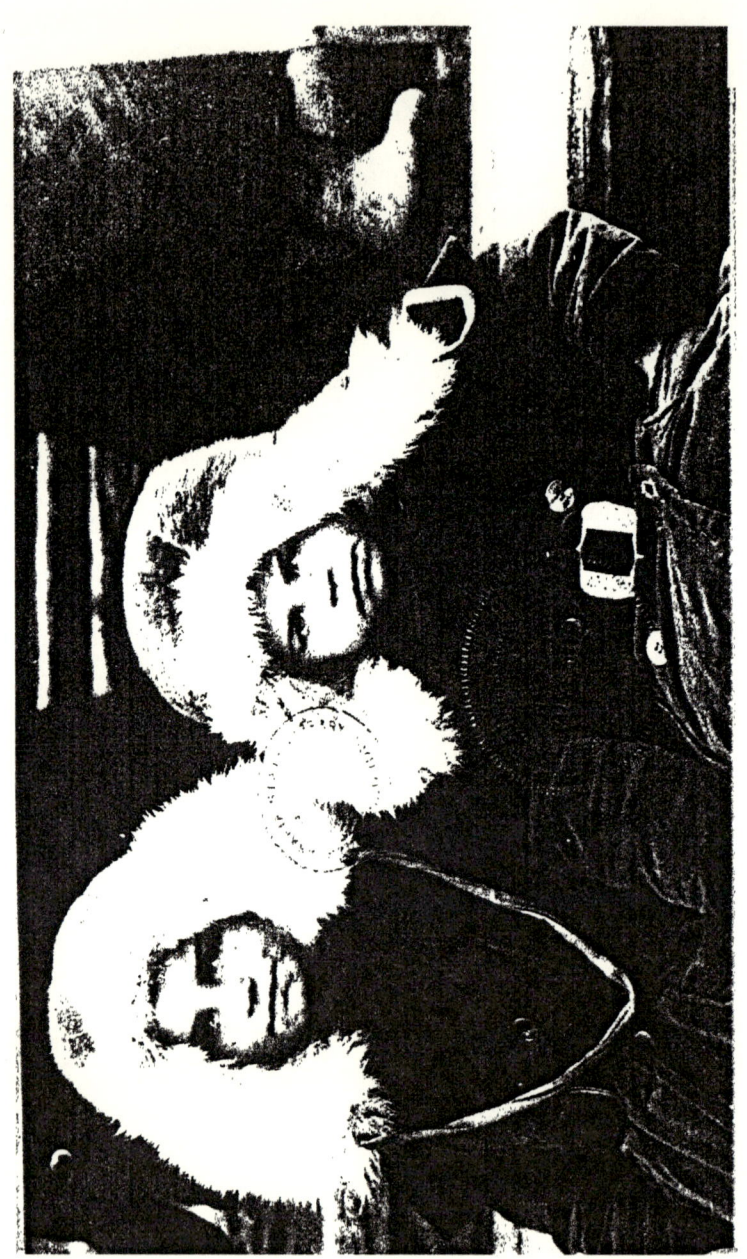

or three chapters which had, she said, 'already been revised and approved by the collective'.

I knew that in the last years of his life Gorki had believed that in Russia, where so much new and significant is happening, where land and people are being changed, not only writers but the people themselves should engage in literature; the simplest and what we would call humblest should put their ideas to paper. And so he gave much time to advising, encouraging and helping his 'amateur writer colleagues'. He became convinced that this activity would yield literature more valuable to the world than his own work.

The Arctic children in Igarka prize this letter from Gorki:

'Hearty greetings to you, future doctors, engineers, tank-drivers, poets, airmen, teachers, artists, inventors, geologists.

You sent me a fine letter. Through its simple and clear words there shone brightly into my room the rays of your courage, the warmth of your hearts, the clearness with which you recognize the road to higher aims in life. There is hardly a place in the world where children live under such harsh natural conditions as you in your Arctic home. Hardly, I think, could we find anywhere else children like you who, by the result of your lives and efforts, will inspire all the children of the world to be equally as bold and proud as you are yourselves.

You write: "At the moment we are living when the sun does not shine on us. We see the light of day only for three hours every morning. The rest of our time is spent in Polar night, in frost and snowstorms." And yet, in the midst of the Polar night, the sun of human intelligence burns unsubdued. Only recently it has won the battle against scurvy, until a short time ago the dreaded curse of the Far North. Under the conquering force of human intelligence the earth, chained with the fetters of everlasting frost, is now growing fruit and vegetables, flowers and grain. All this would have been impossible before the Lenin revolution, for then the right to a full education and to the development and unfolding of knowledge was in the hands only of the land-owning class in Russia.

Great and surprising joys are awaiting you, boys and girls. In a few years, reared in a harsh nature, you little iron Communists will go to work on construction and on further study and, before you, there will unfold the wonderfully varied beauties of our great country. You will see the Altai mountains, the peaks of Pamir, the crests of the Urals, the Caucasus; fields heavy with wheat stretching for thousands of hectares; gigantic factories at work; colossal power stations; the cotton plantations of Central Asia; the vineyards of the Crimea; the astounding towns of Moscow, Leningrad, Kiev, Kharkov, Tiflis, Erivan, Tashkent, the capitals of little brother Republics like Chuvashia—capitals which until the revolution were hardly anything but tiny villages.

With you are snow and frost and snowstorms. I am living in the Crimea, on the shores of the Black Sea. To-day, January 13th, we have had for the first time this year a miserable little sprinkle of snow. It melted away as quickly as it had come. All through December and right down till yesterday the sun shone on us from eight o'clock in the morning until almost half-past five in the evening. Goldfinches, chaffinches, tomtits—all spent their winter here. Spring begins in the second half of February; autumn only towards the end of October.

Until the revolution it was the Tsar, his relatives, the courtiers and millionaires who lived in the Crimea. Now the Tsar's palace has become a Home of Rest for peasants, and on all the southern shores of the Crimea all the palaces are Homes of Rest and sanatoria. There is a pioneers' camp, "Artel". There is much that is very fine and beautiful in the country, in our Union of Socialist Republics, and all of it is growing fast. All of it belongs to us.

Naturally, in order to possess it rightly, to develop it further in an intelligent manner, our boys and girls must learn much, seriously and honestly. We must nourish the love for study in ourselves, develop it into real blossom, so that in the end study will become to us a source of pleasure and joy—a game. The mind and the ability to understand and comprehend can only grow through exercise and training, just like our muscles. Machines are gradually wiping out the gulf between physical and mental labour. But in order to make good machines which will lighten the burden of labour for man we must zealously work to increase our knowledge.

There is nothing in the world which could be useless to know. This is why I approve thoroughly of your desire to write a book about yourselves in the Arctic. While you write this book you yourselves will learn a lot. And if your work will be successful and good you will also teach others. Have courage and energy, be bold. Remember that Pushkin, Nekrasov and Lermontov began to write poetry at your age. Nekrasov's poems looked like this:

> Accept my darling mother,
> This poor work, and see
> Whether it is any good.

You see it does not even rhyme.

But while you should be bold, don't forget that our little book will be read by thousands of children in the Union and it may even go beyond the frontiers. So you must take a serious attitude towards your task.

I would advise you to organize the work like this: First select from the literary circles of the school those who have already shown some ability in writing good prose or verse, work out a plan for the book collectively, and appoint an editorial board of five or seven for it.

It seems to me the plan should be like this:

First chapter: Physical conditions of Igarka, the landscape,

soil, climate, vegetation, sketch of winter, spring, autumn.
This you must write because you live in exceptional conditions that are not familiar to other children in the country.
And you must write as though you were telling of the conditions of your life to someone particularly close to you—
for instance, to your friends Comrade Stalin or Pavel
Postishev (the secretary of the Party in the Ukraine).

Second chapter: Life in the family, work at school, i.e.
your studies, comradely relationships, good and bad in this
regard, and how you fight to eliminate the bad.

Third: Heroic and funny incidents of your life. Don't
be afraid of laughing at yourselves, self-criticism is as necessary as washing.

Fourth: The growth of the town, extension of works, the
impression made upon you by the crews of foreign ships,
and so on.

This, of course, is only a rough outline of a plan, an outline made by someone who does not know the variety of
your life and, of course, you may not take this outline into
account at all.

Personally I think each chapter should be written by a
definite group and all the work should be done collectively.

When the manuscript is ready send it to me and I and
Marshak, when we have read it, will return it to you,
pointing out what is good and bad and where alterations
might be necessary.

Give a place in your book to the children on Dickson
Island and the hibernators at Chorny.

Well now, I am at the end. My letter has turned out
longer than yours.

Be of good health, dear children, be of good health, my
dears.

M. GORKI.'

. . . . . .

Nadeshda was prouder than I can describe as she went
through all this with me, and I felt clearly how she resented

the sudden return of Klimov from lunch. Until that moment she had felt that she was acting as a little ambassadress of Soviet children in initiating me into their problems, treasures and achievements. Now Klimov had to take charge, and although he treated her tactfully and without patronage she felt that her part had come to an end.

First we talked of the children's book. He told me how he had selected seventy of the most gifted 200 competitors whom the 2000 scouts of Igarka had chosen to write their biography. He spent every afternoon with them, setting out the programme for their literary work. Each child took over a particular task of investigation and reporting. Within a month the story was read to the others, who criticized and corrected, called this phrase artificial, that picture unreal, this character untrue to life, that technical detail too poorly explained. All Klimov did was to correct their grammar and spelling, or to suggest a more effective distribution of illuminating highlights and contrasting shades.

I have picked a few items from the book, with the authors' permission to reproduce them here :

CHILDREN'S BOOK

FRIEND NARSO

One day in the summer of 1935 father called for us all to travel to the other side of the Yenisei, in order to set nets there and to capture our own fish. We ran merrily and willingly to the bank and there saw that we were not going alone: in the boat was already a Neniets tribesman, Nikifor Narso, who worked at the factory as interpreter.

We set out. The weather was very still, the sun shone brightly; above our heads from time to time ducks flew and gulls circled. To the measured creak of the rowlocks, Narso told us:

'You may think this is a little river. But from the factory to the other shore is 45 versts. Here in the middle of the

water there is a little land, but there are ten and twenty
such little lands.'

And there was one! It appeared that 'the other bank'
was not the other bank at all, but simply an island, one of
the numerous Brekhovsky islands. What a river! Forty-
five kilometres in width. And in the middle the water was
all cut up by islands, large sea-going vessels travel along
the channels and drag little lighters, carrying goods to the
fishers to their homes.

We also had become fishermen, we were going to catch
fish in nets. We had three nets, while Narso had fifteen.

'Is there a lot of fish in the Yenisei'? asked my sister Nina.

'Oi! Many fish used to be', he replied. 'Terrible many
were, but they were thrown up on the shore themselves when
in the spring they came down like a dam.'

'What, Narso, the fish themselves got on to the bank'?
Nina asked inquisitively.

'Oi, Oi! Lots of beluga used to live here. There were
few steamers, the beluga used to go into the water, the little
fish were terribly afraid of them, and in the shallow places
they got stranded and pushed right on to the shore. But
here we must stop', the Neniets finished.

The nets were swiftly thrown overboard. We returned
home tired, but as soon as it was barely light next morning
we went out again, but without papa, to look at the nets.
We began with Narso's nets. In the first five nets there were
five small pike, in the second five were four pike, and in the
third five there were none at all.

We rowed to our own nets. We drew them up, and every
net was full of sterlet; from all the nets we collected a
hundred good, tasty fish.

Narso was indignant.

'Why is this?' he cried to me. 'The nets you've got are
like mine, but your father must be a Russian *shaman*, you've
got so many fish.'

We laughed merrily, but Narso suddenly stood up in the

boat and began to swear and shout. At his belt at the side hung a horn from which he shook out some sort of brown dust, put it to his lips, then threw it into the Yenisei, while he himself sang with his arms raised above his head.

It was the first time we had seen anything like this, and so, when Narso grew tired and sat down in the boat, we asked him in chorus what he had been doing.

'I prayed to God', he answered, 'to give me a lot of fish.'

'But, Narso, I don't pray, and you see how much fish I have got. The fish come to me', I said.

Narso grew angry, lit his pipe and was silent, but afterwards he abruptly said:

'Why are the Russians such a wise people? Even the fish go more into the Russian nets.'

My sister and I explained as best we could why it happened so.

'You see, friend, we have got nets of fine twine and grey, so that it is hardly visible, while you've got black and coarse nets. So the fish don't go into your net. To-morrow we'll take fine nets and then we'll see how much more you catch.'

He agreed, and we did so. By the evening we had set fifteen good new nets for him, and early next morning we set out to look at them. In the very first nets were lots of sterlet. Nardo laughed:

'Well, to-day the fish have come to me, there'll be none in your nets.'

We looked at his other nets and everywhere there were splendid sterlet. Narso laughed longer, he roared out loud.

'Pity so many fish have been caught, a real pity; what shall we do with them? It's my God has helped me. I prayed a great deal the day before.'

We collected ten poods from his nets. We went to ours, and began to haul them into the boat, and the nets even began to break, so many fish were in them. I said to Narso:

'You said you had prayed to your God, who drove the

stupid fish into your net. But why have we got so many fish?'

Narso laughed at that and again sang his song, and when he had finished he said:

'I've lived many years stupidly, but why have I been such a fool? I always threw out nets of stout twine, now I shall only buy nets of thin twine.'

After that we became fast friends with Narso.

MISHA ZOLOTARIEV.

(Town elementary school No. 3. Born 1924.)

GUESTS OF THE TUNDRA

Gerasimov Kuzya is my great and good friend. I frequently spend time free from school and home occupations with him. We wander on skis out of the town in winter time, catch frogs, lizards and birds in summer, and are rivals in study. I quickly made friends with him. We were brought together by our mutual ignorance of the North, our new comradeship at school, which we entered almost at the same time, and the unusual town in which we had to live.

A year ago we saw a team of reindeer and nomads in Igarka for the first time; they were Zvieniets and Neniets people, who had arrived from the tundra to Polar Igarka.

It happened like this. Kuzya and I were wandering through the streets, thinking of the forthcoming May Day. There was a noticeable liveliness in the streets of the town. For some reason a particularly large crowd was standing by an eating house. Of course, Kuzya and I quickly made our way into the crowd, and found ourselves at the side of . . . reindeer.

The reindeer were grey, with long wool and mournful eyes. Such reindeer are not shown in the zoological gardens, these are much smaller. Great branching horns grow out of their foreheads. In the spring the horns fall off the reindeer.

The reindeer were harnessed to sledges, light home-made ones which the nomads make themselves, without using a single nail. They are fastened together with wood and bound with leather cords or reindeer veins. They have broad runners, so that they should not be turned over in the snow. Close to the reindeer a great, long stick, a staff with a rounded end, was thrust into the snow. This was the 'knout' with which the driver urges on his reindeer.

'Kuzya', I said to my comrade, 'look at the reindeers' hoofs, they're like a cow's. And they are so large because they don't run along roads, but over the fresh, untrodden snow, so they need a broad tread, so as to sink less into the snow.'

Four reindeer were harnessed into each sledge. They were harnessed in leather collars and instead of shafts leather traces stretch from the collar to the sledge. All the harness was beautifully decorated with mammoth bone and vari-coloured ribbons. The oldest reindeer had the very largest, heaviest horns. A great red band adorned them.

The crowd said that guests had arrived from the tundra, from the national collective farm to purchase gifts and food-stuffs for May Day. The collective farmers from the tundra had gone into the dining-room to have something to eat.

Kuzya and I decided to wait, in order to see people whom we had never seen before in our lives. We didn't have to wait long. Soon a swarthy, black-haired, broad-faced Neniets in shaggy clothes, adorned with beads, came out of the dining-room. From head to foot the guest from the tundra was clothed in reindeer skin. On his feet were furskin boots, embroidered with beads. A long-haired reindeer *sakui*, a cloak which is drawn over the head and which is not buttoned in front was over his shoulders. His sleeves, gloves and fur-cap, in the form of a capuchin hood, were all sewn to this warm cloak.

Others followed him, among them women and children. They were all dressed like the first. Only the women had bright, silk kerchiefs on their heads.

They made the reindeer lying in the snow get up, sat in their sledges and with their long staffs beat them on their horns and thrust at them from behind. The reindeer dashed off.

YURA ZHILIN.

(Elementary school No. 3.)

ROAD TO THE NORTH

(Fragment)

Long before we left, when we had only just heard that we were going to Igarka, my school comrades took the news in different ways. Some were jealous, others laughed.

'You've gone out of your mind, Boris, to go to the North. You'll be ill with scurvy,' some said.

'It's always night there, never day, your nose will be frozen off,' others tried to frighten me.

But I was not afraid, for I knew that it was all untrue. What I was most interested in about Igarka was that I should with my own eyes see foreign ships, which come for timber, and also see living Fascist officers, who wear epaulettes and whom I had never seen in all my life.

We travelled by the boat *Yan Rudzutak* to go some 1500 kilometres somewhere beyond Yeniseisk.

During all our journey the banks of the Yenisei were overgrown with the dense wall of the taiga. No wonder the timber factories in Igarka saw up timber to send abroad, there are lots here. The taiga was wild and dense. One day, between the villages of Vorogovo and Yartsevo, as our boat drew near the bank, we saw a great shaggy brown bear plunge back into the taiga.

We took nine days to travel to Igarka. And the further

north we got, the colder it became. The autumn rains were succeeded by a fall of feathery winter snow. October had only just begun. More and more frequently we passed fishing vessels, hauling caravans of lighters and barges with fish and people. They were fishers and hunters after the sea animals, walruses, seals and belugas, returning from their travels. The steamship *Krasnoyarsky Rabochy* was also returning from the northern winter, carrying workers in the scientific expeditions in the Arctic, and those who had been withdrawn from winter quarters in Dickson Island Pasinsky Strait, Cape Loskin and elsewhere.

The *Yan Rudzutak* was making its last journey to the North. There was a danger that if it was at all belated it would have to spend the winter somewhere *en route*.

Together with the falling snow came cold northern winds. Our steamship made its way forward with difficulty, beyond the Polar circle. Its paddle wheels were covered with ice, the water was thickened by snow, or, as they say, the river was putting on its winter jacket.

Our road lay to the north. . . .

BORIS IVANOV.

(Town elementary school, 4 class 'B', born, 1924.)

CHAPTER XV

THE SHEEP THAT WAS LOST

WHEN Nadeshda went back to her mother, Klimov and I settled down to the evening. I liked Klimov from the first moment we met. Except perhaps only Shevelyov I liked him best of all the people I met on my journey. And I collected quite a crowd of acquaintances up there.

He was a short fellow with rich hair, the colour of ripened wheat. Although only twenty-six—as he told me later on—his face revealed a deep knowledge of life, whereas his lively eyes, sparkling as he talked, assured me a thousand times experience had not damped down his interest and love for life. He shook my hand more warmly than anybody else had done. The difference of nations, and of worlds, which was often forced on to me in Russia, vanished during the first half-hour of our acquaintance. When he told me of his wife—he had married, as I had done, at the age of twenty-one—and of his children separated from him by thousands of miles for the greater part of the year, I felt closer to him than to many whom I have known since we trotted together to school.

He was a 'cultural worker', giving lectures on history and letters, arranging artistic circles and editing the literary side of the local newspaper. Every year he wrote a book on his experiences. *The Heart of the Tundra* was one; another dealt with his eighteen months among the natives; a third with the history of the North.

In a pause between making up the pages of local news and waiting for the foreign telegrams and radio messages we drank tea together—in true Russian style, with jam instead of sugar, and in saucers while it was yet too hot.

I asked Klimov about his life.

'I have knocked about the country a great deal since I was a nipper', he said. 'I know the Far East and White Russia, Central Asia and Arctic Siberia. I love the North most of all. It is primitive, clean, virgin and grand. It waits to be awakened by us.'

'How is it that you travelled so much as a child? Did you not go to school?'

'Yes—for two years, from seven until nine. Then I stopped until I was fourteen.'

'And your parents?'

'My mother died in 1919. My father lost me on a road that same year and did not find me again until ten years later.'

Then I understood. He had been a *besprisorni*, one of that army of two million children who had lost their homes and their parents during the civil war and the famines and formed bands of little vagabonds, a pest to the country and a danger to themselves. The *besprisorni* were one of the most urgent problems of Russia before 1928. Stealing, and even murdering, they ranged the country in herds, sleeping in empty petrol drums, smoking opium, sniffing drugs; a prey to venereal diseases, a vast reserve army for crime and vice. It is one of the assets on the active side of Soviet Russia's historical balance to have reclaimed most of these little waifs.

When I asked Klimov straight out, he admitted that he had been one of them. He was born in Ufa, Bashkiria, in the southern Urals, he said. His parents had worked in a munitions plant. In 1919, when the first famine spread over the country like the black plague, the family left their home and went afoot for search of food. His mother died, starved to death. He and his father went on. In Samara old Klimov lost sight of his boy in a crowd, and little Anatoli made for the Volga, to wander down to Saratov and Astrakhan and on further east to Tashkent, where rumour had it there was a paradise of wheat and bread.

'Soon I joined up with a small gang, and we travelled on
the roofs and under-carriages of troop and munition trains.
What I saw was not what a child of that age should see.
What I went through I am trying hard to forget. I have
been able to push it somewhere back far into a corner of
my mind, from where I call it back only as an historical
fact, not as a period of my own life. It lasted five years.
In November, 1924, we established ourselves in some old
rotting timber in a yard in the port of Leningrad. We
built a little stove of discarded tins, got food occasionally
from the crews of incoming ships, and made a few kopecks
at times by going on errands for dock workers.

'One night as we slept, huddled together to keep warm
against the blizzard, men approached our hut. We woke
at the sound of heavy steps. A torchlight flashed through
the wall of a box that formed the door. We were trapped.
There was no escape. Several times before the G.P.U. had
tried to get hold of us; once I had been put into a home, together with forty others, where we learnt boot-making. But
as soon as spring had come we had escaped to wander about,
loafed down the Volga, picking fruit for the monks in the old
monasteries, who gave us food and shelter for it. This time as
we rumbled over the cobbled streets in a lorry—packed together closely with many other boys and girls whom the
G.P.U. had raided in all sorts of hiding-places that night—I
resolved that it would be the end of my wanderings. I felt it
was the last chance to find a way back into quiet and rest,
into an ordered sort of life, less romantic perhaps than the one
I had led up to then—but perhaps making up for this loss in
other values, which I had always affected to despise but
secretly longed for. The Young Communist League, who
devoted much of its activity at that time to the work of
social rescue, organized a little commune for us in the
house of an evacuated convent. It was called "Nova Rossa."
There I spent the winter of 1924-1925. When spring
came the G.P.U. themselves got us on an organized journey

through the country to show that all we loved in the freedom of the open air could be had just as easily as an organized body as in a wild gang. I caught up my education—during those five years on the run I had forgotten everything that I had learned during my first two years at school. The daily struggle for existence had sharpened the wits of all the members in our brotherhood of distress. We were quicker and far more ready to grasp anything we heard for the first time than ordinary school children at our age. As long as our teachers were able to stimulate our pride and play on our sporting spirit we would be ready to follow them anywhere, even into the wilderness of algebra. By 1928 I had learned enough to take me through matric. Seeing that I loved to write little poems or accounts of my experiences they singled me out for a career as a writer and sent me for two years to a school of journalism. In 1929 I took up a job as a reporter on the *Ural Worker*, a new daily which appears at Sverdlovsk. I felt more at home in the Urals—memories of earlier days came back to me. I married a young girl who was also in the Comsomol. The days when I had organized hunger strikes against the G.P.U. in the communes were over. I had learned to discipline myself. In 1931 my first short stories were printed in book form. The paper sent me to the North, to the Yamal Peninsula, as their special correspondent.

'In October a steamer, *Albatross*, coming from the Yenisei, was wrecked in a late autumn storm and broke against the cliffs off the coast. Two of the sailors battled their way through the whole peninsula for 500 miles down towards the south, and in the end reached our settlement, starved, frozen, completely exhausted. It was midwinter when they turned up at our place, Novy Port, the harbour just about to grow into a town on the Arctic estuary of the Obi, and they told us that they had had to leave the rest of the crew somewhere on the way. We immediately equipped a rescue party and found the shipwreck soon enough but no trace of the

men. It was months later that we discovered their bodies—
horrible to look at. They had starved to death, and were
frozen hard, like glass.

'That journey was my Arctic baptism. In spite of the
horror I had seen, I fell in love deeply with the country,
and, after going on a four months' holiday with my wife, I
decided that I would take up work in the Arctic for good.
I learned to speak the native languages of the Samoyed
and the Ostyak tribes and founded a newspaper in the
Nyentze (that is Samoyed) language. It was printed at
Obdorsk and called *Hyarnaya Hyerm*, which means "The
Red North". I studied the life of the natives, always with
one aim in mind: to help to rebuild their national existence
with all its positive elements—their unique abilities to live
and produce in the Polar regions—while giving them at the
same time as much of our technical, social, scientific achievements as would prove useful to them.

'I broke off all contact with Russians, including my
own family, and went into the tundra alone for nine months.
I travelled with a tribe throughout the winter. I wrote
down their songs and legends, learned to drive dog teams,
showed them how to heal scurvy, tried to fight *shamanism*
which was still keeping these peoples in the spell of superstition and fear. Once I met a tribe who did not know that the
Tsar was dead. Their prince was well aware of the fact,
but hid the news from his subjects; his threat of fighting them
with the help of his mighty white ally kept them in fear,
and they obeyed his orders. There I organized a little
revolution to free them from the grip of their evil ruler,
and helped them to dispose of their own miniature
Tsar.

'Gradually I introduced the Red law into the tundra. I
had taken dozens of toothbrushes and packets of soap with
me. In the end I had only my own left. But a man who had
seen my friends using them asked me for it—he wanted
to convert his own tribe to this habit of keeping clean and

healthy.. I gave everything away and had to do without these utensils for four months myself.

'I found Russian traders in some of the backwoods. They had also succeeded in keeping the knowledge of our new laws hidden from the natives, so that they could go on exerting their fur tributes, which they sold to the Government agents once a year as their own booty. I had to fight with them.

'Once in these four years I lived for five months in a winter without tent or hut. I slept in snow-huts only, which I built myself; and I kept myself warm in my fur bags. Throughout I found that my years as a vagabond had taught me many useful things and I was extremely grateful to my comrades of the Young Communist League that they had shown me the way towards a new mode of life.'

After an interruption of half an hour, during which he dispatched the foreign page and the two columns of political and economic news from home to the printers, Anatoli went on with his tale. I did not interrupt him. I had the impression that he told me more than he had told some of the people who lived with him every day.

His pet subject was Mangazeya, the forgotten Arctic town of the seventeenth century. On his journeys along the shores of the Polar Sea he had struck the ruins of this little city, the history of which is so exciting that it is curious to think that no one has written of it before. He is studying all the material available and intends to give us a book about it one day.

'I found documents of Mangazeya's life and death in monasteries in the neighbourhood,' Klimov went on. 'It was founded in 1601 and within a few years became a flourishing town, trading between Europe and China through the Arctic Ocean and by the river system of Obi and Irtish and the caravan roads of Mongolia and Tibet. Staunch Cossacks had built and settled it. It even competed with such important trading centres as Tobolsk and Turukhansk. After twenty years its fame had spread to Holland, and Dutch merchants equipped sailing fleets to fetch precious furs and spices from Mangazeya. In the ruins of its wooden fortress we even found coins with the heads of Alexander the Great and Titus. They had obviously remained in circulation in Asia until even long after the Middle Ages. To compare Mangazeya with Igarka would, I think, be an extraordinary study in social and cultural history. Imagine how people lived there in these centuries. We think our own life up here difficult even now sometimes. And they had no aeroplanes, no radio stations, no electric light. The town must have had a larger population than just that of a little military or trading outpost. There were over a hundred huts, and one record in the library of a monastery nearby tells of the dispatch of twenty-five prostitutes to the town "to make the life of its inhabitants more tolerable".

'In 1648, the year when the Thirty Years' War came to an end in Europe, Mangazeya was burned to its foundations. We do not know the reasons. One theory is that the Cossacks told Tsar Boris Godunov that he had to stop foreigners from using the Northern Sea Route otherwise he would lose all that he held of Siberia at that time. Another supposes that the traders at Tobolsk and Turukhansk had the town fired by secret agents to cut out competition with their own business. One possibility that cannot be excluded is that a native army revolted against the rule of merciless and brutal exploitation which the white men had introduced into the tundra. How differently we are going to proceed in our work of colonization in the North! We shall cooperate with the natives. We are building towns, not to suppress the tundra but to liberate it—not to rob, but to exchange goods and services.'

CHAPTER XVI

SIBERIAN FOXTROT

As I had slept through the whole performance of the Theatre at Igarka during the first night of my arrival I had to go once more to see it with open eyes. My own conscience would not leave me quiet until I had restored my popularity with the actors, and the actors would not leave me in peace until they had established their popularity with me. They were a nice crowd, led by an elderly lady, 'Peoples' Artist' Pashennaya, an actress who was famous before the revolution, the widow of a Colonel in the Tsarist regiment, the daughter of an aristocrat. Two of the men were also well-known actors of the best old type. The rest were younger people, all extremely enthusiastic about this flying tour of the Arctic. They had been invited by Glavsevmorput, and had sacrificed their six weeks' holiday (which they usually spend in fashionable seaside resorts of the Crimea or the Caucasus) to bring art to the workers in the Far North. Pashennaya particularly was conscious of the cultural mission her group fulfilled in coming to the Arctic. 'These people live the most difficult life of all our fellow-citizens', she said. 'In two weeks we have to make up to them the four sunless months of the Arctic winter. We have to bring to them all the beauty they miss.'

She had refused to join the Communist Party, she told me, because she was not prepared to accept all the responsibilities and heavy duties that go with it in Russia nowadays.

'As long as I am a non-Party woman I can go where I want and work whenever I want. The Party is an Army, its members are soldiers; once I joined it I should have to obey its orders blindly, go to any place they send me, accept any job for which they singled me out. It cannot be otherwise in present circumstances. But I am not able to accept such a burden.'

Apart from that one provision, that one-time society beauty was reconciled to the Bolshevik régime. What made her forget all drawbacks was, in her own words, 'the fact that we have now an audience a thousand times larger than ever before, of simple, unspoilt people—with crude tastes I admit—but with an infinitely deeper and more honest longing for true art and æsthetic expression of human emotions than I have met anywhere else or at any other time.'

All the actors had been given the uniform of Polar workers before they left Moscow. The women did not always wear the gold-buttoned military tunics. But they never went out without putting on the officers' caps. That allowed them to return the hundreds of greetings that were fired at them as they walked through the streets; they saluted by pointing their fingers to the badge with the blue Arctic banner. They flew to Dickson Island from Igarka while I was there; they went to play for the people employed in State farm 'Transarctica'—all exiled *kulaks*—and were going down the river one night in a boat to give performances at the reindeer breeding farm of Potapovo. They improvised a stage on one of the barges which carried women convicts to Norilsk.

'A sevenfold murderess sat in the first row as we were playing Ostrovski's *Innocent Victim*', Pashennaya reported cheerfully, 'and she cried at the tragic misfortune of an unmarried mother as I have never seen anybody among my audience cry before.'

The day before I went north—at last, and simply because I bribed the steward of a British cargo boat—the actors left by aeroplane for the south to get home to Moscow in time for the opening of the International Festival season on September 1.

On the night that I watched them play in the tightly packed theatre of Igarka the audience was a motley crowd—

OPERA FLIES TO THE ARCTIC

rough stevedores in wide soft trousers (fastened round the ankles) that have been for centuries the traditional costume of the barge-loaders on Russia's rivers; bearded *kulaks* and their wives who wore woollen kerchiefs round their heads; children in Scout uniforms (blue trousers or skirts and white blouses with red ties); clerks of the Port Administration, of the timber-yard and of the sawmills, all wearing the dark blue Polar uniforms; their wives in black satin dresses; workers from the sawmills in their best suits, with white collars. I was the least elegant of the lot, for I always wore my very heavy boots from early in the morning until midnight. Putting them on and taking them off was an acrobatic performance which taxed my strength.

The theatre, like everything else in Igarka, is made of timber. Inside, every shade of natural-coloured wood gives a quiet decorative variety. The lighting, reflected a thousandfold on the wax-polished, unpainted walls, makes for an air of friendliness in the hall. There is a little room on the same level with the stage, where mothers can 'park' their children during the performance for a nurse to look after them.

After the play—performed in the best tradition of the oldest dramatic institute of Russia—I was Shanghaied into the club; the local *jeunesse dorée* had arranged what in Russia is called a 'fraternization' with the foreign sailors. For the first time in several weeks, I knew again what day of the week it was. The new Russian system of a five-day cycle of work days followed by one free day has done away entirely with all Mondays, Tuesdays and the rest, and Soviet citizens live by dates only. The British sailors explained to me immediately that it was Saturday night.

The programme for the 'fraternization' evening was rather rigid. First of all the guests were treated to a late supper. It started with hors d'œuvre of green lettuce—

a great delicacy in a Polar town, but hardly appreciated as such by the foreign sailors, who did not realize it had rarity value and that a great amount of work and resourcefulness had gone in its making. Then followed pork chops with tomatoes, radishes and cucumbers; and tinned fruit salad. Igarka had offered its best and most expensive—fresh vegetables. The British and Finnish sailors however turned to sweets and chocolates a minute after the banquet, and stuffed their pockets with all sorts of candies and mass-produced acid drops which they bought in the buffet downstairs.

As soon as the meal was over, speech-making began on a grand scale. The club is under the joint management of a Russian and a foreigner. This foreign *maître de plaisir* is a Hamburg-born Australian sailor who had ten years at sea and five years in Soviet ports to his record. He is Russia's host No. 1 for foreign seamen. In the winter he acts as secretary of the Red equivalent of the 'Missions for Seamen' in Odessa; in summer he does the same in the Arctic. Every morning he could be seen going from ship to ship, talking to the sailors in English or German, asking what he could do for them, inviting them to a football match, to an excursion into the sawmills, to a Polar farm, or to a dance. He told them all they wanted to know about Russia—but they were not very inquisitive.

Now he got up and welcomed the guests in the name of the local population, especially the young, and announced that we should have an hour of 'questions and answers' about our mutual countries, followed by two hours' dancing and private merry-making.

As soon as he sat down, a fanatic little Georgian woman shot up from her seat to make a speech about the Young Communist League. As she was speaking, I remembered our frequent discussions at home as to whether the Soviets were clever propagandists. The little country woman of Stalin certainly was not. Instead of telling something of how they lived and worked in Igarka this self-appointed representative of the town's youth excelled in long recitals of Party literature, assured us that she would strangle Zinoviev or Kamenyev with her own hands if she had a chance—92 per cent of the listeners had never heard the name of the accused Trotskyists—and sat down after bellowing: 'Long live the Russian Comsomol! Long live the Soviet Government! Long live our beloved leader, Father, Brother, Teacher, Stalin!'

The *maître de plaisir* was diplomatic enough not to translate this speech too literally; he left out most of the swanky display of theoretical Marxism, interpolated a few sentences about how glad the young Igarkites were to have the foreign sailors among them, and finished in good style with a toast on the guests instead of the host's own Government.

It was now the turn for the sailors to say something. There were bos'ns, engineers, able-seamen and a few officers present. The captains had declined the invitation. A fragile Indian got up first to make a most extraordinary speech. He began by giving a well-balanced account of Gandhi's policy of Swaraj and Swadessi to the audience, whose political *credo* was anything rather than belief in 'non-violence', continued by praising the methods and achievements of the Soviet Union as 'rising star of hope on the sky of the historic future of the working-class', went on to declare that, whatever one might say, the British Labour Party (or rather the Socialist League) was, after all, the real saviour of the proletariat, added a few words on the comparative advantages of a Rooseveltian policy of enlightened reform—and finished gloriously with three cheers for 'democracy in its present form'.

His rhetoric effort was translated to the Russians with the same amount of diplomatic tact—and poetic licence—which the host had displayed in interpreting the Georgian girl's Red catechism. A few people on both sides then said some rather nice and pleasant compliments. The British asked about conditions on Soviet ships, and were given details which I knew from my own investigations on Russian steamers to be correct. The Russians addressed themselves primarily to the Arabs, Negroes and Indians present, who were employed in the stoke-holes of the British tramp steamers. A Somali cursed Italy for gassing Abyssinia and said—as far as one could understand him—that he was happier than ever before in his life when he saw 'how the Russian girls danced with the Eskimo boys'. A second engineer insisted on explaining that the system of parliamentary government in England was really based on the hidden activities of a team of secret advisers to the King, who—whatever the stupid public might believe—did in fact control his Ministers like marionettes. A young sailor from Newcastle broke through the learned lumber of political nonsense by expressing his friendly and hearty desire for friendship and personal understanding between the two nations. He found the real formula instinctively by toasting the Russian girls—'A batch of fine lasses'—he called them. This was translated immediately by the *maître de plaisir* who had suddenly regained his ability to interpret every word minutely according to the dictionary.

Everybody was glad to clear the tables and chairs away as soon as the signal was given. A few of the elder sailors retired to the social room next door, where silk-shaded lamps and soft-cushioned sofas created an atmosphere of refined comfort. There they drank some Crimean wine, played chess and dominoes and told each other yarns. The majority stayed to dance. The second engineer buttonholed me before I had time to invite a girl for the first foxtrot. He insisted on giving me another portion of his brand of political wisdom.

'What I meant to say, when I told those Russkis about our King ruling the country with his secret advisers, was really that it is not at all so very much different with us than with them and their Stalin, or whatever they call

him. Between you and me, I always vote Conservative
—yes, I do. I don't grumble like the other fellows because
I have to serve. If I'd been smart enough I'd be a captain,
too, to-day, or even an owner. But since God has not
given me the brains, I shall have to content myself with my
lot. The way they talked about our ships—and those silly
mugs of our crews telling them we're under-staffed and badly
paid, and don't get enough grub—that's all rubbish. We
have got a bad ship now—last year I had a good one, next
year it may fall in between. It's not capitalism or not
capitalism that counts; it's luck, just good or bad luck.
And if you want to know one more I'll tell you this: our
boys would be better advised not to bother with other
people's affairs so much. You are a sensible man, you keep
your mouth shut. But look at them telling them Russians
how rotten we live, and going back to England telling their
folks how wonderful the Russians are off. I don't care
tuppence what those Russkis do, or think, or want me to
think—to me England is still the best country to live in.'

I was saved from his clutches by a pretty girl who came
to ask me for a dance. Russian girls are refreshingly resolute
in taking the initiative whenever they want anything. We
waltzed round the room and, at a wink from her, the pianist
changed over to a tango—using the same tune in slower
motion. She asked me whether we had any new dance
steps in Western Europe which I could teach her and her
friends. They were very keen on keeping up with the international development of modern dances. Tango has not
changed too much since 1927 (or at least my tango has
not) and so I had little improvements to suggest for her
style. It would have been different with the foxtrot, in
which the Russians are about twelve years behind us.
On went the music, on went I with my partner, round
and round till my feet would hardly carry me further.
No wonder, each boot weighed about four and a half
pounds and I had to be careful not to tread on my partner's

feet in her fragile shoes of thin silk. An idea flashed through my mind which held out a promise of partial relief.

'As a matter of fact I remember one new step of ours, which is very popular in Paris and New York now', I said, and beamed when I saw her eagerness. 'We use it in connexion with most dances you know, particularly with the tango. It breaks the monotony of continuous turning and double stepping.'

'Oh, please do show it me.'

'Well, it's like this. After we have turned round the room for five or six times, we hold our partner by one hand only and march along in the opposite direction to the time of the music but in ordinary walking fashion.'

'Very interesting, let's try.'

It was a splendid step I had invented. We held each other by the hand and walked round the room in the opposite direction to the time of the music. My tired feet found a wonderful rest. But my partner insisted on keeping the orthodox ratio of five to one. Five times round the room in tango, once 'in Smolka'. So we went on for another ten minutes.

The piano-man hammered his sequence of twelve notes into his instrument mercilessly. In the end my exhaustion was greater than my pride, and so I proposed modestly that we might sit down for a while. My partner seemed quite pleased, and took me along to the bandmaster to thank him for his good work.

'Meet my husband', she said; and he welcomed me with 'Ochen pryatno.' We started a friendly conversation on the topic of dance music. After a while my partner offered to get us some lemonade, and in her absence I said: 'Tell me, tovarich musician, do you people in Russia always dance so long in one run?'

He was baffled. 'Well, tovarich journalist, as a matter of fact I wanted to ask you the same question. Do you people in Europe keep the floor so long each time? I was quite

exhausted, but you would not stop.' Words failed me.
He noticed there was some misunderstanding. 'Don't tell
me'—he burst into a roar of laughter—'don't tell me you
waited for me to finish, while I got almost cramps in my
fingers, hoping you would stop any moment? Honestly,
tovarich journalist, I did not know you bourgeois men were so
hypocritical to go on dancing with a girl when you did not
enjoy it any longer? It was my wife you were dancing with.
How could I stop supplying you with the music? All my
comrades would have reprimanded me most severely and
charged me with jealousy if I, responsible for the entertain-
ment—had failed in my duty to supply a guest from abroad
with all the comfort he wanted.' We promised each other
not to tell Masha anything when she came back with the
lemonade.

My next partner, self-chosen this time, was a girl of
nineteen—Claudia by name. She was laughing whenever
I saw her. While we were discussing women's rights in the
Soviet Union, she suddenly asked me: 'Can you guess what
my job is?'

To pay a compliment to her emancipation, I suggested:
'Chief of Igarka's fire brigade.'

'Missed', she smiled, 'much more important!'

'Head of the Radio Station?'

'Oh, that would be nothing—any girl can do that!'

I gave up.

'Registrar'! she screamed. 'I am responsible for all
marriages, deaths, divorces and births in this greatest Polar
city of the world. If you want to marry anybody here, it's
I who have to help you. My figures of production are rising
continuously. I have an average of 5 weddings, 1·3 divorces,
6 births and 4 deaths a day. And I can say that I am a very
influential person. Since I took over, the number of
divorces has rapidly fallen, and births to the couples I joined
have increased by 17 per cent. I am an element of stability
in the social structure of Soviet Russia.'

'How is that?'

'Quite simple—whenever a couple come to be married I don't simply inscribe their names and issue the certificate as the law demands—a job which takes only two minutes— I talk to them and wish them happiness, explain our family laws to them, and tell them how prosperity in Russia is rising and rising, and how children, therefore, are more of a pleasure in life than a burden on their parents. That stimulates their desire for a complete family. I even show them the balance sheet of our post office savings bank: 200 roubles per head of Igarka's population. And when some come to get a divorce I talk to them again, tell them to think it over—"perhaps it is not really as serious as all that"—and suggest that they should come back a week later. Very few ever return.'

Claudia was a charming child. 'Who is going to register your marriage one day, if you are the only registrar?' I asked her. 'Ah, don't think I have forgotten about that. Oh no, I would not risk staying a spinster because of my professional position. I have already trained my best friend for the job—there will be no trouble on my wedding day. But I have not found a suitable husband yet. One or two I met whom I would have considered were among my customers. Too bad.'

Charlie, the stoker of the trampship *Matilda*, with whom I marched off at 1 a.m. that night, gave me his considered opinion about the girls of Igarka.

'They are real ladies—no funny business with them, you know. Look how they dance—two feet away from you. That's no love game—that's a sport with them. Nothing doing, my boy. They've good heads on them, and brains as clear as yours and mine. I can be pretty tough, you know, when I get a couple of shots into myself. But not even when I am under the gas would I risk getting fresh with these kids. It's a rotten place from the sexy aspect, this

230

Igarka. In former years at least they had a few hussies here. Not legal, by all means—they are very silly about that in Russia. But some of those old prisoner fellows here used to send their girls to make some money for them— mainly vodka was what they wanted. I had a system of my own. Silk stockings was my speciality. They were all crazy about them, those *kulak* daughters. And what I did was to give them only one for the first night. Just to make sure they come round a second time to say good-bye to good old Charlie. That did the trick, believe me.'

CHAPTER XVII

ARCTIC STORM GROWS GREEN VEGETABLES

'Of course, if you put a university professor behind each potato to make it grow, you can probably raise them even at the North Pole.'

Grigori Antonovitch Strelyakoff was not much impressed with the idea of Arctic agriculture. To him it was just another manifestation of Soviet madness. Why should he, an exiled *kulak*, join in such nonsense? He comes from the Kuban district which is fertile and rich. No university professor was ever needed in his village to help mother earth to grow food for her children. It was enough to plough and sow to be sure of a good harvest.

Things are different beyond the Arctic Circle. Round Igarka the ice-free period of the year lasts ninety days at the most. Sometimes a mud hole full of rain will turn into a little skating rink over night in the middle of August. Nor is it the cold of the winter alone that makes the ground so hard for plant life. The atmosphere is exceptionally dry throughout the Polar night. There is little precipitation. The earth remains naked, or only poorly clad with snow, and freezes so hard that for many thousands of summers not more than its surface has ever thawed. Six to eight feet below the surface it is lifeless; perpetually frozen. But wherever Nature makes existence difficult for men, university professors are called in to help conquer it. If Nature had not provided so many problems for us throughout the ages, we should not have brought up scientists to get us out of our troubles. At all events as soon as the decision to make town life possible in the Polar regions had been taken by the Soviet Government, the question of feeding the inhabitants off the local soil called for a solution. Natives can live on frozen fish, on uncooked bears' blood, on crude reindeer meat. What Ukrainian, Georgian or South Siberian would feel happy on such a diet? And tinned food makes for scurvy in the long run. Wheat can be stored, flour transported, macaroni brought in paper boxes on ships and aeroplanes. The problem is to grow fresh vegetables in sufficient quantities to provide Vitamin D, the one which is indispensable to man's health, and which cannot yet be bought in tins.

Two years after the first settlers had arrived in Igarka a group of professors and students of agricultural institutes came up from Moscow and Leningrad. Opposite the town on Bear's Island they perched their tents and started rummaging about in the undergrowth. A party of twenty strong men from the town helped them to clear the ground of moss and lichens, small roots and the mass of half-wood, half-bush that bridge the gap between jungle and desert in the Far North. Then, on tiny fields the size of tennis courts they planted potatoes, lettuce, grain, radishes, beetroots. Not only Grigori Antonovitch, the *kulak*, thought them mad. There was hardly a man or woman among their own comrades who believed that they would ever get something eatable out of the tundra. The first two years did certainly little to support their own unshakable belief that anything is possible sooner or later. In 1932 they changed their methods. Instead of artificial they used natural manure. They brought new seeds from Europe. Scientists working in the Institute of Plant Culture of the Ukraine experimented upon many thousands of varieties of wheat to discover which are most suited for growth in northern regions. A system called 'Jacovization' and invented by Professor Lyssenko was established; the seeds are partly saturated with water, and as soon as germination has started they are kept at a constant temperature for 5 or 30 days (according to the kind of seed) and are then planted normally. Their whole life-cycle is speeded up and strengthened. 'Jacovized' winter oats, for instance, were planted in spring and found to have ripened before ordinary spring-sown oats. Their yield per hectare was 30 per cent higher.

When September 1932 approached, the first Arctic potatoes and radishes were harvested in the tundra round Igarka. A handful only was the crop of this first productive year of Polar agriculture, but the handful was enough to warm up the hearts of the persevering optimists and enough to break down the first walls of resistance among the non-believers.

To-day 'Transarctica'—as the farm is called—is no longer news to the people of Igarka. They buy its products on the market and in the shops. Aeroplanes take tomatoes from its hot-houses further north to the Polar islands and to stations in the remotest regions. Its stables give shelter to 350 head of cattle. About 200 pigs were cheerfully wallowing in the mire outside their cots when I visited them. About 250 rabbits were nibbling in their cages. Over 100 horses were working in the fields. There were 430 people living on the farm in 1936. Most of the grown-ups were exiled peasants, happy to do agricultural work once more instead of having to go to the factory. The sowing area is still only a few hundred acres in extent, but the fact that most of the products already grow freely outside the experimental nursery—and without the careful supervision of university professors—suggests that the taking in of more land is only a matter of time and of a sufficient supply of human labour.

I saw potatoes, onions, carrots, radishes and cabbages growing in the open fields; cauliflower, lettuce and turnips—in frames; and tomatoes, cucumbers and asparagus in hot-houses.

A little off the main road of the farm's village, fenced off against intruding animals or humans, extend the fields of the scientific experimental station. A woman professor, Maria Mitrovanna Chernikova, is in charge, together with

four young girl students. They have flower-pots full of tomatoes standing about on the window-sills of their sitting-room, bottles containing minute cucumbers stand next to flasks of eau-de-Cologne in the bathroom. Round their cottage is a garden where pansies grow together with forget-me-nots and pinks. Once every hour two of the girls go out into their miniature fields to do their observation work. I accompanied them, and watched them taking the temperature of the soil, of the subsoil and of the air.

Wherever you go you stumble over thermometers. Long ones, short ones, thick and thin, some even that are not thermometers at all but only look as if they were. They measure and register the daily average of moisture, little glass balls register the sum-total of sunlight for each twenty-four hours.

But does it all pay? This question is really beside the point. Planting vegetables above the Arctic Circle is certainly not a business proposition—least of all for an immense country as rich in fertile soils as Russia. Nobody thinks of extending the cultivation of fruits and greens into the Far North of Siberia merely to increase the food supply of the nation. But once it has been accepted as worth while to open up the North for mining, timber cutting, navigation and aviation, the provision of local settlements with fresh food and to assure that health is safeguarded and transport breakdowns through natural catastrophes will not expose them to starvation—then the cost of producing tomatoes and cucumbers in the tundra is a matter of secondary importance. The people at 'Transarctica' worked out for me that even double the present price of production would still be cheaper than the transport of the produce by aeroplane from Southern Russia.

I could hardly share the enthusiasm of Kossianov, the head of 'Transarctica', when he solemnly assured me that, 'because of the twenty-four hours of sunshine a day in the Arctic summer, the cabbage yield per hectare can be brought up to higher figures in Polar Siberia than in the Central Black Earth region.' But what I did see, and thought worth noting, was that cabbage leaves on Arctic farms are larger than in our kitchen gardens. The leaves are the plants' light-recipients and they do positively profit from the unbroken continuity of sunshine during the Polar summer.

The scientists are now experimenting with apples, peaches, pears and cherries in Igarka. Perhaps this is only another manifestation of the greediness with which Soviet optimism approaches everything new. I dare not call it ridiculous or childish. We have been surprised too frequently in these last fifty years by people who started on crazy ventures and ended up by giving us wonderful technical improvements. The little strawberries that looked shyly out of their dwarf-like bed of leaves were rather sour to taste. Perhaps they will be sweet and juicy at the end of the fourth five-year plan.

Glavsevmorput is about to organize an institute of Arctic agriculture. So far Bogomolkin, one-time chief of the 'Gigant', Russia's largest State farm, is in charge of the farming battalion of the Polar army. He has drawn a chart showing the three regions of climate and geography that divide the area under the rule of Otto Schmidt's 'North Asia Company'. In the first zone, comprising the islands of the Polar Sea and the coastline, nothing except Arctic moss can grow; grain is ruled out entirely; animal life is restricted to reindeer and yaks in some southern stretches; at some Polar stations pigs can be reared and fed on waste food and seaweed. In the second zone two kinds of plant culture are possible, in hot-houses and in open fields; and this region holds out a promise of carrying oats, rye and barley, sooner or later. In the third zone, which reaches down into the 'Subarctic', a region in Northern Siberia which was formerly regarded as quite useless, will grow vegetables of every description and in its southern stretches even wheat. (It corresponds more or less to those parts of Northern Canada where wheat was thought impossible sixty years ago and where some of the world's best qualities are grown now.

Glavsevmorput has opened 4 main agricultural stations in the Far North: In Obdorsk, Igarka, Yakutsk and Anadyrsk. From there 20 smaller experimental points are controlled, 5 of them actually on the coast.

The problems which the 'farming battalion of the Polar Army' must solve are the following:

(1) To drive up grain cultivation as near as possible to the Polar regions in order to have a food base at comparatively short distance of the actual Arctic colony.

(2) To evolve typical specimens of plants with short growing seasons and the power to resist occasional mid-August frosts.

(3) To develop methods by which the ripened plants can be kept fresh over a period of two years.

The last point is essential because most of the plants or cereals are only ready for harvest at a time when the navigation season is already drawing to its close. It would be no good to get crops in October—when the northern parts of the river are covering themselves with ice, and navigation in the Polar Sea can be stopped any moment by a premature winter—or these crops would lose their vitamins, putrify, rot or send out shoots during the winter. After all they are not only needed to feed the local population in the towns of the lower Polar regions. They are of even more vital importance for the crews of Polar stations and air bases high up on islands in the Arctic Ocean. The plants have to be kept intact over the winter, and shipped off safely as soon as the navigation season starts in the following summer. The method, which Bogomolkin claims his department has discovered and which, according to him, has proved successful in 80 per cent of all cases is this: they construct special large boxes in which the plants lie 'asleep' in carbon monoxide. Certain rays, particularly X-rays, do the same trick, and so they are now experimenting with X-ray chambers as storage rooms for Arctic farms.

The agricultural expert would find many other interesting problems which are now attacked by Bogomolkin and his staff. The Arctic—with its bad soil, large expansions and sparse human population—needs mechanization more urgently than any other part of the world. Special machinery to clear the ground, to plough and hack, to uproot the dense undergrowth and get through marshy and frozen subsoil is now being constructed. It was tried out in different places last summer.

Much attention is naturally given to animal life in the North. Our own domestic animals can be acclimatized to the Arctic to a certain degree, I myself saw cows being milked outside the Polar station on Dickson Island and was told that the horse which works patiently for the scientific staff of the station, got used to eating fish and even to drinking alcohol since it came to the North. Pigs do not mind living next door to Polar bears as long as they are given heated cots. Cows will give milk and bear calves on any Polar station. They are being treated with ultra-violet lamps, and the mating is timed so that the calves will be born in spring. Then they grow up in the comparatively warm season and get healthy and strong on the rich light of the Polar summer. Poultry, too, get used to life on Arctic islands. Two years of experience—Bogomolkin assured me—sufficed to prove that hens will live and lay eggs even if they are never taken out into the open air at all. They accept fish and seaweed as part of their diet— but, of course, they, too, insist on getting sufficient light, the sun in the summer, electric lamps in the winter. The aim to be achieved in the next three years is the creation of good fodder bases and stores in the second zone so that all animals can be kept right up into the furthest regions of the first zone, including (theoretically) the North Pole. Once this is achieved the inhabitants even of the most out-

lying Polar stations will always be assured of a variety of fresh meat, milk, butter, eggs. Flour and all preserved foodstuffs will be brought to them by sea once a year—as at present; and they themselves will grow a sufficient quantity of fresh vegetables in subterranean hot-houses.

In Igarka the hot-houses are half under ground. They are built of solid brick and are lined with wooden beams to keep their interior temperature constant. The doors are fur-lined; all fissures are carefully padded with cotton wool, seaweed and textiles. They are heated by large clay stoves with radiators running all along the walls. The plants grow in boxes which stand on shelves underneath the steep glass windows to catch all the natural light available. There is plenty of wood at hand to heat these Aladdin's Caves. The simpler hot-houses and hot-beds in the open air are heated by the addition of certain chemicals to the soil besides the manure. But on Dickson, which is a barren island in the Arctic Ocean, fuel is costly and the driftwood that is fished out of the waves during the summer by no means sufficient. There they have evolved another method. I had fresh cucumbers, tomatoes, cauliflowers and radishes even there—delicacies that had been reared mainly on electricity.

A hot-house entirely enshrined in the ice—isolated against the cold from without and the heat from within (which might melt the surrounding walls of frozen earth) extends below the soil near the radio station. Its roof lies level with the surface of the ground, and is made of thick glass. In winter it is snowed under. Then the inside is lit with 300-candle-power lamps and is heated by electric radiators, worked by windmills. Arctic storms grow green vegetables.

Reindeer culture is a separate problem within the framework of this organization. Fifty years ago the American Government bought twelve thousand reindeer from Russia and imported them into Alaska. The herd has meanwhile increased to a million strong. Enviously the Russians told

239

me that every year fifteen thousand animals of an average dressed weight of 125 pounds are supplied to the markets of the United States. America has applied reindeer culture to a much more economical use than Russia. The Soviets are now trying to catch up. The reindeer is needed in the North for transport, meat, milk and clothing. But the draught animals must be castrated and are therefore lost for breeding purposes. The roaming animal which goes in search of its own moss underneath the snow gives hardly more than a pint of milk a day. And you have to run after it to milk it. If you want to get more milk from them—you have to relieve them of the burden of making their own living—food must be brought to them. It is a whole chain of intertwining problems which have to be disentangled. This is being attempted now. Glavsevmorput has organized eighteen reindeer breeding farms and is trying to persuade the natives to introduce modern scientific methods into their own herds. The company 'controls' one hundred and fifty thousand heads of reindeer. That is to say, this number is regularly examined by veterinaries, studied by experts, supervised in its breeding. The number of heads of reindeer available is estimated to be at least two million, and it is thought that it will be an easy matter to increase their number three or four times by protecting them against snowstorms, by providing them with food and more easily fighting the anthrax epidemics. All these are splendid intentions and admirable work. In this field much that is useful can be expected from the activity of the Soviets in the Far North.

They themselves go much further in their hopes and ambitions. They want to create new types of animals. Selection among fruit trees and a variety of plants has brought them good results in recent years. Now they try out cross-breeding among animals. And for the Far North their ambition is the creation of a new reindeer, offspring of Elk fathers and reindeer mothers. The Elk in the Urals is a beautiful plump and strong animal. The reindeer has made the best of its life in the North; it is wiry and small, has a strong skin and thick fur, but has also lean muscles and not too much meat to cover its bones. Now the Soviets would like to have a reindeer which gives much milk, good meat and plenty of fat without losing its power of resistance against the roughness of Arctic climate. They told me of some results. And I told them a famous anecdote of Bernard Shaw, who is well known in Russia for the praise he has given them and the irony he has exercised on them. A beautiful and charming actress is said to have put before him a serious proposal: 'Your brains and my beauty, Mr. Shaw, ought to produce a marvellous child. Should not we try, for the sake of humanity?' 'But what, madame', answered Shaw, 'but what if the product had my physical appearance and your brains?'

Bogomolkin confessed: 'Well, to be frank, we bred an animal that was as lean and skinny as the reindeer, and on top of all that, displayed weakness and lack of immunity against northern diseases like the elk. But', he added, 'I don't agree with Shaw. There is nothing lost in trying.'

CHAPTER XVIII

BREAKING THE ICE

As Ostroumova would not, or could not, do anything to secure my transport further North I had to organize it myself. I succeeded after several days of anxious negotiations with foreign captains in the port.

It was ten in the evening and the steamer *Stesso*, of Newcastle, was to lift anchor at 4 a.m. The Russians who pitied and had tried to help me succeeded only in stiffening the captain's resistance against the idea that he should take a passenger on board. Finally I persuaded him—defying the guard who, at the point of a bayonet, tried to prevent me from climbing up the gangway. The steward was prepared to give me his cabin at the rate of a pound a day. Food was to be extra—a preposterous arrangement, as you can get inclusive cruising fares on excellent liners in the Mediterranean or the South Seas at that rate. But the steward knew how to profit from his monopoly and I had to give in. After all, the *Stesso* was the only foreign ship which even did so much as hold out the promise of unloading me somewhere in the Arctic Ocean—either on to an ice-breaker or at the station at Dickson Island. All the others were going straight home to England or to Scandinavia. She alone was given a light aeroplane to take to the ice-breaker *Yermak* which was operating in the western half of the Polar basin and which apparently was badly in need of an aerial reconnaissance machine of her own. That was some guarantee that I should get where I wanted sooner or later.

Before I could leave I had to get a written permission from the local militia—the uniformed department of the G.P.U. or, as it is now called, the Department of the Interior. I had only learned of the sailing plans of the *Stesso* at nine in the evening. The militia had closed at four in the afternoon. All that I could do was to call on the sergeant at his home. He was just unpacking his feet before going to bed. He took it all in good humour and, after hedging for ten or twenty minutes, wrote out a permit on a piece of paper from my notebook, and as the official rubber stamp was not kept in his bedroom, simply signed it with his own name. I wonder whether that was according to regulations. If more of his colleagues were as sensible as he appeared to be, travelling in Russia would be even more of a pleasure than it is.

I spent four pleasant days on board the *Stesso*. I was once again treated to an English Breakfast—a great pleasure—although I had nothing to complain about with regard to the food I bought in Igarka's restaurants and at the air bases during earlier stages of the trip. Mr. Ward, the captain, was most kind and hospitable. Once our relations had been deprived of all financial problems through my unconditional acceptance of all suggested terms, he became a real friend. We drank rum together before he went to bed and, although he himself was not in the least interested, he ordered 'Sparks', the wireless operator, to write down all the most important news messages of the London broadcast bulletins to keep me in touch with world affairs. It took us four days to get to the actual open sea, although from the second day onwards I would have sworn we were already far out in the ocean. The river widened so much that its shores usually could not be seen. Whenever they loomed up to our right they might have been a bend in the coastline of the Kara Sea. We changed the river pilots twice—at Ust Port and Golchikha, for the many shoals and sandbanks and very sparse channels require special knowledge and very careful navigation. For four hours each night we stopped; not even the pilot, who had spent most of his life on the Yenisei, would risk going on in the dim twilight between ten in the evening and 2 p.m.

The sun dipped under the horizon only for a very short time. The rest of the 'night' it lingered about, touring the skyline just below the edge of the visible disc of the earth. Delicate shades twined and mingled across the sky— shades of green and purple, silver blue and orange—all turning and changing completely every few minutes. And as this battle of arts between night and day proceeded, so the struggle between cold and warmth was fought until the middle of the morning.

Early on the fourth day we reached the open sea. Mr. Ward translated these Siberian dimensions into more familiar European distances: 'it is as if you could go up the Elbe with Atlantic steamers as far as Central Czecho-slovakia, instead of stopping at Hamburg, or supposing the Thames had wound its way down from Scotland, and you were to find the docks at Glasgow only instead of at London.'

The changing of vessels took hardly half an hour. As soon as we found ourselves in the Kara Sea, 'Sparks', picked up a radio message from the ice-breaker *Yermak*, who informed us of her position, and asked Mr. Ward to heave to. Rocking gently, we drew up alongside the ice-breaker, whose derricks lifted the tiny aeroplane, while I went round the two ships in a sloop and climbed up the bulky hull of the *Yermak* on the opposite side.

I had sent a wireless message to *Tovarich* Krastin, the commander of the *Yermak*, from Igarka, and he received me in a very friendly manner. At breakfast, which was served as soon as the *Stesso* had hooted twice by way of farewell and had left for home, we discussed my further plans. It was agreed that I should go north-east on board the *Yermak* and watch it blast a road for a caravan of Soviet vessels. Two of the ships headed for the mouths of the Lena and Kolyma, two others intended to get to Vladivostok this year —doing the whole of the Northern Sea Route in one season. There was no ice at the estuary of the Yenisei, for the great volume of water brought down by the river warms this·

part of the Arctic Ocean. But the radio messages from further along the route were encouraging—encouraging that is for my hopes of at last getting some of the true Arctic atmosphere; but discouraging for Krastin whose job it was to get his fleet through the difficult spots of the Arctic Sea route with as little delay and expenditure in coal as possible. We went full steam ahead, and behind us at a respectful distance trailed the flotilla of cargo boats. The weather was fine; the sea as deeply blue as the Mediterranean on a sunny day in June. That was in the morning. After lunch, we felt a nip in the air. I suddenly remembered ski-ing tours on the Arlberg. The tang which heralded the approaching ice was the same as in a high Alpine winter sports resort. The sea was no longer blue but dark grey. The sky had put on a heavy coat of clouds—I followed its example a few minutes later by buttoning the extra fur lining into my leather coat. Mist brewed up from nowhere suddenly, and before tea-time we were in the midst of it. There is no reason to be afraid of getting seasick in an ice-covered sea. Your ship does not rock at all. The only compensating disadvantage is that when first an ice-floe smashes against the sides, you are convinced that you are going to sink. But the grinding was only a little friendly greeting with which the Polar Sea welcomed me as a newcomer to its realm. Worse was to follow. By six p.m. we were in 'nine-ball-ice'. This cryptic term was explained to me as meaning that nine-tenths of the water's surface is covered with drifting floes. If you had asked me, I should have said it meant that twelve-tenths of the sea were covered. Nor would I have been utterly wrong. The technicians count only the circumference of the floes; but as pressure is exerted from one side of a *massif*, one cake climbs on top of another, freezes on to it, and may tower several feet above sea-level.

We were making very slow headway now. The caravan had come closer to us, seeking protection in the wake of the ice-breaker, whereas we had to battle against the floes as they came head on against us—or we against them. The cargo boats followed comfortably in the channel we cut for them, like good little goslings behind their mother. Only occasionally they got a light tap from a floe that drifted by. As the evening went on our advance became slower and slower and at dinner-time we stuck fast in the midst of the ice. We went down for food and I had a chance to look round.

The *Yermak* was built in 1899 in Newcastle. On the wall of the messroom hangs a photograph of Victorian ladies and gentlemen in top hats at the launching of the ice-breaker in the presence of Russian diplomatists. To the right of that picture hangs a portrait of Stalin; to the left, in a smaller frame, one of Admiral Makaroff, who was the first to evolve the idea of attacking the ice of the Arctic with ice-breakers. 'Of course', a sailor explained to me, 'in those times he could not find the proper support. The Tsarist Government had no vision for great things. He would have been much better off under our régime, which sees his ideas realized on a grand scale.' Above the mantelpiece are two oil paintings; one showing Yermak, the Cossack conqueror, subduing Siberia by the sword; the other picturing the ice-breaker named after him blasting an open road to the North with the enthusiastic support of Soviet youth.

We could do little that night, the captain explained to me. The fog was too dense for aerial reconnaissance The weather reports from the nearest stations along the shore and on a few islands on the route ahead were not quite in agreement as to the weather to be expected for the next day. We had to wait. They turned the wireless on to hear the news—this is done regularly twice a day on board, and loud-speakers in all parts of the ship allow every member of the crew to listen to the news bulletin without leaving his watch. Since I was anxious to know all about life on board, the second officer introduced me to the woman

YET MORE ABOUT THE WORK OF THE ARCHANGEL ADMINISTRATION

The head of the Marine Department of the Archangel Administration of the Northern Sea Route, Com. Bredis, stated in March last that material held for eighteen months was available for the replacement of the deck of the Siedov.

On May 19th the Siedov *was put into the works Krasnaya Kuznitsa for repairs. For some two weeks the works did not start on the job on the ground that no agreement had been concluded, and when the agreement was concluded it transpired that there was no material for the deck.*

The weather was fine, but they did not remove the old deck for there was nothing to replace it with.

Finally a small deck was sent, but not only was the material completely unseasoned, but it was not according to the measurements; instead of 8-inch, 10-inch planking was sent.

But as the proverb says, troubles never come singly. New holes had to be bored in the iron deck and there was no permission to do this. Permission was received, new holes bored, and then it transpired that there were no bolts.

To complete the tale of woe the rains began. The deck of the Siedov *is warped, the vessel is spoilt and thousands of roubles are thrown to the wind.*

ROMANOV.

Later in the evening we had a sound film performance—perhaps in my honour, because the conditions outside certainly did not call for a particularly cheerful mood on the part of our crew. They had twenty of the latest Russian films on board—'We from Kronstadt', 'Aerograd', 'Party Ticket' were the more famous among them. Frequently when the *Yermak* gets near a Polar station during her operations on the Northern Sea Route—and when there is time because she must wait either for fresh coal supplies or for the caravans to catch up on her—a wireless message is sent to the hibernators a few hours in advance. And when the *Yermak* approaches their island or coastline they come out in boats to meet her; they are treated to fresh fruit, given flowers, and invited to attend a performance of the cinema on board.

The ice-breakers, these Arctic flotilla leaders, are not only technical but also cultural pioneers in the Far North.

They have scientific staffs on board who use all journeys for hydrological observations, making sea-water tests for biological and chemical studies, etc. Navigation on the Northern Sea Route is organized on the basis of posting ice-breakers at those parts which are known to be difficult for ordinary ships. At present the Russians have only three powerful ice-breakers which they can use for this work: the *Lenin*, the *Yermak* and the famous *Krassin*. Besides these they use the ice-cutter *Litke* (a former luxury yacht), and some smaller vessels of suitable shape and reinforced hulls: the *Malygin*, *Rusanov*, *Sibirakov*, *Sadko* and *Siedov*.

In the summer of 1936 the *Lenin* was posted as hall porter outside Novaya Zemlya to clear passages through its straits. The *Yermak* operated in the Kara Sea and had to lead the caravans to the mouth of the Yenisei, but her main task was to break through Vilkitski Straits, the central, the northernmost and always the hardest stretch of the Northern Sea Route. The *Krassin* looked after the tail-end of the route, the Archipelago of the new Siberian islands with their tricky channels, and the Bering Straits. The ice-breakers can only leave their fuel bases for a maximum of twenty-five days. They use up a tremendous amount of coal because their engines have to serve not only to propel the ship along but also to drive its weight against the ice. They are old-fashioned—built originally for the clearance of the Baltic ports. Therefore they will be supplemented by four new ones which are at present under construction in Nikolayev and Leningrad. Two will be ready in 1937 (according to plan), and they will be wonderful ships (according to the models I saw). They will be of 12,000 tons each, with three independent engines developing 10,000 h.p. (the *Yermak* has only 3000 h.p.), and they will work entirely on electricity, generated by Diesel engines. Instead of coal they will burn oil. Two aeroplanes with catapult arrangements will be carried on board for aerial reconnaissance. Their radio sets will keep them in telephonic communication not only with Dickson Island and with the other ice-breakers, but even with Moscow. I should like to see them when they are ready—the last word in Arctic flagships. Once they are put into service the traffic on the Northern Sea Route should quickly be increased. In the summer of 1936, 160 vessels plied in Arctic waters. Some seventy-five of them were actually cargo boats doing practical economic work. The rest were expedition ships, barges in convoy and other smaller fry. On the whole almost 300,000 tons of cargo were carried to and from the mouths of the rivers. Fourteen ships went the whole way from Leningrad or Murmansk to Vladivostok, or vice versa. That is quite a nice achievement. Beyond the Yenisei the Russians are at present only allowing their own boats. I suppose the insurance rates on foreign vessels would still be too high.

The route is of great importance. Its economic value was effectively demonstrated to me by Krastin that night on the *Yermak* when he figured out that it costs 1000 roubles to transport a ton of metal from Moscow to Yakutsk—first by rail through Siberia to Irkutsk and then down the Lena. The cost is only 600 if the load is taken to Murmansk by rail, and then by the Northern Sea Route to Port Tiksi, and by river craft to Yakutsk. The economic value of the Kara Sea (the western part of the North-east Passage) has been established for more than five years. About forty-five foreign steamers—thirty-five of them British —went through it last year. They all carried timber away, and some had brought goods from European Russian ports to Siberia on their way out, like the *Stesso*. Purely arithmetically it is much shorter than the other sea routes between European and far eastern Russia—which go through international seas and many potentially hostile straits, whereas this part of the Arctic is a Russian lake along the north coast of Asia. Murmansk to Vladivostok via the Indian Ocean or through the Panama Canal is a distance of almost 14,000 miles, while Murmansk-Vladivostok is not more than 6000.

But apart from the economic value, the Northern Sea Route has a great strategic importance, which I think is probably one of the reasons why the Soviet Government pushes ahead so energetically with its development. It is open only for three months of the year, but even that would bring a considerable relief to the trans-Siberian transport system in case of war on two fronts—in Europe and the Far East. Beyond that it would guarantee a line of communication by sea to America with which, for all practical purposes, Japan could not interfere. Ships could come up with provisions along the American east coast and be taken in convoy by Soviet ice-breakers at the Bering Straits and be guided to any of the Arctic ports. There the goods could be unloaded and transported on river craft up the Lena to the Far East, or up the Yenisei and Obi to Siberia, and by rail or by the White Sea Canal from Murmansk to the Baltic and Western Russia. Murmansk being quite ice free (while Leningrad is not), the Soviet fleet will have to be shifted there. Murmansk is actually being developed rapidly into a naval base, primarily for the Northern Sea Route, but the wharves and dockyards under construction for this head station of the Arctic can be used for warships just as well as Leningrad.

It was not necessary to put many questions to my hosts on the *Yermak* concerning these strategic aspects. They are quite clear. I refrained from endangering the friendly atmosphere which they, good seamen, allowed me to share. I was tired, anyway, and was quite happy to fall into my bunk towards midnight. It must have been in the early hours of the morning when the rhythmical hammering of the engines woke me up, and almost immediately afterwards came the shuddering crash as we struck ice. I dressed quickly and went on deck. The fog had cleared away overnight, the sun was shining brilliantly, but so far as I could see from the bridge—and as the captain assured me, so far as his observers could see from the crow's nest— there was nothing but ice. Slowly moving, creaking and screeching, we pushed through the ice, that was glittering and sparkling in the sunlight, blinding the unprotected eye.

'We have called Kozlov', Captain Voronin told me. 'He ought to be here any minute now. His base is at Dickson. He can fly the distance in a quarter of an hour.'

Kozlov came an hour later; he had waited for a complete set of weather reports from all stations. Then, having come, he circled above our ship and dropped a note saying that he could not come down because there was too much ice for his floats and no block that was flat enough and large enough for him to land on his skis. To the little parachute with which he dropped the message for us was also tied a bundle of letters. A bunch of them was addressed to the Chief of the Operations, Krastin. The rest were for the crew. Their relatives write them to Dickson Island and, as often as the ice patrol pilot flies thence to assist the ice-breaker, he takes these parcels with him.

Kozlov's machine was of the same type as the one in which I flew with Sadkov—a large Dornier Wal hydroplane. He soon disappeared. Meanwhile some of the men who were just off watch had climbed down on the ice and after testing it with poles had started playing football on a compact *massif*. They were soon called back by two impatient blows from the siren. The ice-field was getting amove, and our observer had seen some cracks opening

I HAD NOTHING TO WORRY ABOUT
ON THE ICE BREAKER

suddenly in the distance. We also started our operations again. The three screws, which are driven by independent engines, were pushing us along.

'We are climbing up on the field, the bow is already out of the water', I suddenly cried out, terrified. Voronin roared back at me—his Old Bill moustache bristling—that I had made a thorough fool of myself—that was just what they wanted. The method of the ice-breaker, which has a very flat and dull bow, is to push its front part on top of the ice and crush it under its own weight. That at least was what they explained to me, whereupon I remembered having read it before I set out. But this time the ice did not crush under our weight and we found ourselves suspended with the front quarter of the ship on the field and three-quarters of it in the water. A rather undignified position for such an impressive ship.

'What shall we do?' I asked.

'Drive the propellors in the other direction and withdraw graciously back into the water', Captain Voronin said.

But either he was trying to fool me or the ice was fooling him, because no matter how hard we tried with full steam to regain our natural element there we stuck with the front on the ice. 'A fine mess', I thought, and for some unexplainable reason, as if I had foreseen all that and known it could be avoided if only they had listened to me, I chuckled secretly, waiting for Voronin to get us out. After all, he is the ablest ice captain that Russia possesses.

Suddenly I felt the ship turning gently on its side. When she had a strong list, and I could hardly control my urge to draw the captain's attention to this new threat of disaster, she straightened herself back into a vertical position. But only to fall again into this newly acquired habit immediately—this time to the left.

'*Perekatchka*', Voronin smiled to me. 'We are playing swings.'

'What, just for fun?' I replied.

'Be sensible, man', he got serious. 'That's the second means by which we try to make the ice give in.'

But the ice did not give in. We were still up in the air. I was beginning to feel rather uncomfortable. The captain had kindly explained that the *perekatchka* was as simple as anything. All they did was to pump water from one side of the hull into the other gradually—there were special chambers for that in the holds. 'That does no harm to the ship', Voronin calmed me once more with a friendly smile.

Voronin now blew his whistle three times, and a few minutes later a party of six men were climbing down to the ice once more. 'Nothing doing then after all', I thought, and said aloud, 'so they can go and play again, eh?'

'Just watch them', Voronin replied.

They were not playing—not, at any rate, football. 'The third degree', Voronin announced. There were four explosions and we sank back into the water. We had at least regained the position of last night. Not geographically, though, because the moving drifts had dragged us along a few miles further north, but in relation to the floes around us.

Now we behaved modestly and waited for Kozlov to return. He came two hours afterwards and again dropped a little parachute. This time it held a small map, showing the position of the ice in an area of about 400 square miles. Little arrows indicated the road towards freedom—N.N.E. of our position, at a distance of roughly 70 miles, was clear water.

We took three days to get through this distance of 70 miles. Once after the midnight watch the entry in the log-book was: 'Moved half a ship's length within the last four hours'. In the morning of the fourth day we were back in the 'Mediterranean'. There was no reason for me to wait for another demonstration of Arctic magic. When Kozlov was free after lunch that day we asked him by wireless to come and fetch me. He sat down on the water a few hundred feet from the *Yermak*; I lowered my rucksack and suitcase into a boat that had come for me and climbed after them down a rope ladder. We flew off to Dickson Island. The *Yermak* went on towards Vilkitski Straits.

There she stuck in complete fog for over a week, as I heard on the wireless later on.

CHAPTER XIX

'RADIO CITY'

MY feet became entangled in a heap of endless tape which had been thrown away after use in an automatic telegraph machine. (The wireless staff were responsible for that.) A minute later I tumbled over two propellors which were lying about on the floor. Of all places the mechanics had chosen the corridor of their dormitory to store their spare parts.

At last I reached my room.

Kozlov had flown me to Dickson. Somehow, although we had left the *Yermak* at 3 p.m. and been *en route* for hardly more than forty-five minutes, we arrived at Dickson after supper. But I had given up wondering at such magic. I knew that in the Soviet Arctic all clocks and heavenly bodies were mixed up. I asked no questions: what is the exact time, please? I moved my own watch accordingly, and left it there until the next jump in time.

There had been a little argument when I arrived. I was taken to the chief of the station, a man between forty and fifty, in naval uniform—'third flagman' or something in the new hierarchy of Red officers. At all events, he had three golden stripes and three red stars on his sleeves and a little beard under his chin. His name was Borovikov. He shook my hand cordially, gave me a glass of wine, and then suggested that I had better live at the other end of the island, at 'New Dickson'.

'It's only 4 miles away from us, right across on the opposite shore, and they have better rooms there.'

I protested. 'Novy Dickson' was only the radio centre. All the life of the station was on this side: the harbour, with twenty-two ships waiting to be taken over the Route, the scientific staff, the dog-kennel, the hospital, the Turkish bath—and the majority of the people.

'Don't you know', Borovikov tried to persuade me, 'that we have got a telephone across the island now? It works. You will be in contact with everything here whenever you want. And you will have a nice soft bed and be much more comfortable.'

I thanked him for his thoughtfulness and added that as far as I had been informed there was a short wave telephone communication between Dickson and Moscow—technically I could be just as much in touch with them from the capital and need not have come out 3000 miles at all. And so I prevailed. As soon as my luggage was tucked away under the wooden bedstead I felt that the day had only just started for me—in fact I had not been up for more than five hours. It looked as if I was going to be paid back the time that was stolen from me on my arrival in Igarka. Fresh and cheerful, I left my room and went into that next door.

Gramophone music came from behind it, and I wanted to see what was going on. They were playing 'Smoke gets in your Eyes'. I felt at home. Far too much at home, considering that I was on a Polar island. I had not had much romance on the trip so far—everything was much more 'normal' than I had expected. That was just what the Russians were proud of. They wanted to make the Arctic 'just another section on the front . . .' 'A Polar station' that sounded 100 per cent Arctic. And now I could hardly see a difference between this smallish room full of dancing couples and a ski-ing hostel in the Tyrolese mountains. I introduced myself informally and joined the party. Within half an hour we all felt we were old friends. There was Olga Pavlovna, the meteorologist, Lydia Dimitrevna, the magnetologist, a fair-haired youngster who turned out to be her husband and scientific assistant, and a dentist with an unpronounceable name. He was spending a busman's holiday in the Arctic, enjoying the invigorating air, while making some extra money by attending the two hundred inhabitants of the island. He did not overwork himself— two hours' drilling each day after lunch was all he would do. He showed up against the real *polyarniki* like a week-end fisherman against the men of Arran. Whereas they wore ordinary town clothes most of the time, he would not go out without at least some parts of his Arctic costume —a ridiculous precaution as it was quite warm.

The girls in the room had dresses second to none that I had seen in the dance-hall of the 'Savoy' at Moscow. As the night went on, with us dancing and chatting away our time, I only noticed that from time to time Olga Pavlovna slipped off her dancing shoes, changed into rubber boots, and disappeared from the room for a quarter of an hour. She did it at intervals of about fifty minutes, and in the end I asked what it all meant.

'I have to go out to make my meteorological observa-tions—temperature, moisture, wind strength and direc-tion, clouds or fog, etc., and send off telegrams through the wireless station. The airmen and ships on the Route and the central weather bureau at Moscow need them. By the way, every four hours our reports go abroad too. They are even picked up at the Air Ministry in London, the meteorological bureaus in Scandinavia, Canada and America. We sit in the weather shop of the world.'

Towards one in the morning a tall youth burst into the room, swinging a telegram triumphantly in his right hand. 'We have won!'

They crowded round him, and I also looked over his shoulder to read the message. It was :

'AFTER YOUR GEORGE TWO TO BROTHER FIVE OUR KING MOVABLE ONLY HARRY SEVEN HARRY EIGHT STOP NEXT MOVE BRINGING UNESCAPABLE MATE STOP UPGIVING STOP THANKS GREETINGS CHESS GROUP ISLAND LONELINESS'.

It was the finale of a game played by wireless collectively

between two groups of Polar workers at stations 1600 miles apart. Usually the chess group at Dickson take part in the wireless tournaments of Polar stations during the winter only—they are too busy during the navigation. But as Zhilin explained to me, this game had started in July and had dragged on for several months. A move a day is the rule. That allows all the players at each station to reach their strategic decisions after careful considerations. Sometimes the radio operators play personally against each other. Then they take the chessboard to their desk and, earphones over their heads, the right hand on the morse-key, the left among the men, finish a game in one evening. A name is substituted for the letter, defining each square on the board. It seemed that the social and amusement side on Polar stations was well organized.

They do serious work, of course, on these stations. There were fifty-seven of them along the coasts and on the islands last summer. Including the weather and radio stations further inland their number is two hundred. Glavsevmorput is still busy opening new stations to sprinkle the whole Arctic with radio aerials and with the young men and women who watch the moods of the earth and its shell of air in these outlying districts. Dickson is the wireless exchange for these stations and the chief meteorological centre in the Polar regions. It serves as a naval base for the Northern Sea Route, passes the forecasts from all parts of the sea on to ships and aeroplanes, and on to Moscow. There are six short-wave radio transmitters on the island, two with universal reach for long-distance telephony and telegraphy and four for the daily communication with sub-divisional stations. The weather bureau collects the reports of all district centres and produces synoptic forecasts based on these many observations.

Olga Pavlovna had a few telegrams from other stations on her desk in her room where she had given the party on the night of my arrival. They work, of course, by code, and I naturally could not make head or tail of the figures of which the whole message consisted. One I saw came from Cape Chelyuskin; it had been sent off at 7 a.m. that morning and read :

155 @@ 48109 20309 14750 9 @602 00011 55009 3 @@@4.

She decoded it for me as follows: There is a strong fog here this morning. We cannot see the clouds and are therefore unable to report on their condition. The visibility is nil, the height of the clouds as well as their quality is unknown to us. There is a north-easterly wind of strength No. 3. Between our last telegram and now the weather was generally fine. The air pressure is 147, the temperature of the sea minus zero centigrades, the relative moisture 90 per cent, the height of the highest cloud unknown for reasons given. There was no precipitation, the sea is calm, we can see fifty yards, not further, the soil is humid and cold, there is a certain amount of snow in the moulds, the temperature of the soil is minus five centigrades, the snow not general, its height therefore of no importance. The maximal wind strength is as we said three. As to the height of the sea we cannot supply any data. The difference between air and water temperature is half a degree. The air is warmer.

If they had a code like that for all subjects I suppose they could telegraph the whole of Marx's 'Capital' in a fifty-units message. The Dicksonians do not only pick up the weather reports from Russian stations but also from foreign observatories. On the morning of September 1st they surprised me at breakfast by telling me that we had the same temperature as London, with the only difference that it was raining in the south of England whereas we had brilliant sunshine for the moment. The weather changes rapidly during the Arctic summer. Fog is the worst enemy.

Apart from the daily weather observations, which supply valuable data for general investigation of Arctic cycles and

are hoped to provide a key to most puzzles that make navigation still problematic in the summer, the Polar stations have biologists, hydrologists, hydrographic experts, magnetologists and geologists on their staffs. Each station acts as a base for investigations in a radius of 300 miles. Most of these roaming studies are made during the winter, when transport is easier. Dog teams, reindeer sledges, on some stations even aero-sledges driven by motor-car engines take the explorers on their trips. They improve the maps of their districts, include more detailed topographical data, collect mineral samples. In fact, they are strategical centres in the battle to tame the Arctic. From year to year their number increases. The net which is woven to hold the Polar region more strongly in the grip of human organization grows tighter.

The staff on Dickson is the largest of all Polar stations. There are two hundred people, twenty-five of them women, who stay there over the winter. A child born on the station is now three years old, two others who came there when they were still sucklings toddle about the mossy ground and seem to be none the worse for their extraordinary life. One of their greatest amusements is to watch the release of stratosphere balloons—a new method of meteorological observation which consists in releasing a set of fourteen balloons which rise up to 18 miles above the ground. They are called Maltchanoff Sound, have little radio transmitters with batteries attached, and send down reports on atmospheric conditions for about an hour or two. Then the whole set is lost somewhere into space. Their observations are useful for Arctic aviation, which the Russian airmen hope to extend into the stratosphere. They found, for instance, that the air high above the Arctic is warmer than that above sub-tropical Central Asia. I don't quite understand why and how that is. But they said they did.

I did not know how long I would be on Dickson. It was just a question of waiting for a chance to catch some boat that would go home via the Kara Sea and stop at Murmansk. Time was moving on, and I, except for occasional telegrams from home (which reached me usually within three hours), felt a little out of touch with what the Russians call my Base of Operations. Upon the invitation of the radio staff at Dickson I rang up an American newspaper correspondent friend of mine in Moscow.

We sent him a wireless telegram first, asking that he should come to the central office of Glavsevmorput in the Ulitsa Razina at three in the afternoon the next day. At this time Dickson had a daily conversation of an hour with headquarters, during which all important questions were discussed between the chief of naval operations and the provision and other departments. At the given hour I sat before a microphone with a loud-speaker next to my chair. Looking out of a window on to lonely ice floes that drifted into the bay of Dickson Harbour, I suddenly heard the voice of my friend come through the loud-speaker clearly as he welcomed me with a hearty, 'Hullo, old boy! how is the Arctic?' At that moment a husky voice butted in on the other side. '*Tolko po Russki, pozhaluysta!*' was the command, and for some quite incomprehensible reason we had to go on conversing in Russian. Short-wave telephony sounds quite familiar nowadays. We know we can talk round half the world by that means from our hotel rooms and ocean liners midway on the Atlantic. Nevertheless, it · was an exciting experience to have the same means of communication available on a Polar island where hardly twenty years ago Scandinavian explorers starved to death in a mid-winter blizzard.

There was quite a bunch of telegrams lying about on the table of the radio station ready to be filed. I glanced through them to get an idea of the variety of news and communications which pass regularly through Dickson, the Arctic radio city.

One was headed, 'On board steamship *Pravda*, Dickson

Harbour,' and was addressed 'Kopusov, chief doctor, Glavsevmorput, Moscow'. It read :

'EXPECTING CONFINEMENT STOP DESIRABLE APPLY PAINLESS STOP PLEASE WIRE EXACT DETAILS NEW METHOD ENSURING ANÆSTHESIA WITHOUT IMPEACHMENT NORMAL DEVELOPMENT LABOURS ACCORDING PROFESSOR LOURIER STOP IF POSSIBLE COMPOSITION MEDICAMENT STOP UNDERSTAND METHOD SIMPLE ENABLING APPLICATION STATION HOSPITAL STOP KAPITOKHIN.'

The reply which had come from Dr. Kopusov at Moscow within two hours was:

'PAINLESS CONFINEMENT ASSURED APPLICATION ONE PER CENT SOLUTION NOVOSCRAINE WITHOUT ADRENALIN STOP AT MOMENT OF CUTTING UMBILICAL CORD INTRODUCE FIVE CUBICS SUB-CUTANE IN UPPER AREA AROUND BRIDLE STOP CHOOSE CENTRE OF LINE BETWEEN GROIN RING AND LINE THREE FINGERS DISTANCE FROM LINE BETWEEN GROIN RING AND NAVEL STOP AT INTERSECTION THESE LINES INTRODUCE SYRINGE FROM BOTH SIDES GIVING FOUR TO FIVE CUBICS STOP ANOTHER FIVE CUBICS IN AREA OF SPINE RHOMBOID HOLE AND APPROXIMATELY AN HOUR BEFORE CUTTING UMBILICAL CORD HAVE ALREADY ONE CUBIC OF MORPHIA INJECTED IN ARM STOP GOOD LUCK KOPUSOV.'

Three telegrams urged the faster dispatch of potatoes from Igarka to a small Polar island; one blamed an official in Archangel for having sent too little drawing-paper to Cape Chelyuskin. Quite a number of messages were private communications between Polar station officials and their families in Russia, such as:

'SHOLOKHOFF DICKSON: VALYA PROMOTED THIRD CLASS ELEMENTARY SCHOOL WITH BEST QUALIFICATIONS TEACHER VERY SATISFIED STOP KISSES NATASHA.' Or

'SHATSILLO DICKSON: THANKS FOR GREETINGS, MONEY RECEIVED, RETURN YOUR WISHES, REMEMBER ME TO PAPA WE AWAIT LETTER A HEARTY KISS SVETLANA AND KOLYA.'

Much is done to make the life of those six hundred young

people who live on Polar stations for two or three years as bearable as possible. They get a ration of fifty telegram words a month free of charge to communicate with their families. Once a month relatives of Polar workers are assembled at the main radio station in Moscow and each family can broadcast one hundred words of personal greetings to their sons or daughters, wives or parents in the Far North. Special concerts are arranged in the capital which are transmitted through Dickson to all the Polar stations and, while the programme runs off, each station may send a wish for a particular piece of music which they like to hear. A number of them are satisfied immediately, the rest have their wishes gratified in the next concert. As the messages arrive at the concert hall during intervals they are read out to the public present, who cheer the Polar workers, to make them feel the country thinks of them and is grateful for their courageous work. A year ago, during a festival parade on the square outside the Kremlin, *Polyarniki* from Dickson sent greetings to the crowds which were relayed to them by loud-speakers in the streets. Dickson itself had tuned in to the Moscow station, which broadcast a sound picture of the parade. They could hear the voices of their own comrades who spoke to the crowds from the microphone next door, mixed with the replying cheers of the crowds in Moscow. These are all quite simple technical tricks, but this instance shows how much feeling of nationwide solidarity can be fed and cherished through our modern inventions.

Living conditions on Dickson seemed comparatively comfortable. Married couples had rooms of their own, single men and women shared dormitories with one or two companions. The scientists had a cottage of their own, to which they referred as the 'academy'. The main building consisted of a large common room, in which meals were taken, lectures held, games played and work discussed and organized. All around doors led into the private rooms.

Almost the entire breadth of two walls was taken up by huge tile stoves. I counted six separate ones and could imagine that they kept the place warm even throughout the coldest periods of the Polar winter.

A separate log cabin contained the baths. I enjoyed them thoroughly. I had a typical Russian steam bath, with an enormous brick stove heated with driftwood, over which you could pour bucketfuls of water, to fill the room with steam to soak you to the bones. Next door was the mechanized laundry—they washed my shirts within twenty-four hours, all by electric machinery. Of course, I did not imagine that this was the general standard of comfort on all Polar stations, but what is possible on Dickson is certainly not entirely impossible on other islands or coastal centres. The Arctic is getting civilized after all.

When I woke up the morning after my arrival at Dickson I heard three explosions at intervals of a few minutes. Dickson is a rocky island with a large bay, almost entirely shut off to the sea by two sausage-shaped arms which leave only just enough space open for three or four ships to come in side by side. This structure increased the noise many times and the echo created the impression of artillery fire. I thought that perhaps a boiler had exploded on one of the ships which lay in the harbour. But then I saw smoke rising up from behind the rocks in a little bend of the bay. I rode out that afternoon to watch the work there. Blasting operations were carried on by 140 workers, who were busy cutting a shelf out of the basalt rock. At that place a mooring line was under construction. The platform was to be brought down to about twenty feet above the water line, panelled with driftwood logs and extended to a length sufficient for two normal-sized steamers to berth alongside. Coal will be stored on this quay so that ice-breakers and steamers passing along the western half of the Arctic coast line of Asia will be able to pull in at Dickson to bunker. That will save the laborious task of loading fuel from cargo steamers on to the ice-breakers in open sea, and also the costly organization of supply fleets for refuelling. The coal will be brought from Spitzbergen and the Taimyr Peninsula—from Norilsk and, later on (down the Yenisei), from the Southern Siberia and Tunguska Basin mines. Dickson will then become the second Arctic naval base after Murmansk.

During my stay on Dickson two doctors of the All-Russian Institute for Experimental Medicine were packing their trunks after two years of continuous study of human reactions to the Arctic. Doctor A. J. Goldkin and his assistant, Dr. I. P. Baltchenko, had been charged to watch how southerners acclimatized themselves during work in the Polar regions; how long they may remain there without suffering dangerous damage to their health; how the women stood the climate. All members of the station were watched at regular intervals, examined for the normal development of all physical processes, and continually urged to communicate all changes they would notice with themselves. The results of these investigations have so far only been registered mechanically and will not be studied and analysed until the doctors return to the Institute. One observation, however, which Dr. Baltchenko told me about is so striking that I would like to mention it here. I must emphasize, however, that no conclusions of a scientific character have as yet been drawn from it. It was noticed that two or three days before the approach of the *purga*—the violent Arctic storm which is frequent during the winter—the human heart reduces its contractions to about half the number per minute that is usual. The pulse is less frequent but stronger so that the individual experiences no disagreeable sensations. This heralding of a meteorological phenomenon by the human organism is the more interesting as it occurs at a time when none of the automatic instruments can register even the slightest warning of the approaching changes as yet.

I had been in Dickson four days when still there was no suggestion as to when I could get away. On the fifth evening I visited the smaller group of people employed at the radio centre Novy Dickson. They are only twenty-three, including three women and one child. In a much smaller circle the atmosphere of friendliness was even more striking than over at the port. The walls of their lounge are adorned with paintings by one of their mechanics and above the reading-table is a poster with a list of books which the Culture Department recommends to workers on Polar stations and which are included in apparently each of their libraries. It was a very carefully selected list of world literature, one representative work of each author displayed as follows:

(1) Classics:

    (*a*) Russian:

        Pushkin
        Tolstoy
        Lermontov
        Gogol
        Dostoyevski
        Ostrovski
        Turgeniev
        Chekhov

    (*b*) International:

        Balzac (*Father Doriot*)
        Boccaccio (*Decamerone*)
        Heine (*Atta Troll*)
        Swift (*Gulliver's Travels*)
        Cervantes (*Don Quixote*)
        Shakespeare (*Selected Dramas*)
        Coster (*Till Eulenspiegel*)

(2) Modern:

(a) Russian:

> Gorki (*Mother*)
> Gladkov (*New Earth*)
> Sholokhov (*Quiet Flows the Don*)
> Leonov (*Construction*)
> Ilf and Petrov (*Twelve Stools, The Golden Calf and A Millionaire in Soviet Russia*)

(b) International:

> Rolland (*Maître Breugnon*)
> Shaw (*Cæsar and Cleopatra*)
> Stefan Zweig (*Fear, Twenty-four Hours in the Life of a Woman*)

Some of the English, German and French books were in the original, the bulk were recent Russian editions by a State Publishing Company which throws a number of representative works of literature on to the market each year in first editions of 200,000 to 500,000 copies. They are distributed all over the country by educational organizations, schools, and the so-called culture departments attached to most of the larger State trusts, factories and Government organizations.

We discussed many human problems. I asked a geologist of twenty-eight, a rather quiet man who had been twice lost on expeditions by foot into the glacier world of Novaya Zemlya and on Franz Josef Land, how he, a convinced Marxist who believed in materialist philosophy, reacted to nearest contact with the danger of death without religion. 'Does Marxism alone give you sufficient replies to all questions, also those ultimate ones of death and thereafter? You have faced dangers so often, as you yourself told me. Did you never feel the urge to have some religious or philosophical system to give you courage and strength in

268

such a critical situation?' He did not reflect for a minute but answered straight and immediately: 'No. Of course Marxism gives no reply to these last questions. It is a historical analysis and the only real economic theory in existence. But it never claimed to answer these last questions. What we call metaphysics to-day—because our scientific work has not yet succeeded in penetrating its intricacies—will be mere physics to-morrow, when our scientific work will have achieved more. I do not believe that science can answer all our questions. Maybe it will never answer the ultimate ones. But at least we have to go on searching all the time. That is a human urge. We feel it, and should organize its satisfaction systematically. Navigating north, we bring the point of our ship towards the Great Bear—but we don't expect to reach this astrological constellation. But aiming for it assures us we get to our destination. I feel something similar about science and the search for the secrets of life. That is my theoretical belief. In practice, and as regards our individual fate—well, it seems to me that the only insurance against physical mortality is striving for spiritual immortality. That is done by works and deeds of social usefulness, through which your memory is gratefully preserved by your fellow-beings. In the small circle of your family, by your friends and children. In a wider sense by the community.'

Towards ten o'clock that night we were rung up from the chief of the station, and Borovikov announced to me that a petrol tank steamer, the *Maikop* from Tuapse, on the Black Sea, which had brought fuel to some of the motor ships in the Arctic, was returning to Murmansk that night and would take me on board if I could be ready in two hours. It was an abrupt end to my stay at Dickson, and I regretted it. To let this chance go by would have been foolish—it might have cost me four or five weeks of waiting, which I could not afford. We went back to the main harbour across the island. The ice on the north coast was coloured pink by the setting sun, but it went quite dark before we got to 'Old Dickson'. My things were packed in a few minutes and I took my leave from everybody in a great hurry.

A bad fog brewed above the island. The *Maikop* lay rather far out, south-west of Dickson. It would not risk the entry into the bay through the rocky straits without daylight. And so a group of sailors who were going to join the ice-breaker *Malygin* took me out in their motor-boat. We took forty-five minutes to pick our way through the fog. Borovikov accompanied us, for he knew every corner of the island and every stray rock that showed up slightly above the water. The ice-breakers, as the crews of the Arctic flotilla leaders were referred to by their friends, had a brass band with them and as we cut through the mist they unperturbedly played cheerful tunes which rang out as our farewell through the tenfold crevasses of rocky Dickson. Their cheerfulness did not ring falsely. The music was no pose of theirs. They felt it was the proper style in which modern men had to pick their way in their motor-boats through the ice floes, rocks and mist of Polar waters, piping triumphantly the hymn of the victory for which forty thousand of their brave companions are striving against the Arctic.

1

CHAPTER XX

THE ICE IS BROKEN

I AM back in my home at London. Behind me is a journey of almost twenty thousand miles, into an Empire of the future.

It introduced me to a variety of people; many enthusiastic, full of love and faith in their work; some unhappy and broken by one of the most decisive turns of human history; most of them kind and helpful, a few narrow-minded and prejudiced. There was very little adventure of the twopenny magazine type, but a wealth of romance and thrill in a higher sense. I saw a great community of men and women struggling against nature, carrying the flag of human victory into a world which seemed untamable wilderness until yesterday.

The first realistic question put to me, by friends and by myself, was: Is it all worth while?

Will it be of standing value to them and to us?

Value is a relative conception. We must make it clear first of all from what point of view we start off, on what standards we base our consideration, on what scales we measure. '*Commercial* value'? Even that is not sufficient qualification in this case. Russia and the capitalist world are organized on different lines. Production both here and there claims to be for the satisfaction of human demand in goods and services. We believe that private initiative and competition, and the motive of individual profit, are the strongest incentive to efficient creative activity. The Russians hold that the high standard of modern industrial organization requires collective effort, social control, planned economy. This enterprise of developing the Polar regions for industry and transport is a tremendous enterprise. It

271

requires enormous expenditure. It requires simultaneous work in many fields: scientific exploration, pioneering in the wilderness, support by wireless and aviation; continuous vigilance on the part of meteorological observers and experts in industry, medicine, social welfare. It would be impossible, or at least it would be slowed down to an incomparably lower tempo, without the closest co-ordination of all these factors. Many of the supporting services will never yield an active commercial balance in themselves. The Polar stations are a kind of police safeguarding the interests of man against the tricks and lawlessness of nature.

It is difficult to measure the whole expenditure in terms of money. The official rouble budget of Glavsevmorput translated into our currency at official rates of exchange was something like £250,000,000 or $1,000,000,000 up to the present.

Still every expert on Soviet economy would point out that there is no real rouble exchange, and that even within the financial system of Russia correct calculation of costs is impossible since all enterprises are state-controlled and no outsider is able to disentangle the cross relation between subsidies, credit advance, and active yields. We must therefore drop the idea of judging this endeavour by our standards. It starts from different premises, is pursued by different methods and animated by different motives. To the Soviet the purpose of colonizing the Polar Empire is clear: it is intended to remedy a geographical deficiency of the country by opening a route for sea transport. It is meant to provide access to a great source of wealth and facilities for communication between outlying districts. Natural riches, discovered and ready for human exploitation but worthless if inaccessible, can thereby be turned to practical use. It is further intended to find and open up new treasures of the earth hitherto hidden under ice and swamp: gold, copper, nickel, coal, oil, salt, tin, rare metals and precious earths.

There is, finally, the consideration for the country's safety against outward attack. It has to be borne in mind that Russia is convinced that she introduces a system of social and economic organization superior to ours in securing comfort and wealth to the masses. At the same time she is convinced that the capitalist Powers will be tempted to attack her once they realize that the Russian system is recognized to be superior. They would fear the effects of her example among their own population. Therefore she regards even uneconomic measures as worth while if they safeguard her frontiers. If this scheme of opening the Arctic thus serves that purpose it is definitely worth all the work spent on it and is fully justified in the eyes of the Russians. It does serve this purpose. There can be no doubt about it. Perhaps after some time, when superlativism, exuberant optimism and romantic enthusiasm have cooled off, certain minor parts of the scheme will have to be modified, some single item dropped or the hopes attached to it cut down to realities. If ice conditions grow worse after the cycle of favourable years turn, for instance, the passage through the central straits between Cape Chelyuskin (Asia's Calais) and the southern tip of North Land (the local equivalent of Dover) may be blocked even in August and refuse to yield also to the cumulative effort of more numerous and more powerful ice-breakers. In that case the journeys from Europe to Obi and Yenisei, and from the Far East to the Kolyma and Lena will still be useful for trade and transport, but the whole route will lose some of its importance for naval strategy. It may also prove too difficult or costly to refine Arctic oil on the spot, in which case it will be of less value to Polar navigation. These were just two of the doubts that struck me as a layman. All these reflections, however, should not and do not prevent the Soviet from trying. They are probably as conscious of them as any outside observer. After all, the utopian impossibilities of yesterday are already the glorious possibilities of to-day and sure to become dull matters of course to-morrow. Who knows what unknown or only vaguely dreamt-of powers and treasures will still be discovered in the Polar regions as the struggle for known and predetermined aims goes on? What visions of future health resorts, new cross-bred animals, special plants hardened for life in the North, what visions of winds and storms on the frozen ice-cap of the world pressed into subservience to man, what possibilities of exploring, and soon using for practical purposes the strange electric and magnetic currents of these regions! The northern Polar region is known to be an ice-covered ocean. Only the belts of Arctic land around, the coasts of Asia and America and the islands in the Polar sea may be of economic value there. But at the other end of the world expands the Antarctic. And this is land, a vast territory, the sixth continent. Surely much of what will be found and learned up north could prove of great value at a later stage to those nations who own a share in the lands of the South Pole! What wonderful possibilites also for co-operation, exchange of information between Russia and Scandinavia, the Soviet Union and America, the United States and the British Dominion of Canada!

Nations can grow rich in two ways: by fighting others for their possessions or by reclaiming new territories within their own borders and no-man's lands. Russia could devote the same energies to conquest and aggression which she now spends on pioneering and exploration in the Arctic. Geographical deficiencies can be remedied by encroachment on other people's thoroughfares, and raw materials gained by robbery as well as by colonization of empty spaces. From that point of view also much can be said in favour and appreciation of her struggle against the Arctic. Providing a nation's youth with an outlet for its energies and romantic desire in a peaceful direction is no less worthy of praise. By all means let us give credit where it is due! And let us forget for a moment what grievances and reproaches we may nurse on other accounts! After all that I have seen on my journey through Russia, and heard in my contacts with the manifold types of its population, particularly the young. I am fully convinced that the country is wholly occupied with itself at present and will be so for a long time to come. It concentrates upon the development of its own resources, its youngsters do not dream of battles against men, but of battles against nature, not of conquest and subjugation of other people's but of their own uncultivated territories; the idea of carrying the torch of world revolution beyond their frontiers, the Islamic belief in preaching the faith (of Communism) to us by fire and sword has subsided to a keen desire to put their own home in order: Why should we not learn and profit in this instance of their work in the Arctic? There I have seen them doing something useful and good. This twentieth-century pioneering in the Polar regions is a wonderful thing. An ice wall of thousands of years standing is pulled down, a road is blasted through it, melted away by the fire of human intelligence. This work is symbolic for man's mission on this earth, and the ice-breaker-Captain's cry from his bridge is battle cry and victory song:

'THE ICE IS BROKEN!'

YOU MAY WISH TO KNOW:

How you could make the same journey?

You have to obtain an ordinary consular *visa* for U.S.S.R.
and a special Arctic *visa* through the Central Administration of
the Northern Sea Route. You can either travel to Moscow and
from there by Trans-Siberian Railway to Novosibirsk, Krasnoyarsk or Irkutsk, continuing by steamer or aeroplane down the
rivers Obi, Yenisei or Lena and from Novy Port, Port Igarka, or
Port Tiksi by cargo steamer to Murmansk or Vladivostok.
Or by sea from London or Leningrad, or from Vladivostok to
any of the Arctic ports and up the rivers to the railway line.

What would the same journey cost?

From Moscow by first-class sleeper to Krasnoyarsk: 500 roubles,
by Avyo Arctica plane to Igarka 800 roubles (to Dickson Island
1000 roubles). The steamer journey to Europe would have to
be arranged on the spot with the captain of a foreign or Soviet
cargo boat and paid for, according to individual arrangement.
I paid £1 a day from Igarka to Dickson Island to the steward
of a British cargo vessel, and from there to Murmansk nothing,
because the captain of the Soviet vessel, *Maikop*, refused to accept
money for taking me along. From Murmansk to Leningrad
I paid 170 roubles for second-class ticket and sleeper on the
Polar Arrow. Hotel prices outside Moscow are about 20 roubles
a night and food per day would cost about the same. In Igarka
itself and on the Polar stations sleeping accommodation would
have to be arranged for in the homes of private persons.

What the journey actually cost me?

A little less than £200, exclusive of drinks.

What equipment did I take?

A tropical suit for Southern Siberia. My ordinary ski-ing outfit for the North. A fur-lined leather coat, fur cap, fur gloves and heavy boots, on loan from 'Arctic Snab,' the outfitting department of Glavsevmorput. I also took a dozen shirts and a great volume of underwear, thinking that there would be difficulty in finding good laundry service *en route*. This was a mistake. I found efficient laundries even on the Polar stations. My medical chest was far too bulky; iodine, permanganate of potash, aspirin and a little reserve of quinine would have been quite sufficient. Delicate persons might be glad to take a home-made bag of some cotton material in order to be always independent of local bed linen or bare rugs. As far as provisions were concerned I came home with all the boxes of cheese which I had taken out. I might have taken more chocolate, as Russian chocolate was still rather poor in the summer of 1936.

Could I see everything, or did they only show me what they wanted?

Russia to-day is like a house in construction. They cannot hide the dirt, disorder and atmosphere of improvization which abounds in all building plots. If you are invited into a finished house, your host may refuse to show you the servant's quarters and the untidy rooms, and will try to boost with his nicely furnished lounge. When some of the walls are not yet more than heaps of bricks and the sky visible through the scaffolding of the future roof, all he can do is to show you his blue-prints and praise his architect's scheme of decoration. If you know something about it, you will be able to dispute his claims. If you don't, you could only notice his good intentions and let your own imagination do the rest. The opinion you will form will depend on your optimistic or pessimistic temperament and your idea of the man's abilities and *bona fide*. On the whole I had to complain more of the lack of interest shown for my curiosity and the apparent preoccupation of people, than of their zeal in guiding and advising me.

Was I spied upon, and watched in my movements?

If I was, it was done in such a way that I never noticed it. Several times, as at Krasnoyarsk, I was in a rage because, contrary to promises, no one had been informed of my arrival in advance.

Did the ordinary people talk to me freely?

Yes, the further away from the capital the more outspoken I found the population. Their criticism of existing conditions and Government measures was even astounding to me at first. In the capital and among officials of the Party and Civil Service I noticed a continuous vigilance over their words and behaviour towards me, as a foreigner and reporter. The ordinary workers and the exiles did not mince their words in conversation with me.

Could I take photographs undisturbed?

Everywhere except in railway stations, on bridges and military premises, aerodromes and barracks. I had to abide by the general rule in Russia that films must be developed before they are taken out of the country and shown to the frontier guards upon demand. They were in fact inspected by a Customs official at the Moscow airport at my departure, but none were taken away.

Could I send telegrams out of the country?

Yes. Press messages are subject to censorship in Moscow, but private correspondence was accepted at all post offices in the English language and in Latin script. Letters and cables from home reached me in normal time. The telephone conversation I had with a colleague in Moscow by short wave wireless from Dickson Island had to be carried on in Russian. No objection was raised against telephone communication with my family from Moscow and Leningrad in my language.

279

Was it cold in the North?

During the months of July, August and September the temperature was never below freezing-point.

Could I buy freely in the shops?

Yes, the system of ration cards is abolished. Whatever goods were available could be had for money in any quantity.

How are prices?

They vary from year to year. Foodstuffs were cheaper by between 20 and 120 per cent in 1936 than they had been in the previous year. Clothes have not come down in price substantially so far except some textiles. Shoes are regarded as expensive by the Russian population themselves. (See also remarks about the rouble below.)

What about the exchange?

The rouble is now fixed at about twenty-five to the pound and five to the dollar. It can only be bought within Russia and must not be taken out. Re-change into foreign currency is not possible normally. At this exchange most goods are twice or three times as expensive as abroad. (Except railway fares, steamer and air tickets, stamps, telephone and telegram fees.)

Is life also so much more expensive for the local population?

Not quite. Their wages are comparatively higher, although they vary greatly according to a man's ability and achievements. Furthermore, a number of services which are somewhat expensive with us, such as theatres, education, certain sports, living quarters, amusements, books, travelling and holidays are partly included in factory wages and given free of charge to selected workers or at prices very much below our level.

What, then, is the rouble worth?

Purchasing power, prices and wages are still in flux in Russia. The development is not completed. Until 1935 the rouble had many different values according to those who held it. Privileged sections of the population could buy in privileged shops at privileged prices. Army and G.P.U., factory workers and civil servants had other sources of supply than intellectuals, peasants, members of the one-time bourgeosie or aristocracy. There were also shops where goods could only be bought for foreign currency or against precious stones and metals. 'Torgsin.' At the same time goods were scarce and rationed. The result was that roubles were offered to foreigners at rates up to ten and fifteen times below the official exchange, by people who wanted to get hold of foreign currency for purchases in Torgsin. The real ratio was then quite clearly visible between 'gold prices' in Torgsin and paper prices in Russian shops. This whole system was liquidated by February 1, 1936. Prices are now the same for everybody, goods can be purchased freely and consequently the 'black rouble' has fallen. It is still obtainable through illegal channels. The sources of supply are foreign specialists and artists who come to Russia temporarily. They are paid very high salaries in roubles, but cannot take them abroad. Whereas in 1935, 150 to 180 roubles could be obtained for the pound, the rate had fallen to 90 and 85 by July and 75 and even 60 by September, 1936.

Some amounts were also offered by consulates of some foreign countries. They have still a larger number of their citizens living in Russia from whom they receive roubles for passport dues and registration fees for marriages, etc.

As prices in Russian shops come down and more goods appear on the open market the home population offer no more of their own earnings against foreign exchange, and the black rouble is bound to fall further, until it will sooner or later approach the official rate.

At the same time industrial development is not fully completed as it is here, and progress in different branches of production goes on by stages and unequally. The systematic building up of the country's economy started first with raw materials, heavy industries and transport. In these categories prices will be found to have come down gradually to a level at which they equal or almost equal world market values in terms of roubles at the official exchange. An aeroplane and a railway engine, coal, pig iron or timber, are quoted within Russia at about the same level or even below their foreign price-equivalent. Lorries are cheaper than private motor cars. Prices for bread and staple foodstuffs were lower by comparison than chocolate and delicacies, these in their turn cheaper than clothes and luxury goods. Articles manufactured from material which is used in war industries, particularly leather (which is scarce because of the mass slaughter of cattle in collectivisation years) are abnormally expensive. On the other hand rents are never higher than 10 per cent of a man's income, books about as much as 5 to 8 kilograms of bread, medical services and sports free for wage earners, holidays and education, including university gratis, and old age pension guaranteed. A larger part of the income is therefore available for general needs. There is very little saving because the absence of unemployment and the shortage of labour, as well as the belief in security for the old, and in good openings in the future for the children, disposes of the care for to-morrow's bread. Nevertheless, some people save and are paid interest on their bank deposits. They can also invest in State loans. The rate of interest used to be between 7 and 8 per cent. Last year Government loans were forcibly converted and interest on them reduced to 4 per cent. The Government's argument that this is justified because the purchasing power of the currency had almost doubled through the development of industrial production, the reduction of prices, increase of wages and larger supply of goods, was more or less generally accepted.

Private property is legal and protected in everything except means of production, machines, factories, land and rent-bearing houses. Rich people—i.e. authors, actors, film producers, inventors and scientists—can own villas and motor cars and can employ servants. Money cannot be used, however, for the establishment of businesses which are based on employment of labour. It has only the power to procure goods and service for consumption. The only yield permissible now is from State loans, through which it is directed into State industries. Fortunes, if any, can be passed on to children and to other relatives after death. Property and State bonds are exempt from, and only cash subject to 3 per cent, death duty. Income tax is always below 5 per cent. Since the State controls all wages and prices it takes what it needs through corresponding regulation of these. Higher output and good brain work is rewarded better than inefficiency and manual labour. Through this provision of an outlet for talent, resourcefulness and diligence, the régime hopes to stimulate initiative, the urge for higher qualification and an increase of production generally. This should not be mistaken for a return to capitalism, the fundamental principle of which is private enterprise in industrial and agricultural productivity. For all these reasons, I have avoided quoting wages and prices in terms of money, but attempted to draw a picture of the actual standard of living among the people I described in this book.

Where can additional information be obtained about the Soviet Arctic?
  General and economic from,

Central Administration of the Northern Sea Route, Moscow, Ulitsa Razina 9.
  Scientific from,
Arctic Institute, Leningrad, Professor Samoilovitch.
  Ethnological from,
Institute of the Peoples of the North, Leningrad, Professor Koshkin.

What publications contain information on this subject?

Sovyetskaya Arctica (monthly magazine in Russian).
Arctic Bulletin (monthly reports on scientific progress in English).
Izdanye Glavsevmorputy, Leningrad (books published by the Central Administration of the Northern Sea Route).

What other books contain information on the Russian Polar regions?

Nansen, Fridtjof. *Siberia, Land of the Future.* London, 1913.
Goldman, Bosworth. *Red road through Asia.* London, 1933.

Matters, Leonard. *Through the Kara Sea.* London, 1931.

Steber, Charles. *La Siberie et l'extreme Nord Sovietique.* Paris, 1936.

Mikhaylov. *Soviet Geography.* London, 1935.

Heller, Otto. *Sibirien, ein anderes Amerika.* Berlin, 1932.

Mirsky, Jeanette. *Northern Conquest* (history of Polar exploration). London, 1932.

The usual standard works on Siberia, Russian history and Polar science.

INDEX

Hutchinson's

IMPORTANT NEW BOOKS FOR THE SPRING OF
1937
BIOGRAPHY & AUTOBIOGRAPHY

Memoirs

These two volumes of "Memoirs" are more than an autobiography. They are an indispensable authority on the origins and rise to power of the Labour movement in Great Britain, written by one of the few remaining leaders who has been in the fight from the beginning and who has never turned traitor to those who placed him in authority. Rightly or wrongly he has stood by his guns.

The story in itself, of such a phenomenal rise to fame, would be as fascinating and vital as any reader could desire, but added to this is the epic of Labour's rise from street oratory to Parliamentary power, and told in the words of one of its greatest supporters.   To be published Autumn 1937.
                    Two volumes. 16 illustrations. Large Demy. 18s. each.

by
THE RT. HON. J. R. CLYNES, M.P.

My Story

In this full and frank diary there is revealed the character and the story of one of the most outstanding public figures of modern times. Mr. Thomas's unique royal reminiscences ; the intimate anecdotes of the ex-errand boy who became the friend of kings ; the secrets of the industrial crises of the past forty years ; the story of his almost incredible years on the railway, are all related in one of the most amazing and dramatic life-stories ever written by a figure of national importance.   *23 illustrations. Demy. 15s.*

by
THE RT. HON. J. H. THOMAS

Dreyfus : His Life and Letters

This remarkable biography which throws so much new light on the life and trial of Dreyfus is divided into two parts. The first, which is by his son, is an account of the case up to Dreyfus's release from Devil's Island and his second condemnation. It contains a most important selection from letters of Dreyfus to his wife (and vice-versa) and to Dreyfus from various celebrities.

The second part is the pathetic and tragic story of the case from the second condemnation at Rennes in 1899 to his final acquittal in 1906, and is written by Dreyfus himself.   *Large Demy. 23 illustrations. 18s.*

by
PIERRE DREYFUS

All prices in this list are provisional and subject to alteration.

I Stand Nude

This is the forthright and very human autobiography of a man who began life in the humblest circumstances and was engaged in a number of odd jobs.

For its rare qualities of naturalness and truth this autobiography will be read as a human document far above the average. Demy. 8s. 6d.

by

JAMES ROYCE

A. E. Housman

A PERSONAL RECORD

Few people enjoyed any intimate friendship with Professor Housman, one of the greatest of classical scholars and a poet secure of lasting fame.

The author of "A Shropshire Lad" and "Last Poems" was popularly believed to have been an unapproachable recluse who lived in a lonely world of his own. This was the legend about him. How far was it true? Mr. Grant Richards, who published "A Shropshire Lad" and "Last Poems", and knew Professor Housman intimately for many years and travelled with him at home and abroad, answers the question in this book. It is a human and intimate account of the author's long association with a man who was only known to most people as the author of "A Shropshire Lad".

Demy. With a frontispiece. About 12s. 6d.

by

GRANT RICHARDS

All the Days of My Life

It is no exaggeration to say that S. P. B. Mais must have brought home the beauties of the English countryside to thousands of people. His books are the stories, one might almost say the diaries, of his travels over the country, whose joys few people can express more happily. His autobiography is a volume that will thus appeal to thousands, representing, as it does, the life story of a man to whom the pleasures and beauties of the English countryside mean so much. Demy. About 16 illustrations. 10s. 6d.

by

S. P. B. MAIS

Author of *England's Pleasance, England's Character*

The House of Curious

In this interesting and readable book Dr. Cecil Alport, author of a most entertaining book on the War, tells of his adventures and association with his father, his own experiences as a doctor, and describes his medical student days with considerable ability. Amusing stories and absorbing reminiscences are features of a sane and well-balanced piece of writing.

Large Demy. About 16 illustrations. 18s.

by

A. CECIL ALPORT

Author of *The Lighter Side of the War*

Lady Houston

*M*r. Wentworth Day has written not only a gracious tribute to, but also a remarkably fascinating book about, one of the most remarkable women of modern times. It is intimate, revealing, and contains many stories and details of the life of one of the Empire's most faithful servants.

Demy. About 16 illustrations. 15s.

by

J. WENTWORTH DAY

Author of *A Falcon on St. Paul's*, etc.

Reminiscences

*S*ir Frederick Hobday is Honorary Veterinary Surgeon to the King ; late Principal and Dean Royal Veterinary College and Honorary Consulting Veterinary Surgeon to the Royal Agricultural Society of England. His life has been spent, one might almost say, in the service of animals. His reminiscences contain many stories and a great deal of information about his most interesting life work. Large Demy. About 16 illustrations. 18s.

by

SIR FREDERICK HOBDAY, C.M.S., F.R.C.V.S., F.R.S.E.

Reza Shah

*R*eza Shah, the Persian Peter the Great of today, must be comparatively unknown to English readers, but his story makes fascinating reading in spite of its obscurity. The author depicts the amazing feudal chaos of old Persia ; Reza's coup ; the farcical Constitution ; the crushing of feudalism, and Reza's enormous achievements on the scale of Alexander the Great.

Large Demy. About 20 illustrations. 18s.

by

MOHAMMED ESSAD-BEY

The Best of Me

*B*asil Maine is well known as an essayist, critic, novelist, and orator. In 1933 reviewers throughout Europe and America were unanimous in acclaiming his biography of Sir Edward Elgar as a "brilliant achievement". More recently his biography of the Duke of Windsor achieved a wide success. He has written brilliantly of the many personalities he has met and the interesting life he has led. Large Demy. 16 illustrations. 18s.

by

BASIL MAINE

Author of *Our Ambassador King*

Swinnerton: An Autobiography

In 1917 *Frank Swinnerton became known all over the world with the publication of "Nocturne", which has been translated into every European language except Spanish. His list of novels is imposing ; he is well known as a critic and as an expert on the publishing trade, in which he has enjoyed a wide experience. His life and his books radiate a sane and balanced philosophy which, indeed, is the keynote of one of the most entertaining of literary autobiographies.*
Demy. 9 *illustrations in collotype.* 10*s.* 6*d.*

by
FRANK SWINNERTON
Author of *The Georgian House* (42nd thous.), *Elizabeth* (15th thous.), etc.

An Autobiography

Mr. W. B. Maxwell is a son of the famous Victorian novelist M. E. Braddon, and although reared in the literary atmosphere of her home, it was not for a good many years after growing up that he became an author himself.

Those literary abilities which have made W. B. Maxwell one of the most important novelists today have perhaps never been better displayed than in this remarkable autobiography. Large Demy. About 8 illustrations. 10*s.* 6*d.*

by
W. B. MAXWELL
Author of *Himself and Mr. Raikes* (10th thous.), *We Forget Because We Must* (61st thous.), etc.

Buffets and Rewards
A MUSICIAN'S REMINISCENCES

Weingartner is, of course, one of the greatest conductors and composers of our time and amongst lovers of music has admirers all over the world. In his book he paints vivid portraits of some of the outstanding figures in the sphere of music. He knew both Wagner and Liszt, and was a friend of Brahms. Large Demy. 17 *illustrations.* 18*s.*

by
FELIX WEINGARTNER

The Romantic Life of Maurice Chevalier

This is essentially a sympathetic study and as such will appeal tremendously to thousands of fans. From a very early age and in his many curious jobs Maurice was always wanting to sing and dance, and in this charming story of his life a very vivid picture is presented of the vicissitudes through which he passed and, later, of the glamorous life that became his.
Crown 8vo. 23 *illustrations.* 8*s.* 6*d.*

by
WILLIAM BOYER

Horse and Hounds

RANDOM RECOLLECTIONS OF A GENTLEMAN RIDER
AND MASTER OF STAGHOUNDS

A great sportsman and known to all the sporting world, Theodore Christy, has written the most fascinating and delightful book, full of good stories and reflecting a witty and refreshing personality.

Large Demy. 16 *illustrations.* 13s.

by
THEODORE CHRISTY

When I was at Court

In this Coronation year there is widespread interest in everything connected with the Court. What goes on behind the scenes? How are the historical and glamorous ceremonies arranged? These are questions which fascinate everybody. Now they are discussed in detail in this intimate book by Lord Ormathwaite, who from 1910-1920 was Master of the Ceremonies. No servant of Sovereigns knows more about Court ceremonial than Lord Ormathwaite, and in these reminiscences of a long life at Court, he tells us much about it.

Large Demy. About 16 illustrations. 18s.

by
LORD ORMATHWAITE, G.C.V.O.

The War Office at War

The author's acquaintance with the War Office extends from 1886—when as a railway official he endeavoured unsuccessfully to find a regiment which the Government had mislaid—to the final stages of the Great War, as Director-General of Movements and Railways and a member of the Army Council. As a civilian at the War Office, Sir Sam Fay had a unique opportunity of forming an unbiased opinion upon the bitter wartime controversy between soldiers and politicians. This opinion he expresses in no uncertain terms.

Large Demy. 16 *illustrations.* 18s.

by
SIR SAM FAY

Romance and Revolution

Born in Hamburg, Iowa, the author of this book soon manifested a desire for the stage. These gay reminiscences of her theatrical and private lives are immensely entertaining. Large Demy. 15 *illustrations.* 10s. 6d.

by
COUNTESS NOSTITZ (MADAME LILIE DE FERNANDEZ-AZABAL)

My Melodious Memories

Herman Finck, renowned wit and British composer, writes brilliantly and with a sharp wit of music, writers, clubs, hotels, and, of course, the stage.

Large Demy. 47 *illustrations.* 18s.

by
HERMAN FINCK

HISTORICAL BIOGRAPHY

"Old Q.'s" Daughter

Here, for the first time, is told the amazing history of the strange family to whom the nation owes the wonderful treasures to be seen at Hertford House.

No small part of Mr. Falk's achievement has been to solve the multitude of riddles arising out of the disputed parentage and behaviour of the different characters.

Mr. Falk has been specially privileged to search the archives of the Wallace Collection, and he is indebted to many of our Peers for hitherto unpublished letters throwing light on the obscure history of a family which, at one time, aspired even to the throne itself.

Large Demy. Frontispiece in colour, 34 illustrations. 18s.

by
BERNARD FALK
Author of *He Laughed in Fleet Street, The Naked Lady, Rachel the Immortal*

IN PREPARATION
Five Years Dead

by
BERNARD FALK
A sequel to *He Laughed in Fleet Street*

Cyrano de Bergerac

Mr. Humbert Wolfe has made a brilliant and original film version of incidents in the life of that immortal character Cyrano de Bergerac. Mr. Wolfe's scenario is based upon Edward Rostand's play "Cyrano de Bergerac", which took Paris by storm when it was produced.

Mr. Wolfe has written a long and provocative introduction to the book which is certain to be the subject of considerable discussion.

Demy. About 8 illustrations. 10s. 6d. net.

by
HUMBERT WOLFE

A Century of Buckingham Palace, 1837-1937

This fascinating anecdotal story of the Palace contains a short sketch of its history prior to 1837, and a fuller account of the Anecdotes and vivid Personalities connected with it since it became a Royal Palace. The story is brought up to 1937. *Demy. Illustrated.* 3s. 6d.

by
BRUCE GRAEME
Author of *The Story of St. James's Palace*, etc.

The Story of Windsor Castle

Bruce Graeme, who has written such widely praised books on Buckingham Palace and St. James's Palace, has now turned his attention to another Royal household. The result is a most interesting and picturesque account of England's most famous castle. *Large Demy. Illustrated.* £1 1s.

by
BRUCE GRAEME
Author of *The Story of Buckingham Palace*, etc.

"Beloved Friend"

THE STORY OF TCHAIKOWSKY AND NADEJDA VON MECK

Here is the truth about the great composer. A book based on conversation with a direct descendant of Nadeja von Meck, who founded the Mecca Conservatory of Music and befriended and inspired Tchaikowsky during the most creative years of his stormy life. This wonderful biography is a fascinating and revealing account that cannot be overlooked by any music-lover.

Demy. 8 Illustrations. 10s. 6d.

by

CATHERINE DRINKER BOWEN AND BARBARA VON MECK

A History of Lloyd's

One of the most brilliant critics of our day, gifted not only with rare critical acumen but also with a witty and pungent pen, Mr. Straus's excursion into a fascinating subject is an event of importance. To the ordinary man Lloyd's is a synonym for efficiency, but the reader is here taken far afield and is shown how from the humblest beginnings in a London coffee-house, this great company, linking land and sea in a world-wide net, has become a household word from John o' Groats to the Horn.

Large Demy. About 20 illustrations. About 21s.

by

RALPH STRAUS

Pauline Bonaparte

From the age of sixteen, and possibly earlier, Pauline Bonaparte's whole life was taken up with the "seizing of hearts". A "gold-digger" of the eighteenth and nineteenth centuries, she was beautiful but never sentimental, which was perhaps the secret of her many amorous successes. Joachim Kühn has brilliantly re-created a vivid and colourful life about which little has been written.

Large Demy. 8 illustrations. 18s.

by

JOACHIM KÜHN

Anne of Austria: The Infanta Queen

This romantic biography tells the story of Anne of Austria during the first years of her marriage to Louis XIII of France, when, to distinguish her from Marie de Medici, the Queen Mother, she was always known as the Infanta Queen.

Young, radiantly lovely, spoilt by her father, Philip III of Spain, Anne found her position in the Louvre, with its intrigues and cabals, almost intolerable.

Large Demy. 16 illustrations. 18s.

by

MERIEL BUCHANAN

HUTCHINSON'S ROYAL BOOKS

In these unique volumes the reader will find intimate and charming details of the lives of Their Majesties and their children. Each book has been carefully brought up-to-date, and forms, we believe, the perfect gift for this Coronation Year.

Lady Cynthia Asquith has written an entirely new and authentic biography of Her Majesty Queen Elizabeth. It will be published in March at 7s. 6d., illustrated.

Queen Elizabeth

Her intimate and authentic life story from childhood up till today told with the personal approval of Her Majesty.

Demy. 32 illustrations. 3s. 6d.

by
LADY CYNTHIA ASQUITH

King George VI

An intimate and authoritative life of His Majesty the King, by one who has had special facilities, published with the approval of His Majesty before his accession and brought up to 1937.

Demy. 32 illustrations. 3s. 6d.

by
TAYLOR DARBYSHIRE

Our King and Queen

An authentic and authoritative story of the life of Their Majesties King George VI and Queen Elizabeth, revised and brought up to 1937.

Large Demy. 65 illustrations. 5s.

The Family Life of Her Majesty Queen Elizabeth

Written and published with the personal approval of Her Majesty.

Size 10 x 7¼ ins. 61 illustrations. 2s. 6d.

by
LADY CYNTHIA ASQUITH

Edward VIII—Duke of Windsor

Being an account of the Duke of Windsor's life and service as Prince of Wales and King Edward the Eighth. *Demy. 32 illustrations. 3s. 6d.*

by
BASIL MAINE
Author of *The Best of Me, Our Ambassador King*, etc.

Air Over Eden

There are many books of travel, but this is an exceptional one. The aim of the authors has been to write a modern air book about Iraq, a country richer in historical associations than almost any other country in the world. The authors describe the country as seen from the air, and they also give a fascinating outline of its history, which began with two people in the Garden of Eden. Large Demy. 69 illustrations. 18s.

by

"H W" and SIDNEY HAY

❧

Airman Friday

As a complete vade-mecum on aviation this book can have no rivals, but it is written by a journalist, in fact the "Evening Standard" Aviation Correspondent, and the popular element has consequently not been overlooked. Mr. Courtenay has many amusing and amazing stories to tell of his wide experience in modern flying. Demy. 69 illustrations. 12s. 6d.

by

WILLIAM COURTENAY

❧

Whirlpools On The Danube

"Whirlpools on the Danube" is an account of a journey made through some of the Danube countries of Europe during the summer of 1936. Large Demy. 39 illustrations. 18s.

by

CHRISTOPHER SIDGWICK

Author of *German Journey*

❧

Changing Horizons

Major Foran started his travels abroad nearly forty years ago, long before the vogue of the "luxury cruises". His wanderings have taken him far and wide on the Seven Seas, both on and off the beaten tracks. Seldom has the same ground been covered more than once. His progress was unhurried, so unusual opportunities came in his path for seeing places and things which are not generally in a traveller's itinerary. Large Demy. 63 illustrations. 18s.

by

W. ROBERT FORAN

Author of *Malayan Symphony*, *A Cuckoo in Kenya*, etc.

The Voyage of the "Girl Pat"

During the early summer of 1936 the whole world was amazed and gasped at the daring of Skipper Orsborne and his crew. The story presented an amazing epic of sheer adventure which will go down in history as a great Saga of the Sea.

Sensation follows sensation in this extraordinary story in which the Skipper tells how, with only a sixpenny atlas for chart and a match-stick for sextant, he and his crew sailed across the Atlantic.

The tale of how they bluffed an agent to secure repairs and fuel and even handsome tips for themselves, how they ran aground and starved, played the mandolin with sharks as an audience, is a stupendous one unparalleled in its sheer daring and gallant pluck. Their adventures are legion, but there is laughter mingled with the anguish of these stirring pages.

Demy. **17 illustrations.** **8s. 6d.**

by

SKIPPER ORSBORNE

An African Travel Book

Mr. Patrick Balfour is no ordinary traveller, for, as "Society Racket" proved, he has a profound knowledge of human nature and is yet able to write racily about it. His ability to write amusingly and intelligently will be once again proved with this new African book.

Large Demy. *About 20 illustrations.* **12s. 6d.**

by

PATRICK BALFOUR

Author of *Society Racket, Grand Tour*

Cricketless Days

Here is no ordinary book telling the secret of So-and-so's bowling or a dry commentary of day-by-day cricket in Australia, but a book with more general interest, and written from the picturesque and social, rather than the technical, aspect. *Crown 8vo.* *About 16 illustrations.* **6s.**

by

BRUCE HARRIS

My Escape from Germany

The author, a German, was put in prison for writing articles about Jewish persecution. He was released, but his passport and papers were taken from him. This extraordinarily book describes his amazing adventures and experiences in escaping from Germany and travelling to England.

Demy. **8s. 6d.**

by

WILLI MELCHERT

Forty Thousand Against the Arctic
RUSSIA'S POLAR EMPIRE

H. P. Smolka, the well-known journalist, whose recent articles in "The Times" on Arctic Siberia have aroused such widespread interest, has now written a most important and extraordinary book. Last Summer he started his journey by ice-breakers and aeroplane to Northern Asia and the islands in the Polar Sea.

During the last four years the Russian Government has embarked on the great scheme of exploiting the vast natural resources of Northern Siberia, establishing a sea passage round the Arctic coast of Asia, and a short cut from Europe to America in the form of a Trans-Arctic air line. There are probably few people who were aware of these developments before Mr. Smolka's recent journey and the subsequent publication of his articles.

Demy. 53 illustrations. 12s. 6d.

by
H. P. SMOLKA

Revisiting My Pygmy Hosts

In his two previous books Paul Schebesta has shown a deep insight into pygmy customs and ways of life. In this fascinating new book the author continues, in more intensive form, his investigations into pygmy culture.

Large Demy. 53 illustrations. 18s.

by
PAUL SCHEBESTA
Author of Among Congo Pygmies, My Pygmy and Negro Hosts
Translated by GERALD GRIFFIN

The Whalers

Unfortunately we are not able to announce the translation into English of a book by Alexandre Dumas. Nevertheless the impress of that great writer is on this book, and it is interesting to discover just where his influence changed Dr. Maynard's pages.

The book represents the diary of a French surgeon on whalers in New Zealand waters during several voyages from 1837 to about 1846. Dr. Maynard, a man of great culture and knowledge, tells in full detail and with any number of human touches the story of the lives of whalers and the killing of whales. Whether describing the natives and their customs, the superstitions of his shipmates, or the dangers faced and endured, Dr. Maynard is always interesting.

Demy. 8s. 6d.

by
DR. FELIX MAYNARD and ALEXANDRE DUMAS
Introduction and notes by JOHANNES C. ANDERSEN, Chief Librarian
Alexander Turnbull Library, Wellington, New Zealand
The translation by F. W. REED

England's Character

In this book of Mr. Mais's recent wanderings round the countryside he has not only described fresh places, he has talked with and listened to all sorts of Englishmen, from gamekeepers to poachers, parsons to tramps, bus-conductors to auctioneers. Crown 8vo. 15 illustrations. 7s. 6d.

by

S. P. B. MAIS

Author of *England's Pleasance*

Australian Fantasy

Taking as his inspiration a gallery of notable photographs, Mr. Dudley Glass weaves around them an Australian fantasy. Its lavishly illustrated pages conjure up a bushland of strange plant and animal life ; paint a scenic wonderland of blue mountains and golden beaches and sunburnt pastures ; show from a new angle a young country at work and at play. The story begins among Stone Age aborigines, and ends with a cavalcade of progress in ultra-modern cities. A colourful Australia is captured in this series of admirable camera-studies accompanied by their complementary pen-pictures. Size 11 x 8 ins. Beautifully illustrated. 10s. 6d.

by

DUDLEY GLASS

Author of *The Spanish Goldfish, The Book about the British Empire*, etc.

Air Mercenary

The purpose of this remarkable book is to describe Lieutenant Wewege-Smith's amazing experiences as an airman with the Bolivian forces during the war in the Chaco between Bolivia and Paraguay. Fact is again proved stranger than fiction—and infinitely more thrilling. Demy 8vo. Illustrated. 15s.

by

LIEUTENANT T. WEWEGE-SMITH

Squash Rackets for Women

In the last few years the game of squash rackets has rapidly increased in popularity, particularly for women players. Susan Noel's book comes therefore at an opportune moment. Women who have achieved a fair competency at the game and those who are only just beginning will find it a source of invaluable help. Crown 8vo. Illustrated. 4s. 6d.

by

SUSAN NOEL

Crowning the King

"*Coronation Day is going to be a day to be remembered for a lifetime. For on that day King George will, with Queen Elizabeth, ride in state to Westminster Abbey to be crowned the undoubted King of this realm.*" Thus the opening words to this fascinating and extraordinarily interesting book in which the author tells the history of coronation and kingship from ancient times. He has sought to give an account of the coronation ceremonies which shall be clear, accurate, and readable. It has been his aim to present the knowledge of historians in a form which young people can read and follow. He also sketches the life of the King and the circumstances leading up to the Coronation. It is a knowledgeable book, written for the purpose of explaining the significance and details of the Coronation to the countless thousands whose interest it will be. *Crown quarto. Four colour plates and 16 black-and-white illustrations. 3s. 6d.*

by
LEWIS BROAD

An A B C Guide to the Coronation

This book is indeed a happy thought of Lewis Broad's, for this year everyone will want information on such an important subject. It has been concisely drawn up, and on account of its size and price is a book that should be in everyone's pocket. Crown 8vo. About 20 illustrations. 6d.

by
LEWIS BROAD

The King: The Story and Splendour of British Monarchy

In "This England" Mr. Shears showed himself to be a man with a very deep knowledge of English customs and places. His book was a masterpiece of patient research and careful selection of material. In his hands the stories of the Kings of England become not only interesting, but also lose that film of unreality with which countless educational works have endowed them. Frontispiece in colour and 24 illustrations 6s.

by
W. S. SHEARS
Author of *This England*

Rex, The Coronation Lion

This delightful book of the Adventures of Rex, who comes down from his place in front of St. Martin's-in-the-Field for the Coronation, will amuse grown-ups and children. His ancient enemy the Unicorn is also in Town on Coronation Day, and the fun is fast and furious. Illustrated. 3s. 6d.

by
SEPP

Sundry Essays

by
MARJORIE BOWEN

10*s*. 6*d*.

Author of *Dickon*, *The Viper of Milan*, etc.

Collected Essays and Observations

*A*s one of the most prominent personalities in England today, Lord Hewart, of course, needs no introduction. A very full life has accorded him little time for the gentler art of writing, but the essays which he has chosen to publish have been widely read and appreciated, and this, his latest volume, will appeal to many readers. Demy. With a Frontispiece. 10*s*. 6*d*.

by
LORD HEWART
(*Lord Chief Justice of England*)

Physic and Fancy

*T*here are many wise and amusing statements in this physician's notebook. The author has jotted down random thoughts and statements on all manner of things, and uses, often very skilfully, medical facts to illustrate the points he wishes to make.

It is indeed a book of parts, for mingled with sound medical advice is a rare and sane philosophy of life. Readable, interesting, and bearing comparison, in its form, with the famous "Notebooks of Samuel Butler", it forms a curiously unusual and inspiring piece of work. Large crown 8*vo*. 6*s*.

by
CHRISTOPHER HOWARD

CRIMINOLOGY

Great Cases of Sir Henry Curtis Bennett, K.C.

*M*r. Grice has succeeded not only in putting on record a series of remarkable pen-pictures of Sir Henry Curtis Bennett, but also in collecting a number of most fascinating and interesting cases. There are stories of murder, robbery and violence, and the sensational trials of the men and women concerned. Throughout the book there runs the vein of masterful cross-examination and brilliant handling of witnesses that were so characteristic of the great King's Counsel. Demy. 24 illustrations. 3*s*. 6*d*.

by
EDWARD GRICE

The Coronation Year Illustrated

One of the most remarkable book values ever offered. The breathless panorama of many world events pictured in a beautifully produced volume. And eminent authorities discuss in illuminating little articles the significance of such all-important happenings in the march of world history. Over 300 unique photographs on fine art paper. 96 pp. (12 x 10 ins.)
2s. 6d.

Edited by
PAUL POPPER

Woman Adrift

In this new book Mrs. Cecil Chesterton has taken the subject of "Woman Adrift" and has once again written a most appealing and knowledgeable volume. Demy. About 8 illustrations. 10s. 6d.

by
MRS. CECIL CHESTERTON
Author of *In Darkest London, Women of the Underworld, etc.*

I Am Going to Have a Baby

It would be difficult to imagine a title that sums up its subject more aptly than this. It is, however, necessary to point out the sane and sensible way in which the subject has been treated. It is a plain and straightforward account of invaluable use to every prospective mother. It contains advice on matters which, if overlooked, may be disastrous.
Crown 8vo. About 16 illustrations. 6s.

by
MARTHA BLOUNT

Company Finance

Famous as a novelist, as a journalist, and as one of the most expert of writers on financial matters, Collin Brooks contributes one of the soundest and most comprehensive volumes on Company Finance yet written.
Crown 8vo. 3s. 6d.

by
COLLIN BROOKS

Claims of the Lesser Creeds

The anonymous editor of this volume is a well-known expert and an author of great repute. His collection of the various Creeds of Great Britain will be a somewhat unique one supplying a great need. The claims in this comprehensive and illuminating volume are set out quite impartially, and readers can judge for themselves of their value.
Demy. About 31 illustrations. 10s. 6d.

Edited by
DUFF DEVINE

The Peril from the Air

In "The Peril from the Air" Sir Malcolm Campbell, himself a war-time air-pilot, warns the nation of the ever-increasing peril of German rearmament and the feverish building up of a powerful Air Force which he believes is intended for aggression and may have for its ultimate objective an attack on the British Empire.

The reader may not always agree with the conclusions he reaches, but the fearless and outspoken manner of stating them must have a very strong appeal to every citizen who believes that the best way of averting war is to be prepared for it.

Crown 8vo. 1s.

by

SIR MALCOLM CAMPBELL, M.B.E.

Author of *The Romance of Motor Racing*, etc.

Road Safety

Sir Malcolm Campbell's great interest in road and car problems is second perhaps only to his interest in motor racing. He has brought his knowledge and experience to bear on one of the most vital problems of today. The lives of every one of us depend on the question and no one should therefore overlook a book by such an authority.

Crown 8vo. Illustrated. 3s. 6d.

by

SIR MALCOLM CAMPBELL

Author of *My Thirty Years of Speed, The Romance of Motor Racing*, etc.

South of the Water

This is one of the most remarkable books ever written by a parson, and will, we think, become a "best-seller". It is the true and frank account of the author's life and work among the poor, not only in the Waterloo Road, but at Woolwich. For years the author has ministered to the needs of the poor and the destitute, and has brought religion into direct relation with life—made Christianity real and practical. This parson in the slums has written a most powerful human document showing how the "other half" struggle against every kind of difficulty and try to live. There has been no book like it since Hugh Redwood's famous "God in the Slums".

Crown 8vo. About 6s.

by

THE REV. C. W. HUTCHINSON

(Vicar of St. John's, Waterloo Road)

Printed in the United Kingdom
by Lightning Source UK Ltd.
123508UK00001B/140/A